THEATRE

A scene from Norman Bel Geddes' "Project for the Divine Comedy", the high point in American dramatic conception.

THEATRE

ESSAYS ON THE ARTS OF
THE THEATRE

EDITED BY

EDITH J. R. ISAACS

With Illustrations

Essay Index Reprint Series

BOOKS FOR LIBRARIES PRESS

FREEPORT, NEW YORK

First Published 1927
Reprinted 1968

LIBRARY OF CONGRESS CATALOG CARD NUMBER:

68-22919

PRINTED IN THE UNITED STATES OF AMERICA

ACKNOWLEDGMENT

SOMEBODY once said that Francis Bruguière was spending his days spreading happy falsehoods about the American theatre, his photographs of a scene were often so much nearer the designer's conception than an accurate record of production would have been. Whether this is true or not, it is certainly true that much of the vividness with which we can recall what has happened in the American theatre during the last dozen years is due to Mr. Bruguière. Since almost half of the photographs in this book are from his studio, we wish, in making our acknowledgment to the authors' of these essays, to include Mr. Bruguière among them.

We wish also to thank the publishers who have permitted us to reprint certain essays: Charles Scribner's Sons for Stark Young's "The Art of Directing" and "On Wearing Costumes" from "Theatre Practice"; Harcourt, Brace & Company for Irving Pichel's "Lighting" from "Modern Theatres", and Charles Brooks' "Fences on Parnassus" from "Like Summer's Cloud"; Alfred Knopf for D. H. Lawrence's "The Dance of the Sprouting Corn" from "Mornings in Mexico."

A special word of thanks goes to *Theatre Arts Monthly* for making the book possible and to Dorothea Baldwin McCollester, who did all but the pleasantest part of the work in bringing it together; and a final word to Montrose J. Moses for his guiding hand.

THE EDITOR

INTRODUCTION

WHATEVER else the theatre is in America today, it is alive. It may be good, bad, or indifferent, according to opinion. At any given point on the theatre highways from New York to San Francisco it may be creative and imaginative, mechanical and imitative, or vulgar and of low intention. It may be all of these at different spots in the market place of the theatre, which is Broadway, and it may even, as in "The Follies" or the Winter Garden, be at the same time something of both extremes, at once brilliant and vulgar, beautiful and of undistinguished aim. But by all the laws of growth and vigor, of striking roots and spreading branches through which we judge of other living things, the American theatre is more alive today than the theatre of any other country in the world. Not so mature and not so elegant, perhaps, but far more " up and coming", as the phrase goes. If you watched closely enough, you could, during the last dozen years especially, almost see this theatre grow. First, out from Broadway to Grand Street and MacDougall, out from New York to Cleveland and Dallas, Pasadena and Santa Barbara, out from professional playhouses into little theatres and universities, into the farm lands of Dakota and the mountains of North Carolina, into the lives of the primitive peoples who are our neighbors and our fellows, deep into the commonplace of our own lives and up into its fantasy, and then back again to Broadway, enriched by all of this with new playwrights and forms of playwriting, new material for plays, new artists and producers, with a whole new pattern of theatre life.

There are plenty of people who can see nothing in the last ten years but the decay of the organized theatre, who look on with horror while the movie absorbs the theatre's audience, and the touring company fades out of life in Wisconsin and Iowa and Kansas before the high price of rents and railroads, and who think therefore that the theatre is dead or quickly dying. That the trade theatre is eating itself alive may perhaps be true; but that is another story. The theatre as an art and the arts of the theatre are just beginning to come into their own in America.

To say this out loud may be overbold. Somewhere, sometime, somebody decided that it was "highbrow" and un-American to count the theatre among the arts, to think of it as anything but a combination of entertainment and big business — literally a show shop. You might almost as well speak of the soul on the floor of the Stock Exchange as to speak of the art of the theatre within radio distance of Broadway, even today. But there the sentence stands. There is no use in our trying to dodge it, for that is, brazenly, what this book is about — this art of the theatre which is beginning to take shape in America beside the arts of American music and painting and sculpture; the art of this American theatre of the twentieth century which we believe may well, before it is done, take its place among the theatres of the world's great days.

There may not yet be, for those who are looking at it from the outside, much to show for such a faith. But as we study the record of the last ten years there seems to be a wealth of implication.

To these years we owe the best work of artist designers like Robert Edmond Jones, Norman Bel Geddes, Herman Rosse, and Lee Simonson; the work of playwrights like Eugene O'Neill, and Susan Glaspell, George Kelly, Sidney Howard, and Paul Green; the growth of organizations like the Neighborhood Playhouse, the Theatre Guild, the Provincetown Playhouse, and the Actors' Theatre — with a host of others through the country aiming to represent the whole of American life in the varied phases of the life of the theatre.

During these ten same years, and at the same time that it was deepening its life from its own inner sources, the American theatre was beginning to measure itself against the standards and traditions of other days and places, to take stock of European progress and to follow closely the words and the accomplishments of the leaders in the theatre of this generation all over the world. Not that it tended to be a mirror or a copy of Europe, except as all fine theatres carry on a permanent tradition from age to age and place to place, but that the courage and high purpose, the clarity of vision and creative iconoclasm of certain European leaders was an example, an aid, and a spur to the young American artists who were trying — with no tradition of their own and little enough help from their fellows — to give form and integrity and native quality to their first experiments toward an American theatre. Just how much the so-called "new movement in the theatre" here was a spontaneous response to the needs of the place and the hour and how much it owed its impetus to Gordon Craig and Adolph Appia, Max Reinhardt, Stanislavsky, and Jacques Copeau, it is impossible to measure. And it is unnecessary. What these men added to the generation's free, straight thinking about the theatre is a debt gratefully acknowledged. And from New York, at least, it brought a quick return, since, as soon as with their inspiration the foundations for a native theatre were laid, we were able, for the first time, to welcome with understanding and appreciation the whole brilliant company of foreign actors, producers, organizations, that have been the high spots of theatre life along Broadway during the last ten years — Eleonora Duse and the Vieux Colombier, the Moscow Art Theatre and the Guitrys. To him that hath shall be given, is one of the fundamental laws of the theatre.

There may not be, even in the record of these vivid years, a way to prophesy what the exact form and style and content of the American theatre of the future will be, but there is much to indicate its trend, to speculate upon its scope, to mark the roads it surely will not take.

It is quite safe to say, for example, that this theatre will not be what it was before, because it has never been American, and a theatre that is alive must just as surely have its roots deep in its own soil as it must surely include the world's theatre in its shade. There is no international theatre that is without marked native quality. But that is a commonplace in art — the artist who digs deepest reaches farthest.

Why we have never had an American theatre before is obvious in our history. It has been said a hundred times but we do not seem to remember it when it comes to judging the process and the product of our playhouses, so perhaps it may be said again : America began at the moment when the theatre in Europe had fallen to its lowest depths and was a source of evil to the body and the spirit. On our first statute books, accordingly, the theatre was called "the ante-chamber of the devil" and actors "the caterpillars of the commonwealth." To both, the art and the artists, the doors of our freedom were closely barred. There was to be no theatre in America. It was the will of our first fathers. When, after a century or more, players and playhouses found their way into our cities, they always came by a back street. And to this day we give the theatre, even at its best, a little of that back-street welcome. Perhaps in no American city would we today, as we did once, stop a performance of "Hamlet" as immoral, and put on a cock fight instead, but if our newer censors have their way this fight may well be renewed as between "Hamlet" and baseball. We need to remember all of this to understand why, even in its best days, about half a century ago, in those "good old days" we hear so much about, all that the theatre in America really had to offer was two or three distinguished groups, the greatest majority of whose actors and directors were born or trained in England, and nearly all of whose plays were imported. As lately as 1916, when the first order lists for the Drama Book Shop in New York were being made up, it was impossible to find enough American plays and books about the theatre (available in print) to fill one shelf. Less than two years ago, when Henry Miller died, it came as a shock even to those who knew it, that within the range of this man's acting life was the whole range of our American drama. He had played the lead in what we call the first modern American play, William Vaughn Moody's "The Great Divide." That was in 1906. And in 1882 he had played the lead in the first important drama of American life and manners by an American — Bronson Howard's "The Young Mrs. Winthrop." It does not seem to me that we can repeat too often or emphasize too strongly this evidence of our youth, because it points so clearly to the fact that, whatever our theatre faults are, they are faults of adolescence and not of decay, they mark the beginning and not the end of an American theatre.

Another thing that we may be quite safe in judging from the facts in hand, is that this new American theatre will not be like the theatre of any other age, or rather that its essential quality will be in its difference from them for the obvious reason that every age makes a theatre in its own image and the theatre of this industrial, mechanical, top-speed, composite civilization of ours cannot possibly be itself and still look like the theatre of the Greeks and the Elizabethans, or even like the theatre of the modern Russians, to whom the struggle for an individual free spirit is the essence of all living.

Every great dramatic period develops its own theatre æsthetic — which includes the approach to the art, the relationship among the component arts, the relationship among the artists, and the relationship between artists and audience. In Greece a great story and a poet were the focus of the theatre; in Shakespeare's day a great poet and an actor. Even in the beginnings of our theatre, one seems to descry the fact that one of its qualities will be the correlation of all the arts on an equality. Already there is fresh vigor in every branch, and experiment and some success — especially in play-writing and design, in music and the dance. And if our theatre is still completely lacking in the leadership it needs to give it form, is it not that very quality of leadership which this age of ours lacks to give it style and body — leadership in politics and religion and social life and creative endeavor? When the American theatre develops leaders big enough to coördinate its energies and its talents, the theatre will take form. Until then, all we see is the trend. This trend towards coördination may seem to be a matter of the time rather than the place, as true of Europe as of America. But there is one thing which differentiates it — the relationship of the audience to the play. The American theatre is sure to be a theatre of the comprehending — one is tempted to say the coöperating — audience. The very fact that the pendulum was so long held back by law and prejudice has already given its swing more force and direction, has in a dozen years linked half a million people actively to the Little Theatres, has carried the study of the arts of the theatre — for the first time in history — through the universities, into the high schools, even to the kindergartens. "The theatre," said Hebbel, "is the only possible pause in a man's life." The theatre, to a people who stand all day at attention before the mass and the machine, is bound to be an increasingly welcome release from the self. The next generation of well-educated Americans will probably be more actively theatre-minded than any other people in the world. But that is still a long way off, with a hard road ahead.

The theatre is the paradox among the arts. It is the easiest to enjoy and the hardest to understand, the most universal and the most special. The material of the dramatist is the material of human life. The medium of the actor, the actor himself, is a man like other men. This closeness to ourselves and to our world is what makes the approach to the theatre seem so simple, what makes so many of us feel so much more at home there than with any other art. We can judge a play as we judge life, and an actor as we judge the man who is our neighbor and be content, quite unmindful of the fact that the thing that makes them theatre really lies just within the range of their difference from life, their heightening and sharpening the process of the story and the lines of the acting to a point that is broader and deeper than life.

Without understanding anything of the art of the theatre, there is so much to enjoy within the doors of the playhouse, so much of color and motion and story, of wit and morals and beauty and grace, so much to share in the actual life of the theatre itself, its gaiety and companionship, its social quality, that the great majority of those who go to a play neither know nor feel the need to know anything of the art of the theatre. To go to a museum without knowing something of painting and sculpture is an ordeal. To go to a concert without an understanding of music is a bore. But there is something live and gay and welcome about going to the theatre with only your senses awake. And so the millions go.

Once the gates of æsthetic curiosity are opened, however, there is a whole new stream of pleasure in the theatre's art and artifice, a flood of new enjoyment waiting upon understanding. This is not, let us admit, altogether in accord with opinion on the subject. It is often maintained that what makes metropolitan audiences so unresponsive is that they know too much about the theatre and are too little subject to its illusion. And there are, no doubt, certain sophisticated theatregoers for whom nothing is any longer good enough, for whom what is done here is never so good as what they saw there, what you applaud not the equal of what they have long since stopped applauding. But these are not the people who really know the theatre, they are the followers of the fashion in the theatre as in clothes and homes and paintings. They are overfed and undernourished. The real lover of the theatre, the man who has searched out its mysteries, no matter how many disappointments he has had, is always hopeful before a rising curtain. He may have his preferences and his prejudices, but he has no sweeping convictions about the superiority of one form of playwriting or one style of acting over another. He does not hunger to annihilate realism for poetry, or expressionism for either. He does not think that all the good acting is in vaudeville, or in the Comédie Française or on Broadway. He does not think that the theatre is good or bad because it has or has not a proscenium arch. He thinks burlesque may be as much theatre material as tragedy, and he knows that a great play never dies. Nothing that is good theatre is alien to him. And the more he knows, the more he wants to know about the theatre's history, its forms and traditions and the arts which unite to serve it; about the ways it has gone and the way it is going.

There is one quality essential to the theatre itself, however, which balks him at every turn. For while the theatre is the most permanent of the arts, it is also the most fleeting. The literature of the theatre, which is the drama, remains from generation to generation, but the theatre itself dies. The painting, music, sculpture, architecture of other ages spread their own living record before us, but there is nothing which can recreate the direction, the playing, the style, the rhythm, the color, and the life of the theatre of another day. Euripides, Calderon, and Shakespeare, well played, may take on a life in our theatre almost as vigorous as that of their own day, but not the same life. Last year's great acting, great productions, great playhouses have no life except in our memory and in whatever record has been made of them on the printed page. Even last night's theatre, if we missed it, has passed us by. We may go to see a part of what is alive in the theatre of our own day, but only the merest fraction of that, only as many performances by a given number of actors in a given city, as a busy life allows. All that happens in the theatre of the next city, of neighboring countries, of the rest of the world we can know directly only through the literature of the theatre which is the drama, and only so far as the drama gets into printed form and is translated into our own language. Or we can partly recreate it in imagination with the aid of whatever record of the theatre has been made in photography and in the writings of critics and essayists, dramatic reporters, and theatre magazines. This is a bad approach at best. But it is what makes a printed record of the theatre's life so much more important than words about any other art in which the work of art itself remains from age to age to tell its own story. It is what makes the record both of ideas and events in any fertile theatre age so vital to the age that follows and inherits its traditions. And if the assumption is correct that the American audience of the future will need to know and understand its theatre life and traditions, it is what gives special import to the records of the years just gone.

To make a record in words and pictures of the American theatre during the first creative decade of its history, and to show this young theatre against a background of the older theatres of the world, has been the business and the pleasure of *Theatre Arts Monthly*. Naturally it is to such a record that we turn to recreate the ideas and the events of this period now that it is gone, to measure the outside influences and the inner forces that most affected it — to illuminate the path of its thinking and to follow it to the point where we meet it to-day.

Some of the writers in this book are American, some European, some are young and some are middle-aged; some conservative, some radical. Many of them are not writers by profession, but artists, philosophers, practical men of the theatre. Their style and tradition and point of view are varied, sometimes in opposition. But they all know and love the theatre, believe in its range and its power, and see the hope of a good day

INTRODUCTION

ahead. It would be an obvious exaggeration to suggest that such a selection from a score of minds and pens as are unified here can make any claim to forming a new theatre æsthetic. But together they seem to us to make the best approach yet made to a formulation of the American theatre idea. In other words, these words and pictures taken together seem to mark out the bounds within which the American theatre will find its life. They indicate who our source-finders and our path-makers have been, what their tradition was and what the problems are that most concern them now. From the top of this book we believe you can see a far way along the road ahead.

EDITH J. R. ISAACS

NEW YORK,
May 16, 1927.

CONTENTS

CONTENTS

LIST OF ILLUSTRATIONS

ILLUSTRATIONS IN HALFTONE

xxi

LIST OF ILLUSTRATIONS

ILLUSTRATIONS IN THE TEXT

LIST OF ILLUSTRATIONS

THE ACTOR

THE ACTOR

In the extensive literature of the theatre, so much of which is concerned with the life and personality of the actor, very little has ever been written about the art of acting. G. H. Lewes' "Actors and the Art of Acting", Talma's "Reflections on the Art of Acting", Coquelin's "The Actor and His Art", are some of the very few writings of an earlier day that remain in mind. Most writers have preferred to assume that acting is not an art with its own æsthetic, like painting or sculpture or playwriting, but a natural gift not to be separated from the person of the actor, and that even its technique cannot be analyzed and understood apart from experience in the theatre. Distinguished modern directors, however, men like Constantin Stanislavsky of the Moscow Art Theatre and Jacques Copeau of the Théâtre du Vieux Colombier, not satisfied with this assumption, have analyzed the successful acting they saw around them, formulated certain principles from which they developed a working theory, and finally tested their results by practice in their theatres. The success they achieved in performance, the exceptionally high level of their individual and ensemble acting, their greater power, by this approach, to achieve exactly the results they sought, have stimulated players the world over to analyze their gifts and develop them. Especially is this true in America, which for many generations had not a well-developed, native acting tradition but which has recently shown its openness to new thought by the diligence and devotion with which many of its

3

younger players have worked, (as for example, Katherine Cornell, Eva Le Gallienne, and Helen Gahagan) and the results they are achieving. Moreover, the experiment both here and abroad has greatly stimulated analytical and critical writing. In 1922 Stark Young wrote "The Art of Acting" (now published in "Theatre Practice", Scribner's) which is an illuminating statement and discussion of the subject and in which Mr. Young gives this definition of acting; "Acting is a business of translating into the terms of human beings, their minds and bodies and voices, certain matter taken either from life direct or from drama of thought and action and appearance that has been created out of life. The completeness of acting as an art depends on the completeness of the translation it makes into its own terms." Acting, in other words, is not life or a reproduction of life. It is not painting or the interpretation of literature — it is a separate art with its own laws, and problems, and methods. What some of the problems are which seem to concern our own theatre most, is indicated — not more than that — in the essays that follow. How much of the art of acting can be taught and by what methods, for example, in Boleslavsky's "The First Lesson in Acting"; what must be added in performance to an actor's own living personality to make it art, in Ashley Dukes' "The Painted Actor", what the details of presence (even so small a detail as the form of speech we use) can mean to the completeness of an actor's equipment in Windsor P. Daggett's "The Lineage of Speech."

Whether you call the theatre a hybrid and an impure art, or a complex and unified art depends somewhat on your appreciation of the essential quality of the art of the theatre. If you think that scene design is impure painting, that drama is a limited form of literature, that the dance is poetry unsung, the art in which all of these are united will not seem to have the simplicity and inevitability of expression which gives the

The Moscow Art Theatre, its repertory, the distinction of its acting, the creative quality of its direction,
had long been tradition in America before this
"world's first theatre" came to New York in 1923
under the direction of Constantin Stanislavsky.
The players of this company were as much at home
in Shakespeare, Molière, and Goldoni as in the
plays of their own country, but their quality seemed
best summed up in "The Cherry Orchard." The
"spiritualized realism" of the play corresponded
perfectly to their acting and gave the audience a sense
of a certain kind of Russian life and its characteristic
rhythms that set our playwrights tingling to find a
form that would reveal American life as simply and
as clearly. Above, Stanislavsky as Gaieff in "The
Cherry Orchard."

other arts their power and their permanence. For the actor at least, however, expression in terms of the theatre is the only possible expression of his art. And so a study of the sources of the actor's art is one of the best approaches to the study of the whole art of the theatre.

Stark Young's other essays in "Glamour" and "The Flower in Drama", Stanislavsky's "My Life in Art", Copeau's essays on the theatre, too long left untranslated into English, and chapters in Ashley Dukes' "Drama" add to the recent interpretative comment on the art of acting. Before many more years go by we will probably have an æsthetic of acting, clear and complete, which may never make great actors but will help good actors greatly along a troubled way.

THE FIRST LESSON IN ACTING

A Pseudo-Morality

BY RICHARD BOLESLAVSKY

Morning. My room. A knock at the door.

I. Come in.

[*The door opens, slowly and timidly. Enter a Pretty Creature of eighteen. She looks at me with wide-open, frightened eyes and crushes her handbag violently.*

THE CREATURE. I . . . I . . . I hear that you teach dramatic art.

I. No! I am sorry. Art cannot be taught. To possess an art means to possess talent. That is something one has or has not. You can develop it by hard work, but to create a talent is impossible. What I do is to help those who have decided to work on the stage, to develop and to educate themselves for honest and conscientious work in the theatre.

THE CREATURE. Yes, of course. Please help me. I simply love the theatre.

I. Loving the theatre is not enough. Who does not love it? To consecrate oneself to the theatre, to devote one's entire life to it, give it all one's thought, all one's emotions! For the sake of the theatre to give up everything, to suffer everything! And more

6

important than all, to be ready to give the theatre everything—your entire being—expecting the theatre to give you nothing in return, not the least grain of what seemed to you so beautiful in it and so alluring.

THE CREATURE. I know. I played a great deal at school. I understand that the theatre brings suffering. I am not afraid of it. I am ready for anything if I can only play, play, play.

I. And suppose the theatre does not want you to play and play and play?

THE CREATURE. Why should n't it?

I. Because *it* might not find you talented.

THE CREATURE. But when I played at school. . . .

I. What did you play?

THE CREATURE. "King Lear."

I. What part did you play in this trifle?

THE CREATURE. King Lear himself. And all my friends and our professor of literature and even Aunt Mary told me I played wonderfully and that I certainly had talent.

I. Pardon me, I don't mean to criticize the nice people whom you name, but are you sure that they are connoisseurs of talent?

THE CREATURE. Our professor is very strict. He himself worked with me on King Lear. He is a great authority.

I. I see, I see. And Aunt Mary?

THE CREATURE. She met Mr. Belasco personally.

I. So far, so good. But can you tell me how your professor, when working on King Lear, wanted you to play these lines, for instance: "Blow winds, and crack your cheeks! Rage! Blow!"

THE CREATURE. Do you want me to play it for you?

I. No. Just tell me how you learned to read those lines. What were you trying to attain?

THE CREATURE. I had to stand this way, my feet well together, incline my body forward a little, lift my head like this, stretch out my arms to heaven and shake my fists. Then I had to take a deep breath and burst into sarcastic laughter — ha! ha! ha! (*She laughs, a charming, childish laugh. Only at happy eighteen can one laugh that way*) Then, as though cursing heaven, as loud as possible pronounce the words: "Blow winds and crack your cheeks! Rage! Blow!"

I. Thank you, that is quite enough for a clear under-standing of the part of King Lear, as well as for a definition of your talent. May I ask you one more thing? Will you, if you please, say this sentence, first cursing the heavens and then without cursing them. Just keep the sense of the phrase — only its thought. [*She doesn't think long, she is accustomed to curse heaven.*

THE CREATURE. When you curse the heavens, you say it this way: "Blooooow wiiiiinds, and Craaaaack your cheeks, Raaaaage Blooooow." (*The Creature tries very hard to curse the heavens but through the window I see the azure heavens laughing at the curse. I do the same*) And without cursing them, I must do it some other way. Well . . . I don't know how . . . Isn't it funny? Well, this way: (*The Creature becomes confused and, with a charming smile, swallowing the words, hurriedly pronounces them all on one note*) "Blowwindsandcrackyourcheeksrageblow."

8

[She becomes completely confused and tries to destroy her handbag. A pause.

I. How strange! You are so young; you do not hesitate for a second before cursing heaven. Yet you are unable to speak these words simply and plainly, to show their inner meaning. You want to play a Chopin Nocturne without knowing where the notes are. You grimace, you mutilate the words of the poet and eternal emotion, and at the same time you do not possess the most elemental quality of a literate man — an ability to transmit the thoughts, feelings, and words of another logically. What right have you to say that you have worked in the theatre? You have destroyed the very conception of the word Theatre. *[A pause; the Creature looks at me with the eyes of one innocently condemned to death. The little handbag lies on the floor.*

THE CREATURE. So I must never play?

I. And if I say "never"?

[Pause. The eyes of the Creature change their expression, she looks straight into my soul with a sharp scrutinizing look, and seeing that I am not joking, clenches her teeth, and tries in vain to hide what is happening in her soul. But it is no use. One enormous real tear rolls out of her eye, and the Creature at that moment becomes dear to me. It spoils my intentions completely. She controls herself, clenches her teeth, and says in a low voice.

THE CREATURE. But I am going to play. I have nothing else in my life.

[At eighteen they always talk that way. But just the same I am deeply touched.

9

THE ACTOR

I. All right then. I must tell you that this very moment you did more for the theatre, or rather for yourself in the theatre, than you did in playing all your parts. You suffered just now; you felt deeply. Those are two things without which you cannot do in any art and especially in the art of the theatre. Only by paying this price can you attain the happiness of creation, the happiness of the birth of a new artistic value. To prove that, let us work together right now. Let us try to create a small, but real, artistic value according to your strength. It will be the first step in your development as an actress. (*The enormous, beautiful tear is forgotten. It disappears somewhere into space. A charming, happy smile appears instead. I never thought my creaking voice could produce such a change*) Listen and answer sincerely. Have you ever seen a man, a specialist, busy on some creative problem in the course of his work? A pilot on an ocean liner, for instance, responsible for thousands of lives, or a biologist working at his microscope, or an architect working out the plan of a complicated bridge, or a great actor seen from the wings during his interpretation of a fine part?

THE CREATURE. I saw John Barrymore from the wings when he was playing *Hamlet*.

I. What impressed you chiefly as you watched him?

THE CREATURE. He was *marvellous!!!*

I. I know that, but what else?

THE CREATURE. He paid no attention to me.

I. That is more important; not only not to you but to nothing around him. He was acting in his work

as the pilot would, the scientist, or the architect —
he was concentrating. Remember this word "Concentrate." It is important in every art and especially the art of the theatre. Concentration is the
quality which permits us to direct all our spiritual
and intellectual forces towards one definite object
and to continue as long as it pleases us to do so —
sometimes for a time much longer than our physical
strength can endure. I knew a fisherman once who,
during a storm, did not leave his rudder for forty-
eight hours, concentrating to the last minute on his
work of steering his schooner. Only when he had
brought the schooner back safely into the harbor
did he allow his body to faint. This strength, this
certainty of power over yourself, is the fundamental
quality of every creative artist. You must find it
within yourself, and develop it to the last degree.

THE CREATURE. But how?

I. I will tell you. Don't hurry. The most important
thing is that in the art of the theatre a special kind of
concentration is needed. The pilot has a compass,
the scientist has his microscope, the architect his
drawings — all external, visible objects of concentration and creation. They have, so to speak, a
"material" aim, to which all their force is directed.
So has a sculptor, a painter, a musician, an author.
But it is quite different with the actor. Tell me,
what do you think is the object of his concentration?

THE CREATURE. His part.

I. Yes, until he learns it. But it is only after studying
and rehearsing that the actor *starts* to create. Or
rather let us say that at first he creates "searchingly"

and on the opening night he begins to create "constructively" in his acting. And what is acting?

THE CREATURE. Acting? Acting is when he . . . acts, acts . . . I don't know.

I. You want to consecrate all your life to a task without knowing what it is? Acting is *the life of the human soul receiving its birth through art*. In a creative theatre the object for an actor's concentration is the *human soul*. In the first period of his work — the searching — the object for concentration is his own soul and those of the men and women who surround him. In the second period — the constructive one — only his own soul. Which means that, to act, you must know how to concentrate on something materially imperceptible, — on something which you can perceive only by penetrating deeply into your own entity, recognizing what would be evidenced in life only in a moment of the greatest emotion and most violent struggle. In other words, you need a spiritual concentration on emotions which do not exist, but are invented or imagined.

THE CREATURE. But how can one develop in oneself something which does not exist. How can one start?

I. From the very beginning. Not from a Chopin Nocturne but from the simplest scales. Such scales are your five senses: sight, hearing, smell, touch and taste. They will be the key of your creation like a scale for a Chopin Nocturne. Learn how to govern this scale, how with your entire being to concentrate on your senses, to make them work artificially, to give them different problems and create the solutions.

THE CREATURE. I hope you don't mean to say that I don't even know how to listen or how to feel.

I. In life you may know. Nature has taught you a little.
[*She becomes very daring and speaks as though challenging the whole world.*˙

THE CREATURE. No, on the stage, too.

I. Is that so? Let us see. Please, just as you are sitting now, listen to the scratching of an imaginary mouse in that corner.

THE CREATURE. Where is the audience?

I. That doesn't concern you in the least. Your audience is in no hurry as yet to buy tickets for your performance. Forget about it. Do the problem I give you. Listen to the scratching of a mouse in that corner.

THE CREATURE. All right.
[*There follows a helpless gesture with the right and then the left ear which has nothing in common with listening to the delicate scratching of a mouse's paw in the silence.*

I. All right. Now please listen to a symphony orchestra playing the march from "Aida." You know the march?

THE CREATURE. Of course.

I. Please. (*The same business follows — nothing to do with listening to a triumphal march. I smile. The Creature begins to understand that something is wrong, and becomes confused. She awaits my verdict*) I see you recognize how helpless you are, how little you see the difference between the lower *do* and the higher *do*.

THE CREATURE. You give me a very difficult problem.

I. Is it easier to curse the heavens in "King Lear"?
No, my dear, I must tell you frankly : You do not
know how to create the smallest, simplest bit of the
life of the human soul. You do not know how to
concentrate spiritually. Not only do you not know
how to create complicated feelings and emotions but
you do not even possess your own senses. All of
that you must learn by hard daily exercises of which I
can give you thousands. If you think, you will be
able to invent another thousand.

THE CREATURE. All right. I will learn. I will do
everything you tell me. Will I be an actress then?

I. I am glad you ask. Of course you will not be an
actress, yet. To listen and to look and to feel truly
is not all. You must do all that in a hundred ways.
Suppose that you are playing. The curtain goes up
and your first problem is to listen to the sound of a
departing car. You must do it in such a way that
the thousand people in the theatre who at that
moment are each concentrating on some particular
object — one on the stock exchange, one on home
worries, one on politics, one on a dinner or the pretty
girl in the next chair — in such a way that they know
and feel immediately that their concentration is less
important than yours, though you are concentrating
only on the sound of a departing imaginary car.
They must feel they have not the right to think of the
stock exchange in the presence of your imaginary car!
That you are more powerful than they, that, for the
moment, you are the most important person in the
world, and nobody dares disturb you. Nobody dares
to disturb a painter at his work, and it is the actor's

own fault if he allows the public to interfere with his creation. If all actors would possess the concentration and the knowledge of which I speak, this would never happen.

THE CREATURE. But what does he need for that?

I. Talent and technique. The education of an actor consists of three parts. The first is the education of his body, the whole physical apparatus, of every muscle and sinew. As a director I can manage very well with an actor with a completely developed body.

THE CREATURE. What time must a young actor spend on this?

I. An hour and a half daily on the following exercises: gymnastics, rhythmic gymnastics, classical and interpretive dancing, fencing, all kinds of breathing exercises, voice-placing exercises, diction, singing, pantomime, make-up. An hour and a half a day for two years with a steady practice afterwards in what you have acquired will make an actor *pleasing to look at.*

The second part of the education is intellectual, cultural. One can discuss Shakespeare, Molière, Goethe, and Calderon only with a cultured actor who knows what these men stand for and what has been done in the theatres of the world to produce their plays. I need an actor who knows the world's literature and who can see the difference between German and French Romanticism. I need an actor who knows the history of painting, of sculpture and of music, who can always carry in his mind, at least approximately, the style of every period, and the individuality of every great painter.

I need an actor who has a fairly clear idea of the

psychology of motion, of psychoanalysis, of the expression of emotion, and the logic of feeling. I need an actor who knows something of the anatomy of the human body, as well as of the great works of sculpture. All this knowledge is necessary because the actor comes in contact with these things, and has to work with them on the stage. This intellectual training would make an actor who could play a great variety of parts.

The third kind of education, the beginning of which I showed you today, is the education and training of the soul — the most important factor of dramatic action. An actor cannot exist without a soul developed enough to be able to accomplish, at the first command of the will, every action and change stipulated. In other words, the actor must have a soul capable of living through any situation demanded by the author. There is no great actor without such a soul. Unfortunately it is acquired by long, hard work, at great expense of time and experience, and through a series of experimental parts. The work for this consists in the development of the following faculties: complete possession of all the five senses in various imaginable situations; development of a memory of feeling, memory of inspiration or penetration, memory of imagination, and, last, a visual memory.

THE CREATURE. But I have never heard of all those.

I. Yet they are almost as simple as "cursing the heavens." The development of faith in imagination; the development of the imagination itself; the development of naiveté; the development of observation; the development of will power; the development of the capacity to give variety in the expression of emotion; development of the sense of humor and the tragic sense. Nor is this all.

THE CREATURE. Is it possible?

I. One thing alone remains which cannot be developed but must be present. It is TALENT.

[*The Creature sighs and falls into deep meditation. I also sit in silence.*

THE CREATURE. You make the theatre seem like something very big, very important, very . . . .

I. Yes, for me the theatre is a great mystery, a mystery in which are wonderfully wedded the two eternal phenomena, the dream of *Perfection* and the dream of the *Eternal*. Only to such a theatre is it worth while to give one's life.

[*I get up, the Creature looks at me with sorrowful eyes. I understand what these eyes express.*

THE PAINTED ACTOR

By Ashley Dukes

An amiable host invited me to take midnight refreshment in an actors' club, where the members rested from the labors of the evening. The grease paint had been removed from their faces, they had washed and changed their clothes, and now they sat at long green tables, with glasses and ash-trays before them, talking of parts finished and parts to come. In the language of convention, they had put off the mask of character, and reverted to their every-day selves. But had this language of convention any meaning? To the casual visitor's eyes, the amazing thing was the resemblance of these actual artists to their stage counterparts. To sit among them was to recall the ghosts of all the new plays for ten years past — or the male part of them, at least. Here sat a complete group from one of Mr. Maugham's comedies; next to them a young man created by Mr. Milne lit his cigarette; in an armchair, one of Mr. Sutro's heavy husbands turned the pages of his evening paper. In voice, in gesture, in presence, they were their stage selves to the life. The atmosphere of this pleasant, smoke-laden room was strangely charged with reminiscence. One caught the eye of a

complete stranger, and felt that one had known him
since the dawn of play-going days. He even nodded
in a friendly manner, under the impression that we knew
each other, though in reality we had always been separated by the wall of darkness that fills the proscenium
to the actor's eyes.

In reality — but what was reality? In the world of
the theatre, is not illusion reality? An actor's voice,
his gesture, his presence — are these not the very
breath of reality? When the actor off the stage so precisely resembles the actor on the stage, how can we
speak of the actor's mask? When private personality
so completely dominates the scene, how can we speak
of an author's character? Where every idiom is
habitual, and every intonation familiar, how can we
speak of a poet's language? Where every movement
is of the street and the parlour, how can we speak of
a designer's scene?

The answer is that such conceptions as the actor's
mask, the poet's language, or the designer's scene,
belong to the eternal theatre, while the actor's personality and all its trappings belong to the exhibitionist
stage. The eternal theatre transforms life; the exhibitionist stage pretends to reproduce it. The eternal
theatre is consciously artificial; the exhibitionist stage
is self-consciously real. We could multiply forever
these contrasts between the theatre of illusion and the
stage of fact; but the immediate question is the actor's
part in the affair. Can he, in truth, make the best of
both worlds? Can he walk the boards of imagination
and reality on alternate evenings?

Actors, no less than dramatists, are the children of

their age. The actors of our own time are the unconscious offspring of Ibsen and Hauptmann and Shaw. Their technique was defined for them by the "free theatres" that arose in Europe toward the end of the last century and so profoundly influenced the stage of ordinary commerce. The actor has been bred up to the naturalistic style. He is forever conscious of the "fourth wall" that is opened between him and his audience. When this imaginary wall was erected a generation ago, the actor's mask became in a new sense a vehicle of personal expression. It became an adjunct of personality rather than a creative symbol. It was merged in the technique of make-up — a layer of grease paint, a touch of the pencil for eyebrows and eyelashes, a heightening of the natural expression to meet the necessities of stage illumination, no longer a mask of fancy, but a mask of fact.

We must distinguish clearly between make-up and the mask. Make-up has the nature of photography; the mask has the nature of painting. Step into the dressing-room of any actor making up for a modern piece, and you will see the photographer's methods in use, with the appearance of youth or age added to the personal portrait. But enter the dressing-room of a dancer of the ballet, for example, and you will see the mask in creation. It is a long, laborious business, lasting perhaps an hour by the clock. Every feature is transformed; the face, as a whole, is harmonized with the lines of costume and decoration. The close view of this artificial mask is somewhat ghastly; but the close view is not the spectator's. What he actually sees is an expressive painting of a face, a work of art that carries emotional significance to the topmost gallery.

And here is surely the main question. Do we desire a photographic theatre or a painter's theatre? The photographic theatre implies the photographic actor, moving credibly in the photographic room represented on the stage, with all his features enhanced by make-up for purposes of natural expressiveness. The painter's theatre equally implies the painted actor, moving with dignity in a designer's scene, and wearing a mask of character that is the joint expression of his own creative spirit and his producer's purpose. There is a complete opposition between these two presentational ideas. It is an opposition, in fact, between the tastes of two different spectators. When we speak of the art of the theatre as a whole, we state a preference for the painter's theatre. But the devotee of the screen, as well as the realist playwright and realist playgoer, states a preference for the photographic theatre. The players of modern comedy are "always the same", as the spectator declares when he has seen them appear in a score of different parts; but it may be he likes them to be always the same. It is quite possible to acquire the taste for plain personality on the stage. The spectator of the films has long ago acquired such a taste. He knows every dimple, if not every wrinkle, on the natural features of his favorite players. For him they actually interpret emotional values as no symbols can interpret them.

Let us grant that most modern plays, being in their nature photographic, require naturalism from the actor. It would be grotesque to introduce masks of human

21

features into the ordinary setting of a stage drawing-room, not to speak of the bedroom of theatrical commerce. But is it not equally grotesque to introduce plain, unvarnished features into the painter's setting for a poetic play? These same actors whom we know in modern comedy are called upon to play Shakespeare before a designer's background, under a producer's direction. They wear their costumes admirably, they speak their lines tolerably well, they are not without emotional understanding of the characters they play, and yet we recognize them as our old friends Smith, Brown and Robinson, good actors all, giving their well-known style, and changed not a whit since last we saw them on the photographic stage. The mask is lacking. The players are, in fact, appearing with their faces undressed; they are exhibiting a state of nature in the midst of a world of fantasy, because they and their producer have misconceived the unity of visual effect, the first of the unities of the theatre.

A few years ago, Mr. Granville-Barker painted the immortals of his "Midsummer Night's Dream", and they were variously described as "bronzed fairies" or "golden angels"; but his mortals were as mortals always are. Painted Malvolios and such-like dandies, I believe, have walked the stage of Max Reinhardt. Mr. Jean Cocteau has lately given "Romeo and Juliet" in a style that is neither realistic nor Elizabethan, but is rather influenced by the conventions of the ballet. If such experiments teach us anything at all, they remind us that the painted actor is inseparable from the painted scene and the painted actor implies not only an outward semblance of the mask, an elaboration of

Nickolas Muray

When Eva Le Gallienne plunged headlong into the director-
ship of the Civic Repertory Theatre in 1926, she made her
home in the old 14th Street Theatre which long ago had housed
Ristori, Adelaide Nielson, and Edwin Booth. The life of a successful star, even a success such as she achieved in Molnar's
"The Swan" (pictured above) did not satisfy her creative
sense of what life in the theatre might mean. She preferred
to go back to the tradition established by Mrs. Drew, mother
of a distinguished line of American players, who ran a repertory theatre in Philadelphia years ago. Miss Le Gallienne
evidently agreed with the American statesman who said that
"the only way to resume is to resume."

the ordinary make-up, a closer harmony with the designer's background. He implies also an inward symbolism of character, an other-worldliness of creation that is needful to transform life into poetic imagery. The painted actor implies style in the theatre, as the spoken word of the drama implies style in conversation. The painted actor implies rhythm and poise and dignity, as the actor of the realistic drawing-room implies the easy gestures of habit and convention. The painted actor is the visible symbol of an imaginative reality. The natural mask that we call his technique and the natural movement that we call his stage presence are only the groundwork of his art. Upon them is imposed his other self, his painted self, which is truly the emotional self of the spectator absorbed in the drama.

We cannot ask of the actor that he should be a poet. If actors were poets, they would not be actors. Nor can we ask of him that he should be a critic, or a man of letters who appreciates literary values in every speech he is called upon to utter. If actors were critics, they would be poor actors indeed. Many a Shakespearean performance has been ruined by too much critical consciousness on the actor's part. We cannot ask of the actor that he should be a historian, a philosopher, a spectator of the drama in which he appears. None of these matters is properly within his province. We demand that he should be a symbol, and this is the only reasonable demand. To our eyes he is a symbol of reality, of poetry, of the theatre. If he be truly a symbol, he will appear before us in the guise of a painting and not of a photograph. He will walk the stage of the artist's theatre, not of the theatre of pretended reality.

How to merge the actor's make-up in the actor's mask, how to harmonize personality with symbolism — these are the eternal problems of stage presentation. They are not to be solved by reaction to the methods of the past. The permanent frown of the villain and the permanent smile of the comedian alike belong to a dead theatre, which has nothing more to say to us. The ironic Strindberg, a generation ago, observed the ghastly consequence of a smile upon the permanently frowning villain's face. But he was for naturalism at all costs, and he declared roundly that "no author has the right to pass summary judgment upon the characters he creates." He claimed for his stage personages the simple right to live in their own fashion, as individuals. After a long experience of the naturalistic theatre, we are no longer able to accept this theory of spontaneous generation in the actor's art. We hold that not only the author, but the stage director, possesses the right of summary judgment upon created symbols. If we seek the painted actor in place of the lifelike actor, it is not that we belittle the actor's art. We believe this art holds possibilities of expression that far transcend personality and realism as they are understood on the stage today. The painter's theatre must be an actor's theatre, if its harmonies are to have meaning.

SOURCES IN ART

By Stark Young

The average man is apt to approach art as he approaches the world around him, with a set desire to make it work, to see that it makes sense, and fits the special scheme that he has come to hold. As to the world around him he is quite right. He must not let it swamp him with its mystery and size, but must bring to bear on it his own thought and philosophy. To rationalize our experience in the world and our contacts within it is our noblest obligation, provided always we recognize the due place and limitation of our reason. The average man's judgment of the world is, except where science has got a hold on him and hedged him within the bounds of the strictly knowable, a vague adaptation of the universe to himself and to his dearest notions. Since he has only himself to go by, only his dreams and opinions and aspirations, he ends by measuring the world by himself.

Art, however, is not only part of this world around the average citizen but adds to his complications by being itself a form of life, quite as a man is a form of life. And with the problem of art and its sources goes all that is mysterious in vitality, and all that is literal, impersonal, and final. So that, if our man pursues the matter of sources in art with anything like the honesty of, in his field, the average biologist, he is apt to come to a most unmoral frame of mind.

This thinking, critical average man approaches the sources of art exactly as he approaches the universe or the vitality in himself or the phenomena of biology. He desires to make out the best case possible for himself, for the universe, and for art. It ought to be true, he argues, that what is good proceeds only out of what is good; and so he goes on, talking about good in two different senses: though he might as well speak of the goodness of the chemical reaction that promotes an affectionate impulse, or of the piety of a muscle that helped St. Francis lift up the leper. He might meanwhile well be asking himself certain useful questions: why is it, for example, that the great artist may not always be considered an admirable man? why is it that the admirable man is not always a great artist? what kind of man in the long run most benefits society? and so on, but he does not ask them. Confront him then with the artist, say Byron, and see what happens. Byron is obviously a great poet. He left records of his power and he created many expressions of human experience, in themselves magnificent and for magnificent human ends. Our thinker is troubled in fitting the creator of these admirable fruits to the pattern of excellence that seems to satisfy his ideas. Byron's life is full of things that he cannot properly endorse — Byron's pettiness, his hair in curl papers, his vanity, his temper, his avarice and extravagant generosity, his affairs with women, his impatience — these are not the qualities that one might recommend nor are they excellent traits of character. Something has to give way; either our thinker's philosophy is discredited or Byron is. What shall the thinker do about it? Well, after all, the test is the fruit; by their fruits we shall know them. If our thinker's admirable man contributes to the future some superb expression in art of experience, or in some action, or in his social relationships expresses himself in terms of other men superbly, he may be as great as Byron. But without something to his credit of creative fruits in art or thought or social relationships, the case is against him. He may have had the most excellent intentions and — for the sake of a good illustration let us say — opportunity also, but the result has not been significant. The difference that has arisen between him and Byron, then, must have been traceable to some original source. And our thinker must therefore ask himself all over again what the sources are of a great artist's work.

The sources of art have at their origin no more to do with character or morality than biology has; they are as single in themselves as the colors are on a palette. The original and fundamental endowments for art parallel exactly what we commonly acknowledge as endowments for boxing or soldiering, the difference being that the artist's endowment — except for certain obvious natural gifts like a fine voice — is subtler and less discernible. An artist's fundamental endowment, no matter what else may be later implied, is one of vitality. In him there is a fountain of life welling up. And certain raw elements, temperamental ores, elements that we might speak of as richness and complexity and depth of feeling, passion, vividness of impulse, cerebral vigor, elements that we might speak of as force and sensitiveness, these are the things that constitute the fundamental source of art. And from this fact arises what comes at last to be the fundamental test of all art, I mean power.

It by no means follows, of course, that the possession of this well-spring, this vitality, this essential power, makes a man an artist. It may at the contrary extreme make him only a great liver of life. But the point here is that it is the basis of the artist's gift and the sustaining substance of his talent. And in the end whatever other elements are involved, either to perfect or impede the success of his art, the possibility of his being an artist at all or not depends on the amount that he may have of this natural gift.

When we have once placed this stress where it belongs, we may go on and say that, after all, the art is the whole man. This pressure of vitality, this abundance of life, this sensitive and forceful response to experience in the world, emerging into expression, pours through the artist's complete self and, molded and tinged with ideas and habitations and influences, takes its final shape. And it depends for the final form of its expression on the ideas alive around the artist, the conceptions, the mode of living, the artist's chance for experience and his digestion of it.

A considerable part of this chance of the artist's for experience, turns on the matter of external influence. And nothing bears more distinctly on the discussion of these fundamental sources in art and nothing more happily illuminates the nature of them, than does this subject of the external influences to which the artist is subjected. Take the art of the theatre, by way of example. Of mere names and titles and stock situations and stock characters borrowed by the theatre of one epoch or one country from another, the instances are innumerable. Everyone knows them in scores, though other centuries — Molière, Shakespeare, Ben Jonson, the dramatists of the Restoration — have borrowed more openly than ours, lifting persons and plots with little change whenever desired, while we tend to imitate and adapt. But an influence if it goes no further than such borrowing is of small significance. The significance of an influence on an artist is measured precisely by the extent to which it achieves in him a release of power, of the life pressing up from within him. The influence of ideas, either large ideas like heredity and the problem of justice, for example, or more limited social ideas like questions of marriage relations and taxation, is significant for art only in so far as it carries the artist to new ground and extends the expression of himself. The influence of an art form on the artist is really significant only in so far as it can release something in him that other forms do not serve so well, only in so far as it provides a statement more expressive of him. And a borrowed form that does not do this is only a piece of imitation or a copy, a mere outer accident in art. But from any profound standpoint, form and idea are largely inseparable, since, as Spencer said, soul is form and doth the body make. In art an idea passing over as an influence from one time or place to another carries with it a form or method that expresses it; and a form carries an idea that meets

29

the need of some matter waiting for expression. The Renaissance ideas of love, of splendor, of the tragic, brought with them when they came from Italy to England patterns of art to embody them. Plautus and Terence took over from the Greek both typical forms and their accompanying comment on human society. In Marlowe's mighty line Shakespeare accepted and carried to deeper proficiency a release for the audacity of his imagination. Ibsen showed Pinero how to think — in so far as he really had any urgency of thought — in new terms. Tchekov's realism may show some artist of the theatre among us the approach to a more poignant and quivering revelation of our visible and audible life, may suggest a means by which what seemed dumb and silenced with the limitations of the realistic method, may be given its release in expression. From French drama, Molière especially, we may learn how to express the haunting sense we have that every man seen at his unique truth, freed of all characteristics but his own, becomes the type as well as the individual. The Spanish theatre can show a way of passing without self-consciousness from prose to verse and back again as the emotion of the scene dictates, and so of bringing the rhythm of expression closer to the flux of our experience. The Italian theatre may exemplify the possibilities of a unified and vivid body as a dramatic medium. There are many such influences. But influence can in the end only release what is in the artist. It can give him intentions, channels, forms, freedoms, and new patterns; but afterward everything must depend on the artist's gift and its essential power and abundance.

Henri Manuel

When in 1917, under the direction of Jacques Copeau, the
Théâtre du Vieux Colombier came to the old Garrick Theatre
where Harrigan and Hart had played, it made a bridge between the old theatre and the new. The American imagination was just ready to be fired by the practice and ideas of this
distinguished director who was, at the same time, actor, designer, and playwright. Above, Copeau as Felix Deronge
in his own play, "The House Into Which We Are Born."

SOURCES IN ART

This external mass of conceptions, ideas, influences, relations with the world, may be called the artist, quite as much as may the inner source of his talent, the fundamental endowment that makes his art possible at all. And these ideas and relationships and this character may be quite as much determined by this fundamental natural endowment as his art is. And without the idea, the character, the mold of circumstance, the art could, obviously, not come into existence. Indeed the desire of all art is to achieve in the passing some permanence, to arrest the transiency of fleeting things by fixing on them the idea, and so bringing into what might otherwise be but temporary material and sheer accident, some formal intention; even as in the natural world the chaos of atoms is moved perpetually toward ideas or forms of things. In all this transient incident and material of his power, in all this pressure of life in him, this cerebral and passionate activity, the artist wishes to create a pattern and duration. What is in him he wishes to perpetuate in terms of idea.

All that is true enough, but the accent should fall first on the artist's endowment at the source of his art. A triumphant piece of art is at its first source a sheer animal triumph. If this fact is not remembered, we may be lively and highly contemporaneous lovers of art but are poor judges. Not to know this leads us into all sorts of absurd positions.

If he does not know this, our average thinker — to return to him — is first of all put in a position of forgiveness; he must constantly explain and make allowances, before artists and forms of art may be approved. With this Byron of his — to return to Byron — he must

31

forgive much. But why? His business is to understand. And to understand Byron implies first of all
knowing that the elements of genius in Byron were the
elemental sources of life in him, and that the things that
enabled Byron to let himself go in poetry produced the
abandon less commendable in other directions. The
same thing that made Byron feel the quality of his
experience as he did, made him subject to the distractions and violences of living, as the tips of our fingers
may experience both the surface of a marble and the
blistering of fire, or as fire is by the same quality radiant
and consuming. Our thinker may forgive the universe if he likes, but he will not get very far in art
by forgiving Byron.

Our thinker's next step, under his malicious fortune,
will be to become theological about the world. He will
deny this and rearrange that, to make all suitable. He
will be led into some position like that of the college
presidents who discussed not long ago the question as
to whether every young man had a right to a college
education; the answer being, yes, certainly, just as
every chambermaid has the right to be a prima donna,
the real question being has she the throat? If he has
not this straight about the sources in art our thinker
will land where he cannot bring himself to understand,
or to admit, that it is possible enough — if we carry our
principle to an extreme illustration — that many young
lady musicians would, from the standpoint of their
musical volume and flexibility, be greatly improved if
they went to the dogs. Certain phases of such a life
might very well affect unpleasantly their taste and
style in music, but so far as the sources of music are

concerned, the sensitive power and abundance, this utter break-down in the young lady's life might be highly valuable.   And there are plenty of actors who, so far as the volume and current of their art is concerned, might act better if they killed a parent before going on the stage, since this might serve to release in the actor a certain flux of the material out of which acting arises, that he was otherwise unable to bring to the moment.   But that would be the last thing our thinker could admit.   In sum, if the devil should happen to have a physical ear for music that advanced him in it more rapidly than a deaf saint, our thinker, theologizing this world of his, would end either by denying that this artist with a good ear was the devil, or by denying that this devil was an artist.

Without knowing this about the sources of art our thinker runs the chance of confusing intentions with accomplishments and mere willingness with talent. And by trying thus to force the hand of art and make it fit with his own moral and ideal standards and prejudices, he gets his whole range of artistic judgment out of scale and full of incidental error.   In such a state he might think it impossible that Boston drawing-rooms, for all their high-minded concern in the matter, may have contributed less to art than the cabarets of Montmartre, for all their smoke, nudity, and fumes of wine. He might not know that D'Annunzio brings more to the theatre in "La Citta Morta" than Galsworthy has done in "Loyalties."   Galsworthy has an honorable enough intention of portraying the working of various class loyalties and assumes to establish a vast fairness in his consideration of the matter.   But the play ends by bringing very little into living form, and it remains only an expert, thin melodrama that as convincing art is never quite created at all. D'Annunzio, regardless of the stage limitations of his piece, regardless of its static quality, brings to it an immense poetic endowment, and creates a region, an event, a state of soul that is beautiful and superb.

All this talk about sources in art may seem obvious, and ought indeed to be, as the finalities of rain and our own blood and nerves are. But among serious people dealing with art, the ignorance or obliviousness of, or the refusal to admit, this point concerning its fundamental source is the cause of most of the overrating of poor art. There is something evidently unpleasant about the business, as there is about nature frankly seen. One is loath to believe that some work that says what one wishes to find said, that some effort so admirably exerted, some pious intention toward noble achievement, makes in the end so poor a result as art. And yet we are driven to face the cold fact that art, being a form of life, has the same ruthless exigency and unescapable conditions that underlie all vitality. No philosophy, no honest purpose, no sheer strength of will — except in so far as will is propulsive image, an energy of the imagination — no sentiment and no idea, can in itself become a work of art. All these may complete and direct and exalt a work of art, if you like. As art they do not even begin to exist until they are created and filled from some elemental power and life.

THE LINEAGE OF SPEECH

By Windsor P. Daggett

AMERICA is on the look-out for a standard of speech. The regional dialects of North, South, East, and West and their half-hundred variants have gained their foothold through custom and local pride. Each regional standard adopted by the upper classes in that regional division is considered "educated" in its own home. These differences add local color and a certain vigor to American speech, and for the ordinary commerce of communication they have a practical unity. But English is a language of literature and of art. In the speech education of our schools and colleges, in the theatre, and in the assimilation of the foreigner the regional divisions are a severe handicap.

The educated foreigner whose ears are keen complains that no two Americans give him the same answer regarding individual sounds of English or the best form of cultured usage. He turns from one to another until his mind and his tongue are equally addled. In the theatre a mixed standard of speech that has no relation to the scheme of the play is distracting. In education a child of good pronunciation is sometimes classed as "defective" just because his teachers happen to know nothing in English but a single local dialect.

Super-added to this varied regional pride is a national-istic system that makes "The American Language", as separate from British English, assume importance as an ideal of geographical independence.

This refusal to look over the fence of regional and national boundaries gives a provincial outlook. A world language and an educated standard of pronun-ciation usually have an historical prestige of rather fixed importance. To teach English speech reasonably well necessitates knowing the history of English speech as the point of departure for estimating what the influence upon it of a national life in new territory may have been. What is the status of English as a world language? is a reasonable question, as well as what was standard English when America put her finger into the pie? To idealize spoken English as an art language for the singer and actor and the man of cosmopolitan culture, necessitates an evaluation of English that has out-grown any line-fence and any national geography. This delocalized English must cease to be "their" English or "our" English and become a universal English that is the servant of men's thoughts. This is obviously the ideal for an art language, and its merits as an ideal of education are worthy of consideration. The acceptance of such a standard is the surest means of minimizing the regional skirmishes and the antagonis-tic formation of line-fences.

One approach to the question is to ask how other lan-guages have arrived at a standard of speech. In France, an idealized speech of Paris is standard usage, its superior purity being carefully conserved at the Théâtre Français. An idealized speech at Madrid, a sort of purified Castilian, is accepted the world over as the standard dialect of Spanish. In Italy, the speech of Tuscany, starting in the speech of Florence, holds the honored place. Italians who understand hardly a word of the standard dialect will throng at a public meeting to hear their language well pronounced. In Germany, no local dialect met the requirements of a standard speech, but a committee of linguists, actors, and managers in 1898 agreed upon a theatre pronunciation with the result that the Bühnenaussprache agrees with the best usage of German pronunciation.

English has its traditions, and a cultured dialect of English was already in world use when America was born. Chaucer had lived and died a century before the new world was discovered. Yet if he walked into our midst out of his fourteenth century we would be able to converse with him, and if he heard Ethel Barrymore in *Declassée* talk about April in England, he would know that he was hearing the English language, the pronunciation a little altered by time. The *Atlantic Monthly* once published an account of the murder of Christopher Marlowe. It quoted from old documents of 1600 and earlier, and though the spelling is a little antiquated, the English is the same English in which the *Atlantic Monthly* and the morning paper of Detroit (with its verses by Edgar Guest) are printed month by month and day by day for any English reader in the civilized world. The print is in Chaucer's orthography. From his pen and generation standard English emerged. He wrote and spoke in the dialect of the English court which set the standard of London speech. His orthography was nearly phonetic. The setting up of Caxton's printing press in the Almonry at Westminster in 1476 and the popularity of Chaucer established his London dialect as the literary and spoken standard of English over the world.   Later changes have unified the spelling, modernized it as each generation has left the marks of its living upon it, but the bodily foundation is Chaucer's.   The following lines from his pen are easily read by any American boy :

> My peyne is this, that what so i desire,
> that have I noght, ne no thing lyk thereto,
> and ever set Desire myn herte on fire
> ek on that other syde, where so i goo :
> what maner thing that may encrese woo,
> that have i redy, unsoght, everywhere :
> me ne lakketh but my deth, and than my bere.

The speech of the American theatre is a direct descendant of this line from the time of Garrick.   In the drama, the English-speaking union has been strongest, most enduring and most progressive.   William Hallam, "father of the American stage", was a London actor, successor to Garrick's cradle at Goodman's Fields. "The First American Company" selected its repertory and cast its plays in London.   While sailing for America it rehearsed on the quarter deck of the *Charming Sally*.   It made its début in Williamsburg, Virginia, in 1752.   For the next hundred years the American stage was recruited from London and in 1827 it was a recruiting agent that brought John Drew's mother to American shores.   Maurice Barrymore, educated at Harrow and Oxford, father of Ethel and John and Lionel, made his American début as late as 1875.   To mention a Booth, a Jefferson, a Sothern, a Hackett, a Drew, a Barrymore, a Wallack, or a Holland is to mention American actors of English origin. All the Powers family, A. E. Warner, and dear Mrs. Whiffen were born in England. English actors oriented on the American stage are legion.

The art of the theatre has helped to preserve the unity of English as a world language. The speech of the theatre is an unofficial arbiter of American regional differences of sound and distribution of sound. Edwin Booth was American born, an exclusive American product if you will, but as he wrote in 1881, his pronunciation and enunciation "amazed the English" although he was frequently criticized by Americans. John Barrymore in his turn has amazed the English by his pronunciation free from regional influence.

Enough remains to be done to improve the speech of the theatre, its carelessness, its indistinctness, its mixture of dialects among the young recruits, and a lack of certainty regarding preferable use in certain classes of words. The actor, like the school-boy, needs historical education to know what he is about in a revival of Sheridan or in the dialects of "Trelawny of the 'Wells.'" But the best speakers on the stage, whether British or American, in a modern play are in pretty close agreement in delocalized pronunciation, and intonation as well as other national differences are liberated into a universal art form.

The beauty of spoken drama depends on two things, genius and the magic word, and the magic word is the work of genius. No scheme of elocution, no book on the etiquette of speech can take the place of emancipation of the mind, tongue, and voice. No school of thought, no organized effort can do more than encourage the individual creative impulse and stir the individual ambition. The magic word is a combination of voice and speech and of the actor in all his being. It is created by myriad forces and can be described only in its details and by such qualities of its creativeness as can be suggested. But a very practical and fundamental part of the magic word is pronunciation. Here there must be some standard to go by, some scale of values from good to bad, from well-bred to vulgar, from modern to out-of-date, from general to local. A theatre without a standard of speech is more or less an orphan, not to say a child of questionable parentage.

"The best speech in America is heard on the stage." That is the unanimous judgment of the best scholarship in the country. True it is that some of our older actors neglect what they know and some of the younger ones do not know what they neglect; that our actors would not always have an authoritative answer if questioned about disputed pronunciation of certain words, and that there is no tribunal or superior court to turn to in such cases. But with educated actors there is a remarkable degree of uniformity in the dialect of English which sets the standard of Good Use in the American theatre. This dialect makes no pretense at being an "American Language." It gives the power of communication a wider clarity than geographical boundaries, and it is neither *pro* nor *con* in the narrow confines of nationality. It enables an actor, be he English or American, to speak English without raising any question about his birth certificate or the date of his passport; it makes a perpetual cry of "Federal Language" or "American Language" seem rather foolish. Emancipation of language is a throwing off of belittling localisms and regional mannerisms and a finding of a common denominator of universal acceptability. Every language has such a common denominator and it is the business of the stage to stand by it. Without a norm of this stability there is no means of gauging the varieties of English that are appropriate to fluctuations of time and place.

There are among the "American Language" boosters two theories about the variations that have grown up in American speech in different parts of the country. One is that they are the natural outgrowth of differences in living in different communities. In certain minor ways this is true, not so much in pronunciation as in the creation and adaptation of words to new uses of climate, industry, and trade. And as far as it is true it is an expressive, if not always a beautiful, growth.

But the chief contention, strongly held and vehemently defended, is that the differences are an inheritance from different social castes, each region defending the superiority of its own early aristocracy by defending their dialectal speech. The truth of the matter is that practically every dialect of American speech is a dialect of English speech marked not only as to the quality of the folk who brought it, but especially as to the date of their coming. The purity of the thing in its archaic splendor is heard in the out-of-the-way places. The seventeenth Century English-English of the Carolina Mountains in Lula Vollmer's "Sun Up" has been greatly relished in London where the only two words that missed fire were "crap" and "blockadin." The Middle English "hit" for "it" probably struck home much quicker in London than it did in New York.

Our American ancestry did have its smatterings of aristocracy, but these belonged to no particular region or set of colonies. The distinction between Cavaliers and Roundheads, either in England or America, had no real significance in respect to lineage or social rank. John Fiske makes this perfectly clear in his history of Old Virginia and her neighbors. Peerage and commonalty mixed and overlapped in the old country and mixed and overlapped further on the new soil. Differences in American speech are far more a matter of isolation and stagnation than of differences in caste.

An American actor from the Coast was discussing his problems in pronunciation. He says "ahffice" for "office" and "ahpportunity" for "opportunity." When he came to New York he considered his pronunciation good; he had had the standard teaching in the region he came from. It was "natural" to him, and he refused to become self-conscious in his speech by learning new habits. But experience taught him that he was turned down on good parts when a more modern pronunciation, according to standards of the theatre, was required. This sent him back to study the lineage of Chaucer. "Dog", he found, was originally "dog" in pronunciation, then it changed to "dahg" in western England. During the seventeenth century this ah-pronunciation became fashionable and widely spread, and during this time it was introduced into America. Today it may still be heard in the south-west of England and over considerable territory in America. John Daniel Kenyon gives this ah-pronunciation of "o" spelling in his book on American speech. He claims that this usage represents the cultured speech of his locality in the Western Reserve of Ohio and believes that it is fairly uniform in the speech of the North from New York State west. Be that as it may, to the New York stage, the pronunciation is not only regional and dialectal but seventeenth century, and it keeps a first class "western" actor from playing first class parts in good speech. To make "dahg" the standard of the theatre would be to turn history and drama upside-down.

"Dahg" was restored to its original "dog" in the eighteenth century by the purists, partly to suit the spelling, and it has remained there ever since. With the ah in "dog" came the ah in "hot" and "God" and "opportunity." Granted that this ah-pronunciation is wide-spread here, what shall be done about it in determining standards? Shall the stage go back, or Western Reserve come forward?

The old Charlestonians were capable of a gallant and intellectual gesture. When Henry James visited there not many years ago, he listened to reminiscences of lace-capped old ladies whose English, he said, reminded him of the rhymes of Pope. Here was an aristocracy of American culture, but a southern dialect "in the rhymes of Pope" is hardly the thing for Walter Hampden to use in playing Cyrano even in Charleston. And the lace-capped old ladies who talked to Henry James were not talking, beautifully, an American language, but eighteenth century English, a heritage from

43

their grandfathers' speech, which — away from the rush of social (which includes linguistic) progress — had become the regional dialect.

The state of Arkansas has produced Davy Crockett and has also added to our store of comic legend and native humor. Senator Jones, one of her famous speakers, began: "Mr. Speakeh, God damn you sah, I've been trying for half an hour to get your eye," and he then proceeded to condemn a bill proposing to change the name of Arkansas to Arkansaw. Is that, perhaps, our American language?

These United States are united by railways and a central government. In artistic and social tradition they are segregated. The early centers of aristocracy were independent and local. With colonial self-interest and new boundary pioneering, however rapid and grandiloquent, a good deal of American life has been provincial. American speech habits are largely concerned with the territorial expansion and the frontier lines of the historical atlas.

The outstanding Eastern pronunciation of the North and the outstanding Southern pronunciation, together with smaller regional differences old and new, have been shuffled over and over again in the democratic mixture of hitting the westward trail and settling new territory. The speech of Oklahoma, for instance, where everybody came from somewhere else all of a sudden, is a modification of a little of everything that the country offers. And so in different degrees of mixture and accentuation the dialect of each State is explained. But when it comes to a standard, local pride and desire for supremacy are expressed in the

THE LINEAGE OF SPEECH

attitude of Mr. Kenyon's book on American pronunciation: "This is the way we pronounce it at the Western Reserve of Ohio."

Now, between Mr. Kenyon's "American Pronunciation" and Henry Cecil Wyld's "History of Modern Colloquial English" there is a vast difference in attitude of mind and historical scope. Mr. Kenyon talks about Ohio in the year 1924. Mr. Wyld talks about five hundred years of speech lineage. He shows, for instance, that the pronunciation of "house" has gone through eight or ten changes from the time of Chaucer to Tennyson, that "blood" has gone through five or six changes, and so on through "chair", "heart", "fruit", "tune", and practically every word in the language. Here is the testimony of ages that makes today's pronunciation of Ohio assume a position of only relative importance.

The stage is already exerting an influence in the direction of establishing a lineage of speech. In every university dramatic club and in every Little Theatre of importance someone is entertaining the thought of playing on Broadway. But word comes from those who have tried it that the local pronunciation will not do in New York. And sometimes the teacher of speech or the Little Theatre director is soundly scolded by the man who comes back because he has had to unlearn his pronunciation before he could play in a first class company.

The lineage of speech on the stage is of purer strain and less archaic than the speech of the South or West. Mr. Wyld traces the pronunciation of "house" through eight changes from Chaucer to Tennyson and the

45

final modern pronunciation will be found to be the standard of the stage. Any deviation from that pronunciation in American dialects will represent an earlier or a variant usage. That is why the educated American actor and the educated English actor practically agree, just as other cultivated Americans and Englishmen agree; and that is why the boy from Ohio disagrees.

It is the theatre that is up-to-date. The dramatist, whether he be a Pinero, a Zoë Akins, or a James Gleason, knows his dialectal scale of values. It is only by knowing the universal standard of English of Chaucerian descent that he can give grandfather an old-fashioned pronunciation and point his character in regional dialect. A relatively absolute standard English is the point of departure for setting off period, class, profession, slang, vulgarity, and the back country. Even where departures are relatively slight, the situation is pretty well defined in what the farmer said to William James: "There's mighty little difference between one man and another, but what little difference there is is mighty important."

THE PLAYWRIGHT AND THE DRAMA

THE PLAYWRIGHT AND THE DRAMA

THE material of each generation's plays, and the shape in which they are cast, change with the spirit of the life and the times they represent. "The soul is form and doth the body make." There is the same pioneering — in matter and manner — that is characteristic of progress in the other arts, and in science and politics and philosophy: first a battle for new ideas and then when these do not seem to fit into the old mold, a struggle for new molds to fit them. In all the arts, and all over the world, this after-the-war generation is felt to be a generation in transition and it seems impossible today to be objective enough to isolate either the material or the forms which will, in the future, most nearly represent our times. In the theatre especially, which always serves in the double capacity of record and of prophecy, it is easier to recognize iconoclasm and experiment than to measure the permanence of achievement. Critics are in agreement as to the fact that the old forms and the old matter are breaking down, but there is a wide divergence as to the meaning and the value of what is taking their place. We can ask ourselves about our own dramatists, for example: Is George Kelly, who makes a photograph of character and then adds his dramatic comment on it, more true to his time than Eugene O'Neill who paints only so much of a character as he needs to express an idea? Is O'Neill more notable as an iconoclast than as a playwright; is his gift of freedom from the "well-made play" more per-

manent than the contribution he has made to the gallery of
created characters? Is a play like Paul Green's study of
negro life, "In Abraham's Bosom", important because of the
poetry of its intention, or John Howard Lawson's "Processional" because it despised the use of poetry to portray an
unpoetic, mechanistic life? Is Ivor Brown of the *Manchester
Guardian* and the *Saturday Review* right when he makes a
fight for his own English idea of the theatre as the Kingdom
of the Dramatist; is Edouard Bourdet, the author of "The
Captive", right when he says a new code of morals and religion
has outmoded all the old dramatic conflicts? Or is it, perhaps, something broader than the drama that is changing; not
only the literature of the theatre but the theatre itself. As
Ashley Dukes says, "The theatre has a collective mind of its
own. It has a collective way of regarding the pageant of life
which is its everlasting subject.... And this mind changes,
this taste varies." One needs only to go back to Montrose
Moses' "The American Dramatist", which remains the best
record of the past in our theatre, to see how far the change has
carried us. That is why it seems wise here to supplement all
these arguments with essays on "Tragedy" and "Comedy"
and so to come back to permanent dramatic values, to the
qualities that have made the greatest plays of other days and
that have kept them alive through many generations.

THE PLAY IN TRANSITION

By Edouard Bourdet

In Europe today the opinion is quite generally held that the stage is going through a period of depression. Those who are concerned with the theatre, whether because of their profession or because of a more general interest, are forced to the melancholy conclusion that the standard of plays now being produced is steadily becoming lower and there are few competent dramatic critics who do not complain, at the end of every theatrical season, of the poor quality of the plays on which they are required to pass judgment.

The constant increase in the number of theatres, with the consequent multiplication of stages available to young authors; the very considerable and well-merited support that is given to the experimental theatres, which serve to introduce to the public the work of playwrights as yet unknown, or known only to a few — these things make the number and range of plays offered to the judgment of the press and public greater each year. But this profusion of plays should not give us any illusions as to the small number of really fine playwrights. If a boy who vaguely flourishes a pen in the ill-founded belief that he has something to say decides to write a play, I, for one, see no reason why he should be prevented. But it is necessary to do far more than tell some trifling story to earn the name of playwright. To write plays, the ability to give life to your characters, to create living beings on the stage, is essential.

The mere fact that very few authors of today possess this gift should not lead anyone to the premature conclusion that the theatre has reached a state of complete decay, because at any given period the really great playwrights have generally stood alone; so it was with Shakespeare and with Calderon; and (with the exception of the Seventeenth Century in France, where Racine and Molière flourished at the same time so it was with Ibsen and with Tchekov. However, even if the theatre is not altogether dead, one would be blind indeed not to recognize the fact that it is for the moment in a condition of decline. I should like to consider the nature of this decline, its importance, and its causes.

The real playwright, as I have just said, creates first and foremost living characters. But that is not enough. To merit stage production these characters should also interest us. To achieve this the author chooses some particularly arresting moment in their lives. That is to say, he brings them into conflict with someone or something, whether it be the conflict of man and woman in love, the conflict of the individual with society, the conflict of the individual with himself, or, finally, although more rarely in the theatre, the conflict of the individual with God. In the fact that it is becoming more and more difficult to produce this sense of conflict is to be found the main cause of the present decline in Europe not only of the drama but of the novel as well.

One of the greatest French novelists of the day, François Mauriac, has some singularly illuminating words to say on this subject. "If," he says, "the novelist were required to define this post-war day in which we live, he would signalize it as an age where all those conflicts to which, up to now, the novel owed its very life were constantly diminishing in importance." What François Mauriac says in connection with the novel is equally applicable to the theatre, with perhaps even greater truth, as I will try to show you in a moment. In further explanation of his point of view, Mauriac adds: "One can no longer expect the present generation to be satisfied, as were those of the eighties, with the faint fragrance that may linger in a broken vase. The young men and the young women of today refuse to consider themselves in any conflict either with a religion to which they no longer adhere, or with the code of morals that has developed from that religion, or with those formal conventions of society that are, in turn, built upon that code of morals. Their passions recognize no effective barrier; they stop at nothing. In other words, for them these conflicts no longer exist."

It seems to me that this is most concretely put — although it is at the same time distinctly disturbing so far as the actual sources of present-day literature are concerned. A young woman, the other day, before whom Racine's "Phèdre", one of the greatest works of French classical literature, was being discussed, admitted that she could not be in the least impressed by the remorseful lamentations of this unhappy queen.

"Why all this fuss about nothing?" she said. "As though it was n't the most ordinary thing in the world to fall in love with one's step-son!" The sufferings of Phèdre and Hypolitus could not provide the basis of a tragedy today. At the most it would seem, to five out of seven of our sophisticated moderns, legitimate material for some cheap burlesque. Mauriac concludes his reflections by saying, "How could an age where everything pertaining to the flesh has lost so tremendously in significance be a productive period for writers?"

Here it is, if I am not mistaken, that we find the main reason for the present decline in the theatre. The other causes of conflict that have for so long nourished whole categories of plays are equally enfeebled or are in process of disappearing entirely. With the growth of cosmopolitanism, the doctrine of political and social equality, the intermingling of races and of classes, little remains today of all those suppositions upon which the most striking dramatic works of the last century (with the possible exception of the Russian theatre, for reasons that are too long to go into here) are founded. The remarkable dramatic construction of many of these plays makes it still possible to produce them from time to time, but the moral, human, and social foundations upon which they depend, tend to make us smile and are chiefly interesting to a present-day audience as historical studies of a period that is past. Confronted with the society of today, where the familiar conflicts of both the novel and the drama are becoming less and less important, what is left for the novelist or the playwright to do? Their respective situations are quite dissimilar. The novelist without going any further can follow the famous definition according to which "a novel is a mirror set up in a crowded thoroughfare." And without troubling himself with any more questions, he can limn his epoch quite as it seems to be, following scrupulously his profession of expert witness, of observer of society. In this case, the characteristic absence of conflicts instead of embarrassing him can serve as the very subject of his delineation. In France, for instance, Paul Morand devotes his unquestioned art to this type of observation. His books "Ouvert la Nuit" and "Ferme la Nuit" show us men and women of all races and of all classes that pursue each other, take each other, leave each other, and find each other again, knowing no barriers, obeying the impulses of the moment, recognizing no other law than that which drives them to a constant search for a further and further refinement of their sensations. Morand succeeds with singular felicity in putting before us a picture at once pitiless and savage. He has found in France and elsewhere a great many imitators. The followers of this school find their literary material constantly replenished by the evolution of that society which they describe and the more rapid this evolution, the more material for the novelist.

The playwright, however, is in a very different case. He lives, it is true, in the midst of a society that could and should serve him as a model. It is a society, however, that, while it no longer respects most laws and is, moreover, quite willing to accept a completely realistic portrait of itself in a novel, cannot endure to see itself represented with the same realism upon the stage. The reason for this is, doubtless, that the novelist addresses himself to us as individuals. When we read a book we are alone with the author. No matter what our reaction may be on reading his book, this reaction concerns ourselves alone and we are not accountable to anyone else. In the theatre, on the other hand, our judgment is no longer completely free. It becomes a part of the judgment of those around us. For the reaction of the individual is substituted a crowd-reaction — that mysterious crowd that we call the Public. If there is any passage in a play that takes us by surprise or shocks us, we resent not only our own shock and discomfiture but the sum of the shock and discomfiture sustained by the entire audience. If the playwright ventures even a trifle too far in pursuit of the truth of his subject, the spectator who might have read before dinner, without turning a hair, a novel ten times more audacious in theme and form, will leave the theatre indignant with this presumptuous writer who has had the temerity to put such a thing on the public stage.

It has been said that the theatre is before everything an art of deletion. Nothing could be closer to the truth. Take the most trite circumstance, such a thing as you might read of any morning in your newspaper, and try to put it on the stage in strict conformance with life, conceding nothing to the customs or prejudices of the public. Hardly anyone would put up with the spectacle.

It would, however, be a mistake to believe that this public that will not submit to be shocked by what is presented on the stage — and that has a perfect right not to submit — will bestow its favor on plays of an old-fashioned type that simply handle honestly uncontroversial subjects. We live in an age when people can no longer become excited about anything unless it is exceptional. Old methods are no longer in vogue. Something new everywhere and all the time is what is wanted. The audience says to the playwright, "Go, seek, find me something that I have never yet seen. Bring it to me. Life is bitter and weary. I go to the theatre to forget. Do something to distract me, to astonish me, or to move me; but beware! I will only tolerate the unexpected up to a certain point. My emotions may be aroused for certain causes only. If you lose your way or if you go too far, I will denounce you."

It is thus that the playwright of today, harried, pushed by an obscure feeling of what is expected of him, no longer able to consider the moral, social, or religious conflicts on which his predecessors thrived because they are no longer founded on real life, finds himself at the same time up against the danger of not being followed by anyone at all if he ventures too far into unexplored regions.

A French humorist has defined the successful author as "one who possesses a special gift for laying his fingers on subjects that are neither excessively novel nor threadbare." If this definition is accurate, it is not a very encouraging outlook for the theatre. For while the desire for success is a dangerous mirage for any genuine playwright to follow in his work, it is none the less true that a play has no existence until an audience confers it. A novelist can, if he must, give up being understood or approved by his contemporaries. The future remains open to his books. The written word does not die. The spoken word, on the other hand, has an ephemeral existence and endures only as long as there is someone to listen to it.

A society that has ceased in its actual living to observe certain laws but has not given up demanding a respect for these same laws upon the stage, such seems to me to be the principal cause of the present decline of the European theatre. It is, to be sure, a decline of limited scope and which of course does not affect the literature of fantasy or of pure imagination. It is also a temporary condition, the inevitable consequence of an age of transition and one that will cease when this transition is completed. But it does seem worth while to delve somewhat into the origins of this condition.

Two designs for projected scenery by Herman Rosse — the first a pattern of lines and circles, the second a background of changing form and color for a grotesque dance.

THE DRAMATIST IN DANGER

By Ivor Brown

It is a curious thing that the rise of the cinema from a place among the toys to a place among the arts should be accompanied by a movement in the theatre that threatens to bind the spoken word in unhappy bondage to the spectacle. The cinema can express up to a point psychological subtleties and individual reactions: but this delicacy of facial and bodily play, great as it may become with the finer arts of the studio, can never be as great as the combined delicacy of speech and motion that is realized upon the stage. The cinema has its own advantages: it can put a girdle round the earth and keep pace with Puck himself. It can deal in mass-effects and crowd-effects that are far beyond the scope of even the mightiest play-house. It can create, by the technical trickery of the camera, atmospheres that defy the stage-director, though his equipment be charged with the full powers of electrical invention. The cinema can cultivate its own kingdom with science and imagination; it is, in fact, doing so. But it cannot extend its kingdom, since its own silence stands, like the angel with the flaming sword, to keep it from straying. No dramatist whose spoken word is worth listening to can be effectively filmed, because the virtue of his language must ooze away in the process. Therefore, one would imagine, as the cinema gains ground the theatre will defend itself by concentrating its own strength and fighting on its own position. It will make human speech its fortress. It will not try and imitate the new stuntsmanship of the studio: it will not set the dramatist in thraldom to the producer whose mind is a league of effervescent notions: it will rather rely upon the old craftsmanship of pen and voice. It will fight with rhythm and beauty of speech, with deftness of dialogue, with the melody of poetry, and with the music of the actor's voice. Experience supports this view, since the greater the dramatist the less can be filmed.

So far the theatre has met cinema competition by yielding to it. In the drama vaguely called "Expressionist" the debt to the cinema is obvious and the kind of play that comes from Central Europe, either actually or by imitation, that is to say, the kind of play which is fashionable with our intellectuals on both sides of the Atlantic, is just such stuff as the best films are made of. Whenever I see or read a play by Kaiser I cry out for the producer of German films. The essence of Rice's "The Adding Machine", of Kaiser's "Gas", and "From Morn to Midnight" is nothing individual: the dramatists deal with forces, masses, economic systems, factories, Salvation armies, velodromes, spectacles. Accordingly the whole thing might be better realized in the idiom of the up-to-date cinema. But instead of telling the studio-producer to prepare his bag of tricks and get on with the job, the expressionist (or it might be more accurate to say the antirealist) takes up the bag of tricks and brings it into the theatre. And so the one thing in which the theatre is unique, its command of polished or of mighty speech, of the color that lies in rhythmic utterance, and of delicate tonal variations, is made secondary to spectacle which a man can get for nothing from nature, or for very little from the picture house. The dramatist, in short, is surrendering to the cinema, not defying it.

The dictatorship of the dramatist in the "realistic and argumentative theatre" has been deplored and a condominium between author, producer, and actor demanded. The playwright has even been informed that "to write for the theatre is to write a libretto that may be made into an opera." Yet individuality is the essence of any work of art and a man who thinks that the passport to theatrical activity is a document of surrender to actor and producer may help to create a spectacle but can hardly succeed with a play. A play is made in the mind of a man and is then handed to the stage for the most effective representation, in which task various specialists collaborate. But if it is a work of art at all and not just a piece of raw material for commercial exploitation, it must have had a finality when it left the author's mind and hand. That is its value; accordingly that is what producer and actor must preserve. They should be the honored servants of the author: here, as elsewhere, equality of power means anarchy.

A written play is frequently thought of as something "plastic": I think of it as something formed. The translation from paper to stage is a process in which technical skill is needed. But that is no reason why the technician should conceive it to be his right or his duty to add his own notions of mood or form. Once admit that the author's business is only to hand to the play-house executive a malleable lump of thought and speech and the author's position as an author becomes insufferable. Writing librettos means laying foundations for another man's architecture: it is the job of a hack in many cases. Is the dramatist to be reduced to a scribe-in-waiting for the empurpled regisseur? That seems to be the position of the scenario-practitioner. Does any artist envy him his crouching, if profitable, stance? In any art, as in any state, sovereignty must be acknowledged and precise. Art is order, not anarchy. And if we want good drama we must place the responsibility on the dramatist, and give him his appropriate rights.

During the nineteenth century, the sovereignty of the theatre did pass very largely into the actor's hands. It was the age of "parts." And what "parts"! The great performers tossed these glittering opportunities from one to another, a Duse, a Bernhardt, a Mrs. Campbell would pick up these gages and enter the tournament of personal virtuosity. It was all very entertaining, no doubt, and produced some astonishing feats on the players' part. But it was shockingly bad for drama as a whole. The old plays are dead: they were only librettos and when the actors' music had left them, they deserved to die. Then Ibsen came and the true art of the theatre came back with him. He killed the libretto theory and reëstablished the dramatist as a person of artistic importance, thus driving Sardoodledom out of any play-house with the slightest claim to intelligence. The theatre lived again. It became an accepted and powerful medium of people who had something to say, which simply means that it was a medium of art and not an arena in which a Bernhardt could kindle the most marvelous bonfires out of anybody's stale faggots. In England intelligence flowed into the theatre because it knew it could do so without being subject to the tyranny of vainglorious actor-managers who considered a play in terms of "fat" for themselves, and "lean" for other people. It is significant surely that Shaw, the strongest of the new recruits, has always guarded his text most jealously, refusing to permit "cuts", and supervised his own productions. The theatre would be intolerable to him if his work was called "plastic" and handed over for other people to mold — and probably maul.

The post-Ibsenite movement gave the English theatre more vitality than it had ever had since 1700. This vitality was made possible because the dramatist had come into his own. He was allowed to write plays instead of librettos for star performers. He usurped the traditional function of the poet and became an unacknowledged legislator, and this without loss of the comic sense and quickening flame of wit. But the fashion passed on, as fashions will, and theatrical sovereignty began to pass with it. The producer who had been an executive agent became a ruler, a regisseur. Reinhardt was the pre-war master of his craft and he has had many followers. In Russia, Stanislavsky stood firm and his productions of Tchekov remained the perfect models of respectful interpretation of masterly writing. But Central Europe became infected with the notion that the first business of a theatre was to be something else and that there is no stage like the the stage that is n't there. We were taken back to the circus, the arena, the platform. Simply to let the dramatist speak his mind was not enough : architects, electricians, and designers were busily engaged upon what Francis Bacon in his essay on "Masques and Triumphs" called "petty wonderments." The root of the new movement was a materialistic conception of art : the light of Schwabe-Haseit was held to be more illuminating than the light of the mind. The human factor was dwarfed by the constructional and mechanical and amid a general outcry of "Hats Off to Gordon Craig" one saw his design for "Hamlet" in which a midget stood amid soaring spaces. Here indeed was "Hamlet" without the Prince.

I have not the least objection to spectacular invention or to soaring columns with dwarfish manikins crawling at their feet or to a circus for the cultivation of mass-effects or to any of the apparatus of the up-to-date regisseur. These things have their corner and the dramatist has his. But they are not the same corners. The dramatist is distinctly in danger if he may not speak for himself, simply, quietly, and directly. The actor also is in danger from the dominance of spectacle and the increasing powers of the producer. I do not pretend that the thing has reached such a pass yet or nearly reached it. But the menace is there and should the strength and beauty of the spoken word be made subject to petty wonderments (which the cinema will always execute more wonderfully) then the play-house may add to its trappings but will assuredly lose its life.

Ernst Toller's play of revolution, "Masse-Mensch", at the Volksbühne was a notable achievement. Strohbach's designs were fundamentally enhanced by the use of light.

NEW FORMS FOR OLD

By Rosamond Gilder

Of all the arts that enliven and release the heart of man, the art of the theatre has the greatest tendency to crystallize, to turn from form to formula, and to accept a lifeless repetition in the place of dangerous and dynamic invention. The reasons for this are not far to seek, for the theatre is not the expression of a single daring individual. Plays cannot be tossed into the world like those flimsy first editions of "Leaves of Grass" — dynamite wrapped in paper to explode a world of pretty verse. The theatre is a painfully elaborate mechanism, requiring the coöperative effort of many individuals in order to bring to life the unembodied spirit of the script. The written word is a mysterious hieroglyph that to be understood must be interpreted by a band of initiates, directors, actors, scenic artists, musicians, and all the troup of craftsmen that work the ponderous machinery of the stage. The sculptor can hew his marble, hard as it may be, the painter can wrestle with canvas, brush, and pigment, the wielder of words needs but the barest of raw materials wherewith to clothe his vision, and each can obtain a certain permanence for his creations by his own unaided effort. Not so the playwright, for his play is literature and not theatre unless he can find a director, an actor, or a born fool who will put it upon the stage, and pay the heavy toll that production entails. No artist is so constrained by the economic necessities of his art as the playwright, and in consequence no artist is so driven and controlled by the accepted codes and formulas of his profession.

The tendency toward crystallization is strikingly evident in the theatre today. By far the largest number of plays on Broadway are patterned on the neat and effective formula of the "well-made play." Exposition, narrative, climax, dénouement — we sit for two hours and a half and are led gently along an expected path. We know just where attention may relax while the obvious is being explained; we can rest comfortably in our chairs while custom-made dialogue fills in a necessary stage wait; we know when and how we should be moved; we feel at the proper moment the proper ecstasy. With the rising of the curtain and our first glimpse of kitchen, dining room, or parlor we accept the inevitable march of pre-ordained stage events, and — if we are in any way alive to life and beauty and adventure — we are not amused. Familiarity with this particular form breeds not contempt but indifference. And familiarity with an accepted and successful cliché engenders an army of hack playwrights who have nothing to say but merely a method of saying it.

But the true artist is not content with repetition. He seeks instinctively a weapon that has not lost its cutting edge. Bound down as he is by material handicaps, the playwright of today is struggling against stultification. Yes, the young men are about their

God-given task of breaking up old formulas to make new forms of beauty.. So far, perhaps, the broken shards of the old are more in evidence than the beauty of the new, but the process is no less vital and life-giving for being as yet incomplete. Essentially, too, as far as the actual productions of the newer school of play-writing in America are concerned, we have to do with a re-adjustment of detail rather than a break in tradition. In Europe a more violent and radical experimentation has found its way into the theatres, but in this country the change is coming by peaceful penetration rather than by revolution. The re-adjustment is the more valuable and important for being gradual, for it proves itself to be the healthy outgrowth of a living theatre rather than the result of a streak of freakish inventiveness.

Considered from the purely technical point of view, the striking feature of what Mr. Lawson calls the new showmanship is its return to a pre-Shakespearian scene sequence — the liberation of the playwright from the confinement of the three, four, and five act form which has held the legitimate stage for so many years. Where Jones and Pinero built the slow ascending curve of the "well-made play", creating a steadily increasing tension and rising to a single climax, the modernist lets off his Gatling gun of experiences — a volley of scenes in rapid succession, each one complete, climactic, independent, connected only by the thread of life itself — the life of the human being whose individual and typical experience is being unfolded. So in 1588 Christopher Marlowe told the "Tragical History of Dr. Faustus" in fourteen consecutive scenes each complete in itself, each taking place in a different locale, each characteristic of some phase of Faustus' experience, without forcing that experience into the limitations of time and space that a three-act form, founded more or less on the classic unities, would require. It is the Everyman technique and it re-appears today when dramatic biographies are in vogue, in such astonishingly divergent forms as Lawson's "Roger Bloomer", O'Neill's "The Great God Brown", and Sidney Howard's "Lucky Sam McCarver." In the field of romantic drama Shakespeare's scene sequences are the direct progenitors of what is today referred to as the movie technique in play construction. We are so accustomed to thinking of Shakespeare in terms of a five-act tragedy molded to fit an equal number of portentous scene sets heavy with archæology and gorgeous trappings that we forget the twenty scenes of "Hamlet" and the forty-two breathless shiftings of time and place that build the immortal tale of "Antony and Cleopatra." During the reign of the well-made play Shakespeare as a playwright was looked upon with pity and compassion, and generously remodeled to fit the prevalent idea of form. Today the younger writers find in him, unconsciously, an ally. The quick-fire staccato effectiveness of the short scene, the flexibility and variety of the changing locale, the clarity of presenting rather than reporting events, all these qualities of vigor and sincerity have been recaptured by a reversion to scene sequence in the telling of a rapidly moving dramatic tale.

Not only is the formula of the three-act play being rejected where it is found inadequate, but the formalism of the three-walled stage is also being attacked.

Here again an amusing analogy is evident. The steel-girder, built-in set of the modern stage, with a changing back-drop and the barest suggestion of properties to indicate different scenes, with several acting levels and a generous equipment of exits and entrances, serves the same purposes and can be used in the same manner as the typical Elizabethan stage. Then a single platform was given variety and flexibility by the use of a permanent balcony and inner stage, tapestries and hangings were changed to fit the occasion, and the property man set the scene with a few indicative and decorative pieces of furniture which would suggest the time and place of the action. The modern scenic artist would find, indeed has found, no difficulty in Shakespeare's many scenes and by his freer and more imaginative methods he has allowed them to reëmerge in their intended order. The playwright today is no more hampered than was Shakespeare by the necessity of keeping within a prescribed number of interior, street or garden sets. He can flit as far and as fast as he chooses and a shadow, a spot light, the frame of a window, a silhouette against a cyclorama sky will indicate the place to which the imagination of the onlooker must follow him. Such a setting was that of Robert Edmond Jones for Hasenclever's "Beyond", which by the reduction of each scene to its ultimate irreducible meaning, by a masterly use of line and light, of color and form, created an atmosphere of remote loveliness for the twenty-three scenes of that strange odyssey of the human soul. Such a setting, to take an extreme contrast of content and therefore of treatment, was that of Donald Mitchell Oenslager for Faragoh's

"Pinwheel", where sixteen scenes of typical New York life were impaled on one permanent setting, suggestive of subway and skyscraper, but which, by a rapid adjustment of detail and the focussing of light on different sections, was made to carry the action from factory to tenement, from pool room to cabaret as the tale required. The extraordinary fluidity of such stagecraft will in time become as integral a part of the new forms of play construction as the fixed Elizabethan stage was part and parcel of Shakespeare's dramatic technique.

With the breaking up of the carefully elaborated pseudo-realistic play, many of its accepted smaller conventions have also gone by the board. Today a certain impatience is felt with the verbal *feu de joie* of the drawing-room comedy. Brightness *per se*, repartee, witty dialogue, obscure the issue and serve as padding to fill an evening's entertainment. A play centered on one climax can carry such light freight and still achieve its object, but when the pilgrimage of the soul of man is to be unrolled in the two hours and a half usually allotted to one episodic love affair, dialogue must be as stripped and telling as elimination can make it. In this effort toward a sincere and direct expression of the essential reality underlying a given situation a number of divergent methods have been evolved. On the one hand we have the long rhythmic outbursts of Yank in O'Neill's "The Hairy Ape" or the monologue of the Emperor Jones — direct expressions of the laboring subconscious minds of these bewildered men, on the other the newspaper headline jargon of "Pinwheel" dialogue limited to the few phrases, the constant dull repetition

Modern mechanistic life and all the cross rhythms of a modern
city are the theme of much of America's expressionist playwriting and production. "The Hairy Ape" of Eugene O'Neill,
John Howard Lawson's "Roger Bloomer" and "Processional",
"Skyscrapers", a ballet by John Carpenter and Robert
Edmond Jones, produced at the Metropolitan Opera House,
and "Sooner and Later", a dance satire by Irene Lewisohn
are examples of this. In the setting above, Donald Mitchell
Oenslager caught the satiric and picturesque flavor of "Sooner
and Later." It is a murky day when the puppet inhabitants
work at their different trades feverishly until the whistle blows.
A motorman cranks a machine endlessly, a tailor, squatting
cross-legged, cuts baby clothes futilely with enormous shears,
and a man in a traffic tower shrieks ceaselessly through a mega-
phone over the terrific noise of whistles and percussions.

which is the actual language of such people as the Guy
and the Jane. In this play the theatrical license of
building with words, of creating the impression of reality by an unreal effectiveness and resourcefulness of
speech is sacrificed in almost every scene in an effort to
convey the barrenness of these lives by an equally arid
barrenness of language. Two or three scenes, however,
resort to that "primary magic of the theatre, the magic
of the spoken word" so effectively that in this case
the tabloid method of expression is still left unproven.
In Hasenclever's "Beyond" we have yet another
method of approach. Here two people, present in the
flesh, drinking a cup of tea together, talk, not those
platitudes which are commonly exchanged over the
trivial affairs of the day, but the strange, groping, and
divergent thoughts which are present in each one's
mind. We hear this man and woman think, and as the
play progresses, their thinking becomes as it were
audible to each other, their words tend to converge
upon the same objects, only to part again on their fundamentally different points of view. Again, "Le
Tombeau Sous L'Arc de Triomphe" presents three
individuals whom the author has endowed with a cosmic gift of speech. We have a sense of the soul itself
receiving the gift of tongues. These people do not
speak with the subconscious mind of Yank, the conscious mind of the man and woman in "Beyond", or
in the street vernacular of the Jane in "Pinwheel."
Theirs is a language not of men but of angels. It is
the inmost spiritual essence of typical yet entirely
individual characters. Paul Raynal has had the courage to attempt verbal expression of a spiritual conflict

and not merely to suggest it by outward and visible signs in action and ordinary speech. Finally we have the purely poetic expression of abstract idea which does not attempt to approximate colloquial idiom but creates its effect through the emotional force of rhythm and harmony. The new freedom which permits the use of every resource of theatric expression from dull or violent realism to philosophic meditation and lyric outbursts has given the young playwright a wide field from which to select his medium of expression. He will perhaps learn once again the lost art of passing from prose to poetry, from poetry to song and prose again as was done in an older and more generous day. The rich store of language is released from the constraint of a fixed type of attempted realism and lies ready for the craftsman who can mould it to his uses. Slang and poetry are equally colorful and effective weapons and wielded as they are today with a new fearlessness, they have swept the merely clever dialogue from its pre-eminent position in the middle of the stage.

A natural corollary to the disruption of the accepted code of play-making has been the introduction into the newer forms of certain elements of theatre fare which have for a long time been considered out of place in legitimate drama. We have grown accustomed to carefully segregated types of entertainment, song and dance in one place, tears in another, moderate laughter and an occasional thought in a third, crime, passion, and adventure in the last stronghold of melodrama that still remains in a pulseless land. The new playwright will not tamely accept the limitation of a single species. Youthfully he attempts omniscience — and makes mince pie. But the pie has at least the spice of the unexpected and an evening of "Processional" is worth a year of tamer fare. In Lawson's combined maze we have vaudeville, tragedy, jazz ballets, murder, and the "Blues", a bit of "Hamlet", a bit of passion, a lyric interlude, and much noise, all uniting to make a satiric comment on the American scene. This mixture of elements makes for variety if not for harmony, and again, as in all points of technical equipment, depends for its success on the skill with which it is handled. As a tendency it is of the greatest value to the theatre, helping to restore to drama its original integrity, to re-unite action and word, song, sight, and rhythm in one dynamic whole.

Behind all these shiftings of emphasis, these revolts from formula, these experiments in theatre technique and dramatic craftsmanship there is a definite psychological movement. Artistic expression is inextricably linked with the social order which passes through a series of cycles from chaotic origins to a matured and balanced completion. Each time that a way of life, an ordering of elements, has been achieved society tends to become static, fossilized. Again and again that state which was once a hard-won dream, a longed-for ideal, becomes in a few generations a hardened and hindering rule. This is equally true of art, for in the realm of creative thought two currents are in constant conflict: one which has its source in a universal urge toward balance and proportion and tends towards the elaboration of a mould which will encompass beauty; the other a demoniac force seeking truth through a destruction of the outward shell, a trampling of the grape, a pursuit of what might be called the atomic structure of reality. . . .

> the mold to break away from, the crust to break
> through, the coal to break into fire. . . .

This need of destruction and re-creation is felt in every generation, but today it is more vocal than usual. Leaving aside its manifestations in political and social life it is strikingly evident in all the arts today. Poetry, painting, sculpture, music, and literature have been radically affected. The theatre in America, that stronghold of the safe and sane, has at last felt its breath. The results, inevitably, are chaotic, but from that chaos new forms will rise to take the place of the old, and to be in turn destroyed. The new craftsmanship demands, and on the whole has not yet received, as expert handling as the "well-made play" in the strictly limited sense of the term. Moreover the structural form associated with this phrase is so excellent and effective a medium for the expression of certain ideas and emotions that it will always hold its own upon the stage. Today we have such shining examples of its immediate value and effectiveness as Edouard Bourdet's "The Captive" and Sidney Howard's "The Silver Cord." But side by side with these neatly articulated, highly polished, and adroit specimens of the fine art of the theatre as we know it, we will have an increasingly dynamic and varied dramatic fare. As the public forgets its predilection for the type of play that it has known so long, and learns to look and listen with open eyes and ears and a receptive attention, we shall find in the theatre a renewed source of stimulation and delight. Even now new forms are evolving from the old to fit the kaleidoscopic needs of an incredible generation, and in the theatre as everywhere else we are once again assisting in the eternal drama of renewal and re-birth.

FENCES ON PARNASSUS

By Charles S. Brooks

We are still waiting for the great play or novel of American life to be written by an American. That is the customary formula, but it needs amendment if we would summon a diversity of talent. What we really want is great writing of any kind by anybody of any nation and we should not insist that it be of contemporary life or that it concern itself with America. Any one who is worth the prize has brains enough to choose a subject and the manner of its treatment. It is better for us, of course, if it be written in English, for then its value does not diminish in translation, but if we limit the field to American life and exact a closer realism we tie a hobble on the vagrant foot of fancy.

It is natural, perhaps, in a period when fashion smiles on barest fact that we should forget the less rigid fashions of the past — fashions that produced greater work than ours — and think that the only field proper to an author is the one that lies nearest to his eye. And most of us, therefore, to meet this current demand, become notebook writers, eavesdroppers with pencil sharp for scandal. We set an ear to the golden clink of profit and look incessantly at objects near at hand.

FENCES ON PARNASSUS

We lay our nose closely against a smell, because stench has become the fashion; and our brains, like the quick shutter of a camera, record a litter of detail but smudge all colors into gray. And even if we are not mercenary to catch an echo of popularity, we fear to follow another path and seem perverse, and a kind of shame impels us to do as we are told and march in the procession. Our critics, by asserting this narrow formula, would persuade us that literalness is the only truth and they cry down the rangier romantic methods of the past. These customs have bred a squinting, waspish school of writers.

There is a place, of course, for the camera in literature. I grant it right that a man who has dwelt in any village of Ohio — in any State you please — that such a man may with propriety give us an exact picture of the houses on its streets, of its tin-roofed shops, the gossip of its grocery steps, its people, the ox and ass and the stranger within its gates. If there be scandal, let him make the most of it in royalty! Or if there be something of gentleness and village beauty in the scene — material now neglected — these are his province, too. Or if a man's window reveals a crowded street where smells arise, where fire-escapes are shabby nurseries and there is noise and chatter all day long, let him make the worst of it by concealing its better aspect and suck thereby a bit of wealth from the dirtier side of poverty!

But if our whole reward is for books that deal with barest fact — with things that lie entirely before our eyes — and fancy is cried down, then we pinch our field and build fences on Parnassus. Material residence, whether of town or of city uproar, is but a husk upon our lives and, when we write, it is the outlook of the heart and brain, rather than the outlook of our eyes, that is the best guidance to our pens.

I have never lived in the sweating districts of the poor, or for that matter in Chuckville, let us say, but I am persuaded that one may live in either place and write honestly — with a touch of beauty, perhaps, upon the things before his door; or if these do not engage his sympathy he may let his fancy wander and be within his rights. He may properly choose a broader outlook than is afforded by his cluttered roofs or any range of village shops. For there must be a mist at twilight even on common hills and any crowded street may be a sufficient springboard for a leap. I must not give vent to absurd statement, but it is my belief that a novel or drama of the Italian Renaissance — any prodigious thing far off — the Last Judgment or the Fall of Rome — may very well be written by the right man any-where, in the thick of sordid smoke, in crowd or open space, in cellar or attic or fire-escape, on desk or knee. It is the flight of fancy, its journey across the brain from ear to ear, that reveals the world. And this holds for Chuckville and for the thicker streets of New York.

For a work of art arises from within and not from a local setting; and an author's eyes may lift themselves from vulgar circumstance and look across the wide spaces of romance. If a man thinks of poverty and pigs he should write of poverty and pigs, but it is quite possible that from a seat beside a trough he may see the evening candles in the sky that lead him on the singing paths of fancy. For it is protest, sometimes, rather than whole immersion, that starts the wheels of thought. And there are persons who need an outlook on a factory, the smoking stack, the whistle and the tides of sweating labor, to climb best to some fantastic peak of unreality. It is the plain that breeds the mountain in their thoughts. It is monotony that starts them running to adventure, and racket and storm of circumstance may turn them inward into quiet.

Nor should it be forgotten that Chuckville, in its essence, stands on every map. It is a state of mind and the grayness of our thoughts. It is vulgarity, as we find it everywhere. It is the pettiness of common circumstance and it belongs to London, to New York, and Paris, as well as to any swampy town beyond the pavement. All places are common, if we take them so; and all places are prisons of barest fact to a spirit that declines to break its bars.

But chiefly it is neither whole immersion nor protest that fashions us. We grow from inner circumstance, from a dim inheritance perhaps. We touch the God of nature somewhere and, like a puppet, we obey the pulling of a string. We are what we are, despite our fine or gross surroundings. We think and work outside our wish, on guidance beyond our power, in direction predetermined. A mystery resides within and heeds not our outward place. And from the whir of this uncomprehended gearing our thoughts rise on compulsion either to tread the familiar paths before our doors or to run on wayward whim across the world. This by consent is true of genius and, in a measure, the rule serves with sharp talent. When a critic tells us what we must write and what we must not — pigs or castles,

butcher-boy or prince, now or yesterday — he becomes
a teacher in a barren school.

This, however, should not give unrestrained license
to Chuckville or our fire-escape to go entirely on the
loose and to flaunt an ignorance and inexperience.
Nor does it insure that far-off romance springs inevitably to a pen that is reared in a village setting. And
yet, when all is said, there is divinity in a masterpiece,
and by no rule of the critics can its manger be foretold.

For, to repeat, if there is value in writing of what is
nearest to the eye, there is value, also, in writing of
what is nearest to the imagination. And imagination
seldom resides at home. It has a roof somewhere, but
it spends its whole life travelling. "Tell me where is
fancy bred?" It is bred on one's own street, but it is
often away upon a visit. There was never a night of
stars that did not lay an invitation at its door. It is
made of the stuff of dreams. A fact taken from a book
is its passport around the world, but fancy buys the
ticket. And a gingham kiss creates a princess in the
heart. This truth was once believed, and writers felt
themselves freed lawfully from a narrow setting.
Vagrant pens have been used throughout the centuries
by the best writers of English. Nor did Sophocles
hold his muse to the streets of Athens, but he ranged
on high Olympus. Homer and Dante did not stay at
home, Victor Hugo or Dumas. Every noble writer of
the past has packed his grip and gone on journey.
Look as you will among the books and plays that have
endured and you will see how large a number lie in the
cottage or the castle of an alien occupation.

No one can be really sure why a monstrous bear

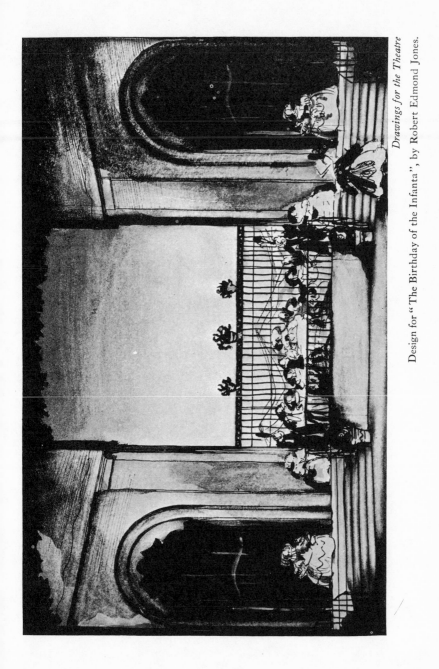

Drawings for the Theatre

Design for "The Birthday of the Infanta", by Robert Edmond Jones.

thrives on blueberries or how an elephant gets its bulk from peanuts. Upon what meat doth this, our Cæsar, feed? But no one answers. Nor can we know why the poet of the ages lived behind a dunghill in dirty Stratford and ransacked eternity for metaphor. Genius and even talent have never studied dietetics or perused a geography in school. The mind leaps all barriers; and if its window looks upon a woodpile, by no necessity must it write of woodchucks.

The list of truancy is tiresome. Historical romance, as an instance, is now for a space taboo. But run through the names of the great novels and learn how large a number of them drew upon the past and trafficked with matters outside their authors' lives, with events acquired from books, with slimmest plots of other days that they colored to a semblance of the truth. "Vanity Fair" and "Esmond" are historical romance. Barchester was seen not as in reality, but a stranger saw it through a mist at night hanging on an ancient tower. Much of Dickens, Stevenson, and Defoe, the best of Hewlett and all of Scott are the product of fancy that wandered off from home. England has always ooked through a rainy window into Italy. Shakespeare gazed from a dingy London lodging into the golden kingdoms of the past. Ibsen, even, who is the father of our present realism, wrote in the main his Scandinavian plays of shadow and gloomy discord when he lived in gayer countries, and his plots turned to the colored south when he resided again in the gray and sunless north.

There is danger — there is hope for all of us who live in common, even in ugly circumstance. If there is ugliness in our hearts we must write with a dirty realism. If we have a turn toward sympathy and understanding we will see beauty and romance in things about us. Or in looser mood we may fling our curtain wide at twilight and look for fiery castles in the west.

I have rambled on too long and obscured my argument. Flatly, it is well to write of what is nearest to the eye — the tin roof, the patter of the village, and the crowded street. But it is better to write of what lies nearest to the imagination. And if one really sees vividly the Fall of Rome, that is a proper subject for the pen despite the dictates of our narrow fashion.

TRAGEDY

By Edith Hamilton

When a poet takes tragedy for his subject he enters a field peculiarly his own. Only poets have "trod the sunlit heights and from life's dissonance struck one clear chord." The intuitive insight we recognize as poetical is the endowment without which no tragedy can be written. For tragedy is nothing less than pain transmuted into exaltation by the alchemy of poetry, and if poetry is true knowledge (truer than history, Aristotle said) this transmuting of pain has arresting implications.

Pain changed into, or let us say, charged with, exultation. It would seem that tragedy was a strange matter. There is indeed none stranger. A tragedy shows us pain and gives us pleasure thereby. The more piteous and terrible the events depicted, the more intense our enjoyment. There is food for wonder here, not to be passed over, as the superficial have done, by pointing out that the Romans made a holiday of a gladiator's slaughter, and that even today fierce instincts, savage survivals, stir in the most civilized. Grant all that, and we are not a step advanced on the way to explaining the mystery of tragic pleasure. It has no kinship with cruelty or the lust for blood.

On this point it is illuminating to cons der our every-day use of the words "tragedy" and "tragic." Pain, sorrow, disaster, are always spoken of as depressing, as dragging down — the dark abyss of pain, a crushing sorrow, an overwhelming disaster. But speak of tragedy and, extraordinarily, the metaphor changes. Lift us to tragic heights, we say, and never anything else. The depths of pathos but never of tragedy. Always the height of tragedy. A word is no light matter. Words have with truth been called fossil poetry, each, that is, a symbol of a creative thought. The whole philosophy of human nature is implicit in human speech. It should give us pause that the instinct of mankind has perceived a difference not of degree but of kind between tragic pain and all other pain. There is something in tragedy that marks it off from other disaster so sharply that in our common speech we bear witness to the difference.

All those whose attention has been caught by the strange contradiction of pleasure through pain agree with this instinctive witness, and some of the most brilliant minds the world has known have concerned themselves with it. Tragic pleasure, they tell us, is in a class by itself. "Pity and awe," Aristotle called it, "and a sense of emotion purged and purified thereby." "Reconciliation," said Hegel, which we may understand in the sense of life's temporary dissonance resolved into eternal harmony. "Acceptance," said Schopenhauer, the temper of the mind that says, "Thy will be done." "The reaffirmation of the will to live in the face of death," said Nietzsche, "and the joy of its inexhaustibility when so reaffirmed."

TRAGEDY

Pity, awe, reconciliation, exaltation — these are the elements that make up tragic pleasure. No play is a tragedy that does not call them forth. So the philosophers say, all in agreement with the common judgment of mankind, that tragedy is something above and beyond the dissonance of pain. But what it is that causes a play to call forth these feelings, what is the essential element in a tragedy, Hegel alone clearly defines. In a notable passage he says that the only tragic subject is a spiritual struggle in which each side has a claim upon our sympathy. But, as his critics have pointed out, this excludes the tragedy of the suffering of the innocent, and a definition which does not include the death of Cordelia or of Deianira cannot be taken as final. What one definition, indeed, can cover Antigone, the high-souled maiden who goes with open eyes to her death rather than leave her brother's body unburied, and Macbeth, the ambition-mad, the murderer of his king and guest? Yet these two plays, seemingly so totally unlike, arouse the same response. They have something in common, but the philosophers do not tell us what it is. Their real concern is with what a tragedy makes us feel, not with what makes a tragedy.

When was tragedy first made? The recent writer of a most distinguished book on the subject,[1] answers: "The spirit of inquiry meets the spirit of poetry and tragedy is born." Make it concrete: early Greece with her godlike heroes and hero gods fighting far on the ringing plains of windy Troy; with her lyric world, where every common thing is touched with beauty, her two-fold world of poetic creation. Then a new age

[1] "Tragedy," W. Macneile Dixon.

85

dawns, not satisfied with beauty of song and story, an age that must try to know and explain. And for the first time tragedy appears. A poet of surpassing magnitude, not content with the old sacred conventions, and of a soul great enough to bear new and intolerable truth — that is Aeschylus, the first writer of tragedy. Other poets may, the tragedian must, seek in the visible world signs of the invisible; seek, that is, for the significance of life.

Only twice in literary history has there been a great period of tragedy, in the Athens of Pericles and in Elizabethan England. What these two periods had in common, two thousand years and more apart in time, that they expressed themselves in the same fashion, may give us some hint of the nature of tragedy, for far from being periods of darkness and defeat, each was a time when life was seen exalted, a time of thrilling and unfathomable possibilities. They held their heads high, those men who conquered at Marathon and Salamis, and those who fought Spain and saw the Great Armada sink. The world was a place of wonder; mankind was beauteous; life was lived on the crest of the wave. More than all, the poignant joy of heroism had stirred men's hearts. Not stuff for tragedy, would you say? But on the crest of the wave one must feel either tragically or joyously; one cannot feel tamely. And the temper of mind that sees tragedy in life has not for its opposite the temper that sees joy. The opposite pole to the tragic view of life is the sordid view. When humanity is seen as devoid of dignity and significance, trivial, mean, and sunk in dreary hopelessness, then the spirit of tragedy departs. "Sometime let gorgeous tragedy in sceptred pall come sweeping by." At the opposite pole stands the "Spoon River Anthology."

But it is not the outside that matters. That may be exactly the same in tragedy as in Spoon River. We do not, to be sure, go to Mr. Sinclair Lewis any more than to Mr. Masters for tragedy, but the reason has nothing to do with the familiar sordidness of either Main Street or Spoon River. There is no inherent reason why Babbitt's house in Zenith should not be the scene of a tragedy quite as well as the Castle of Elsinore. The only reason it is not is Babbitt himself. When the Moscow Art Players presented the "Brothers Karamazov" there was seen on the stage an absurd little man in dirty clothes who waved his arms about and stamped and sobbed, at the farthest remove possible from the traditional figures of tragedy, and yet tragedy was there in his person, stripped of her gorgeous pall, but sceptred truly, speaking the authentic voice of human agony in a struggle past the power of the human heart to bear.

The dignity and the significance of human life — of these, and of these alone, tragedy will never let go. Without them there is no tragedy. To answer the question, what makes a tragedy, is to answer the question wherein lies the essential significance of life, what the dignity of humanity depends upon in the last analysis. Read the great tragedies. They themselves offer the solution to the problem they propound. It is by our power to suffer, above all, that we are of more value than the sparrows. Endow them with as great a potentiality of pain and our foremost place in the world would no longer be undisputed. Deep down, when we search out the reason for our conviction of the transcendent worth of each human being, we know that it is because of the possibility that each can suffer so terribly. What do outside trappings matter, Zenith or Elsinore? Tragedy's preoccupation is with suffering. But, it is to be well noted, not with all suffering. There are degrees in our high estate of pain. It is not given to all to suffer alike. In nothing do we differ more than in our power to feel. There are souls of little and of great degree, and upon that degree the dignity and significance of each life depends. There is no dignity like the dignity of a soul in agony:

> Here I and sorrow sit,
> This is my throne, bid kings come bow to it.

Tragedy is enthroned, and to her realm those alone are admitted that belong to the only true aristocracy, that of all passionate souls. Tragedy's one essential is a soul that can feel greatly. Given such a one and any catastrophe may be tragic. But the earth may be removed and the mountains be carried into the midst of the sea and if only the small and shallow are confounded, tragedy is absent.

One dark page of Roman history tells of a little seven-year-old girl, daughter of a man judged guilty of death and so herself condemned to die, and how she passed through the staring crowds sobbing and asking, "What had she done wrong? If they would tell her, she would never do it again" — and so on to the black prison and the executioner. That breaks the heart but it is not tragedy, it is pathos. No heights are there for the soul to mount to, but only the depths

Drawings for the Theatre

The Hopkins-Jones-Barrymore production of "Richard III", in 1920, was a brilliantly unified achievement — saturated with the spirit of a personality and of a place — The Tower of London, within and around which the tragedy was lived and the walls of which Jones used as his permanent background.

where there are tears for things. Undeserved suffering is not in itself tragic. Death is not tragic in itself, not the death of the beautiful and the young, the lovely and beloved. Death felt and suffered as Macbeth feels and suffers is tragic. Death felt as Lear feels Cordelia's death is tragic. Ophelia's death is a tragedy only if Hamlet's and Laertes' grief is tragic grief. It is not the conflicting claims of the law of God and the law of man that is tragic in the "Antigone." It is Antigone herself, so great, so tortured. It is not Hamlet's hesitation to kill his uncle that is tragic. It is his power to feel. Change all the circumstances of the drama and Hamlet in the grip of any calamity would be tragic, just as Polonius would never be, however awful the catastrophe. The suffering of a soul that can suffer greatly — that and only that is tragedy. What else is the supreme tragedy, the tragedy of the Cross?

It follows, then, that tragedy has nothing to do with the distinction between Realism and Romanticism. The contrary has always been maintained. The Greeks went to the myths for their subjects, we are told, to insure remoteness from real life which does not admit of high tragedy. "Realism is the ruin of tragedy," says the latest writer on the subject. It is not true. If indeed Realism were conceived of as dealing only with the usual, tragedy would be ruled out, for the soul capable of a great passion is not usual. But if nothing human is alien to Realism, then tragedy is of her domain, for the unusual is as real as the usual. "Desire under the Elms" is a tragedy. A drearier setting, a more typically realistic setting, it would be hard to find, but to see it is to feel pity and awe before a very ordinary type of man and woman, commonplace in everything else but made great by what they can suffer. Ibsen's plays are not tragedies. Whether Ibsen is a realist or not — the Realism of one generation is apt to be the Romanticism of the next — small souls are his dramatis personae and his plays are dramas with an unhappy ending. The end of "Ghosts" leaves us with a sense of shuddering horror and cold anger against a society where such things can be, and these are not tragic feelings.

The greatest realistic works of fiction have been written by the French and Russians. To read one of the great Frenchmen's books is to feel mingled despair and loathing for mankind, so base, so trivial, and so wretched. But to read a great Russian novel is to have an altogether different experience. The baseness, the beast in us, the misery of life, are there as plain to see as in the French book, but what we are left with is not despair and not loathing but a sense of pity and of wonder before mankind that can so suffer. The Russian sees life in that way because the Russian genius is primarily poetical; the French genius is not. "Anna Karènina" is a tragedy; "Madam Bovary" is not. Realism and Romanticism or comparative degrees of Realism have nothing to do with the matter. It is a case of the small soul against the great soul and the power of a writer to see "*clair dans ce qui est*" against the intuition of a poet.

Why is the death of the ordinary man a wretched chilling thing we turn from, while the death of the hero, always tragic, warms us with a sense of quickened life? Answer these questions and the enigma of tragic pleasure is solved. "Never let me hear that brave blood has been shed in vain," said Sir Walter Scott; "it sends an imperious challenge down through all the generations." So the end of a tragedy challenges us. The great soul in pain and in death transforms and exalts pain and death. Through it we catch a glimpse of the great Stoic's Dear City of God, of a deeper, more ultimate reality than that in which our lives are lived.

COMEDY

By Edith Hamilton

"Comedy has been particularly unpropitious to definers," said that eminent definer, Dr. Johnson. From Aristotle, with whom everything begins, whose definition of the comical is "a certain error and turpitude unattended with pain and not destructive", to the chief moderns who have attempted the task, Meredith who calls it, "The first-born of common sense, the genius of thoughtful laughter," and Bergson who defines it as the corrective of mechanization, all who have ventured on the perilous ground seem to have justified Jean Paul Richter's airy fling at them, that the only value in the various definitions of comedy is that they are themselves comic.

There is no single formula for tears. Both tragedy and pathos may draw them forth and no one definition can embrace these two. So also with laughter. It is on this point that the definers have come to grief. A formula that covers all the comic is of the nature of the enveloping blanket. As soon expect light and air in the folds of the one as point and illumination in the muddlement of the other. Three divisions of the comic are generally recognized: humor, wit, satire.

COMEDY

Properly understood, there are but two; satire, and irony also, belong to the domain of wit. But whether the division is two- or three-fold, every all-inclusive definition fails to define. In point of fact the only illuminating definitions have come from those writers who have instinctively recognized this fact and have considered only one of the two. In these cases it is always wit that is considered and humor disregarded. The reason is that wit, being of the mind alone, has the clarity and sharp outline that tempts to definition, while humor is of the heart as well as of the head, a combination hard on those that love the pigeon-hole. The union of mind and heart has ever produced stumbling blocks to the definer. Religion and poetry are their products as well as humor, and the pursuer of the definition is wise to turn aside from them.

If this two-fold division is accepted, wit covering the purely intellectual side and humor that which is emotional as well, it is apparent that under the latter must be placed all that we understand by slapstick and the like. These are clearly not of the mind. The point, however, is immaterial in a consideration of the comic in literature where the question is considerably limited and the discussion of it facilitated. What causes a laugh when a fat man falls, what makes the new-born baby smile, and all like matters, so delightful to the psychological searcher into the comic, can be completely dismissed by the critic. The divisions in the drama are clear cut: there is comedy, which is either comedy of wit or of humor, and there is farce, so-called comedy of situation, which belongs in another category and is comedy only by courtesy. The fun of farce is

93

neither of the mind nor of the heart; it is the fun of circumstance. Comedy is concerned only with human beings, "the way they are, the way they talk, the way they walk"; everything not human is alien to it. Farce is concerned only with what happens to people; it might be called the comedy of events. Such divisions as Romantic Comedy, Learned Comedy, Comedy of Intrigue, and the like, are not based upon distinctions in the nature of the comic. Romance is not comic. A romantic play with comic scenes is a comedy only so far as these predominate, and in so far as it is a comedy it belongs to the division of wit or of humor.

Poetic Comedy can also be dismissed. Poetry and comedy have no meeting ground. It is true that there is in Shakespeare a kind of poetry which is frequently confused with humor and is remotely allied to it. Jaques often gives it utterance, as when he meets the fool who says:

> . . . very wisely, "It is ten o'clock:
> Thus we may see," quoth he, "how the world wags:
> 'T is but an hour ago, since it was nine;
> And after one hour more, 't will be eleven;
> And so, from hour to hour, we ripe and ripe,
> And then, from hour to hour, we rot and rot,
> And thereby hangs a tale."

The familiar "all the world's a stage" will occur at once as an instance. This poetry is near to humor, and yet it is not humor. It is whimsical; it arouses not laughter but thought. The spirit of fun is so far from it that it is, above all, pensive. It is poetry, not comedy.

The same thing may be said of another kind of poetry also often met with in Shakespeare. Mercutio's
speech is an example :

> O ! then I see Queen Mab hath been with you.
> She is the fairies' midwife, and she comes
> Drawn with a team of little atomies
> Athwart men's noses as they lie asleep.
> Her waggon-spokes made of long spinners' legs ;
> The cover, of the wings of grasshoppers ;
> Her traces, of the smallest spider's web.
> And in this state she gallops night by night
> Through lovers' brains and then they dream of love —

This poetry of the fairy tale has a delicate delightfulness
which must bring a smile, but there is nothing in it
that approaches the comic. It springs from neither
mind nor heart but purely from the fancy. Laughter
is too robust for it. It is "so thin of substance as the
air", — a poet's dream. There is no poetry that is
comic. Molière is called by common consent a great
comic poet, but he has nothing of the poet in him unless
the word is used to cover all creative genius. The
entire range of his comedy of wit, irony, and satire is
by its very nature unpoetical. It is the creation of
the crystal-clear intellect, at the farthest remove from
that which allies the lunatic, the lover, and the poet.
If Aristophanes is a poet, it is only in the lyrical parts
of his plays ; there is nothing that could conceivably
be construed as poetry in the humorous parts. Shakespeare's comedy is written in prose, not blank verse.
It must be so. Comedy has to do with the surface of
life. Beneath the surface there is that which is not
comic, and poetry's concern is only with the reality

that lies beneath. Comic poetry is a contradiction in terms. When comedy enters, poetry departs.

Molière once said that it was more difficult to write comedy than tragedy, and he added wistfully: *"C'est une étrange entreprise que celle de faire rire les honnêtes gens."* He meant he could have made them weep more easily; sentiment was in his mind, not the heights of tragic exaltation where only poets walk. If he had said that great comedy is rarer than tragedy, the facts would bear him out. It is not to be supposed that it is harder to make people laugh than to lift and exalt them, but it is a fact that many more great dramatists have turned to tragedy than to comedy. To run through the list is to become aware that geography has played a part in the matter. The Comic Muse has her favorites among the peoples of the earth; she prefers the south of Europe to the north. In Italy the Commedia dell'Arte testifies to her presence; Spain has her own comedy of breathless adventure with tragedy hovering near; France with Molière is pre-eminent. But in the north, laughter comes less easily. There are giants of the stage there: Ibsen, Strindberg, Schiller. There is Goethe, a very god. But these have no commerce with comedy. The northern playwrights, it would seem, see life austerely, a landscape snow-covered, wind-swept. Gleams of comedy are very few; the most notable is the Danish Holberg. Lessing, the chief German, has been placed forever by Meredith's wit: "he tried his hand at comedy with a sobering effect on spectators." Russian comedy is negligible save for one name, Gogol. The list, it will be seen, is very small. England remains, but if Shakespeare is as

Drawings for the Theatre

Robert Edmond Jones made the chandeliers and mirrors of his setting for "Love for Love" heighten the brilliance of Congreve's comedy.

always the *exceptum excipiendum*, her best comedy writers have not been of the undiluted British stock, but rather of John Bull's other island. Of the Restoration dramatists one was Irish; another was brought up in Ireland; all five had lived long in France. Goldsmith was Irish; Sheridan, too. So were Wilde and Bernard Shaw. The self-conscious Nordic does not seem congenial to the Muse of Comedy, but the reason is perhaps only that wit is of the south chiefly, and humor of the north, and that literary comedy is pre-eminently comedy of wit.

The comedy of wit derives from one man who has dominated the stage for well on to three hundred years, the supreme master, the embodied genius, of thoughtful laughter, Molière. He has dominated not only the stage but the very idea of the comic. Read any definition of it: ten to one you are reading a definition of Molière. Bergson says: "The comic arises when a group, silencing emotion and calling only intelligence into play, concentrate upon one of their number." This is not a description that applies to the birth of Pantagruel, or to Falstaff's paternal lecture to the prince, or to Don Quixote and the wind mills; it is an exact description of "Le Tartuffe", "Le Misanthrope", "L'Avare." Goldoni holds that the underlying idea of the comic is to correct faults and foibles; Diderot says: "Gay comedy's purpose is to ridicule and chastise vice"; Hazlitt's statement is that the comic genius takes the mask from ignorance and conceit; Meredith declares that it springs "to vindicate reason, common sense, rightness and justice; for no vain purpose ever"; Bernard Shaw says that it exists "for the correcting of pretentiousness, of inflation, of dulness." All are descriptions in brief of Molière.

A Molière comedy has for its avowed purpose instruction in the moralities. It is a sermon, not always in disguise. Vices, weaknesses, faults, are held up to ridicule. The world of his stage is the world of society, and he is forever showing up the inconsistencies and absurdities and hypocrisies of the social scheme. Seriousness is always very near. It is satire, gentle satire for the most part, sometimes bitter satire. This description clearly fits the modern makers of the English drama of ideas quite as well as it does Molière. It might stand without the alteration of a word for Shaw, Galsworthy, Granville-Barker. Wilde's comedy is essentially of the genre. English Restoration comedy is Molière as the court of Charles II understood him. Goldsmith and Sheridan are his followers. It needs not to be pointed out that he created French comedy. He set the model to which all French playwrights turn. The fact is recognized and requires no buttressing, but he did the same thing for the stage of the civilized world. All comedy everywhere since Molière harks back to him, in Russia as in Spain, in Italy as in Germany. Benavente is Molière's descendant, not Calderon's; Gogol's "Revizor" is built on his model; Goldoni used to say when he saw a new play of his on the stage, "It is good but it is not yet Molière"; Lessing avowedly took him as his master. Had ever any genius such a following? He made the world forget that any other kind of comedy was possible.

In what does the peculiar greatness of Molière's comedy consist? To describe the superlatively excellent in superlatives is easy, but how describe it when all superlatives, all glowing language, must be rejected as not consonant with the subject. There are no sweeping flights in Molière, no purple passages. He is the lover of the golden mean; he is common sense incarnate. *Goût et mesure*, so valued by his countrymen, are his beyond any other writer. He is the exemplification of nothing in excess, a Greek in his art of omission. He is not quite the laughing philosopher but perfectly the smiling philosopher; he looks at life with detachment. His comedy is elegant comedy, brilliant comedy. There are no undertones "where more is meant than meets the ear." All is clarity, the clear light of keen, calm reason. Each of his great characters is at once an individual and a type, a supreme achievement. Tartuffe is an individual, a big fat man with a very red mouth and a soft cushiony tread and a trick of persuasive speech; a *bon viveur* and a sensualist; he is also not a hypocrite but the hypocrite. His maker has not only depicted his hypocrisy with such complete fidelity that the vice is stamped clearly forever more, but he has at the same time so heightened it — *l'exagération juste* is the French phrase — that hypocrisy is embodied in Tartuffe. He is more a type than an individual; his truth is that universal truth which Aristotle said was truer than the particular, individual truth of history. He is a great artistic creation; he is not a living human being. Like all of Molière's characters he moves on the stage, not in real life. Always, above all, Molière is a master of the stage. Take M. Jourdain, for instance, receiving his dancing master in night cap and dressing gown, displaying proudly the magnificent waistcoat and "shorts" underneath, and when the dancing master insists that a gentleman must carry a hat in a minuet, not understanding and putting it on top of the night cap, and so dancing the stately measure. The comedy, as so often in Molière, is directed to the eye, not the ear. It is masterly stage craft. We are used to it by now. Every comedy we see depends on it. But Molière created it. The comedy of wit at its perfection is then a moral pointed by delicate satire against a social vice embodied in a clearly depicted individual set off by brilliant talk and by a consummate stage technique.

"Laughter," said Lord Chesterfield, "is illiberal and illbred." He was voicing the Molière tradition. The comedy of wit had taken possession of the stage and the days of rollicking, irresponsible fun were gone. In the two supreme ages of the drama, Elizabethan England and the Athens of Pericles, the step from the sublime to the ridiculous had been easily taken. Uproarious comedy had flourished side by side with gorgeous tragedy, and when one passed away the other passed away too. There is a connection between the sublime and the ridiculous. The comedy of humor, which is Aristophanes' comedy and, pre-eminently, Shakespeare's comedy and theirs alone, has a kinship with tragedy. "The drama's laws the drama's patrons give." The audiences to whose capacity for heightened emotion "Lear" and the "Œdipus Rex" were addressed, were the same that delighted in Falstaff and in Aristophanes' maddest nonsense, and when an age succeeded, in no wise less keen intellectually but of thinner emotions, great comedy as well as great tragedy departed. Aris-

tophanes had no followers. Shakespeare stands completely isolated. His descendants are not on the stage.
They are to be found in the great English humorists,
and also in the writers of that delightful, unmiti-
gated nonsense which is the bewilderment of the foreigner and understood only by the Anglo-Saxon mind.
"Alice in Wonderland" came from one of Shakespeare's
family. But their medium has never been the drama.
The two supreme geniuses of the comic stage have had
a singularly different fate: no comedy has ever been
modelled upon Shakespeare; all comedies have been
modelled upon Molière. The comedy of wit has dominated the comedy of humor.

The reason for this — numerical — supremacy is to
be found in the nature of the comedy of humor, that is,
in Shakespeare's comedy. This is not to say that all
his comedy is humorous, but his great comedy, his own
comedy, is comedy of humor. Almost any one of Falstaff's speeches could be given as an example. In the
second act of "Henry IV" he assumes the part of the
king and reads the prince a paternal lecture:

FALSTAFF. Harry, I do not only marvel where thou spend-
est thy time, but also how thou art accompanied. . . . There
is a thing, Harry, which thou hast often heard of, and it is
known to many in our land by the name of pitch; this pitch,
as ancient writers do report, doth defile; so doth the company thou keepest. And yet there is a virtuous man whom
I have oft noted in thy company, but I know not his name.

PRINCE HENRY. What manner of man, an it like your
majesty?

FALSTAFF. A goodly portly man, i' faith, and a corpu-
lent; of a cheerful look, a pleasing eye, and a most noble

carriage; and, as I think, his age is fifty, or by'r lady, inclining to three score, and now I remember me, his name is Falstaff.

That this is high comedy no one would deny, but it teaches no lesson, it points no moral. Has it a purpose at all? Only, it would seem, to amuse. It is gay, irresponsible fun. No brilliancy of wit is there, and never a hint of satire, only laughter, the laughter of those who love what they laugh at.

In "A Midsummer Night's Dream", Bottom would act every part in the play:

Bot. Let me play the lion too: I will roar, that I will do any man's heart good to hear me; I will roar that I will make the duke say, "let him roar again, let him roar again."

Quince. An you should do it too terribly, you would fright the duchess and the ladies, and that were enough to hang us all.

All. That would hang us every mother's son.

Bot. I grant you, friends, if you should fright the ladies out of their wits, they would have no more discretion but to hang us; but I will aggravate my voice so, that I will roar you as gently as any sucking dove; I will roar you an 't were any nightingale.

There could be nothing more comic than this but the laughter it evokes is not thoughtful laughter; there is not a trace of "mechanical, automatic inelasticity contrasted with human flexibility"; it is not directed against any social vice. It has no place in any of the categories of the comic. It is just enchanting nonsense; nothing more — and nothing less — than super-excellent fooling.

Are we so made that we cannot place great value

upon pure fun unless we find some trace of high truth in it? To the earnest minded this may be said in its behalf: it frees us for a precious moment from our tiresome selves. Great tragedy, great music, the world of out-of-doors, have also this freeing power but not a whit more than whole-hearted laughter. Touch it with the least bit of derision — wit, irony, or satire — and we are self-conscious again, but unalloyed fun that never looks before or after is of those that open the prison doors.

The "Merry Wives" has all the matter for a Molière play. The virtue of two honest married women attempted by one who is the embodiment of sensual lust, the plot that foils him and reveals his villainy, — it is a perfect setting for a comedy of thoughtful laughter. Molière would have treated it after the manner of the golden mean, holding the just balance between seriousness and gayety until the end, when the lustful knight would have been shown in all the loathliness of sensual vice and punished with whips of scorpions. Thereafter Falstaff would be a synonym for fleshly vileness. None of all that moral earnestness so much as touches this comedy of humor. Not only we ourselves but the people of the play laugh very kindly at the wicked fat man. His evil designs are foiled, of course; he is shown up in the end to all; but the only result is an invitation to him to sup a posset with them and laugh at those that now are laughing at him. It has just been sport, says Mistress Page, fit for a laugh around a country fire. There stands Sir John, very crest-fallen but with a twinkle in his eye, and the spectator's heart goes out to him in his deserved affliction. The comedy of humor never sits in the seat of judgment; it never condemns. Judgment is for the disinterested spectator, and philosophic detachment is not more alien to the poet than to the humorist.

Bergson, writing again with Molière in his mind, says that tragedy is concerned with individuals and comedy with classes. Shakespeare is not concerned with classes or with types. His characters are individuals, people in real life, and we never think of them as personages of the stage. Falstaff sits at his ease in his inn; he walks the London streets; it is always the background of life he moves against; it is inconceivable that he should be placed forever on the theatre boards. Is it a stage wood and moonlight of the electric arc that comes to mind with Bottom and his crew? The green plot is their stage, the hawthorn brake their tiring-house, the chaste beams of the wat'ry moon their light. To think of Beatrice and Benedict is to be transported to an orchard as inevitably as to think of Alceste and Célimène is to be in fancy seated before the footlights.

Set thus side by side, it can be seen why the comedy of wit has been favored to the exclusion of the comedy of humor. Wit is born of thought; humor is spontaneous. A formula for the comedy of wit is possible; a receipt can be made out for it. But as well try to imprison poetry in a formula as humor. The type, the class, can be generalized, but no formula for the individual has ever been discovered.

Life is the key-note to the comedy of humor. Its aim is not to clarify the mind and help it to knowledge — that is for the comedy of wit. It helps us to under-

COMEDY

stand. *Tout comprendre, c'est tout pardonner.* It seeks not more light but more life. The comedy of wit is the white light of the unbiased intellect turned upon human follies. The comedy of humor is the laughter of "the mighty master of the human heart." The comedy of wit is true to art; the comedy of humor is true to life.

THE DIRECTOR

THE DIRECTOR

THE feature by which the world theatre of this generation is chiefly distinguished is the rise of the director, not only as the coördinating, but as one of the great creative factors in production. Twenty years ago, the director was an apologetic person whose business it was to evoke a working harmony between an egotistic actor and a stubborn playwright. Tact and patience and humility were his chief requisites for success. Today he is the guiding, the unfolding, the unifying spirit in the theatre. The greatest men in the theatre today are all directors. Many of them have other theatric gifts — they are designers too, or actors, or playwrights: but all of them have that sense of unity, of the theatre as an art which all the arts unite to serve, which most characterizes the trend of our production. Gordon Craig, in his "The Art of the Theatre", "Theatre Advancing", and "Scene"; Adolph Appia in "Music and Stage Design" and in "L'Œuvre de l'Art Vivant" have put their practice and their theory into words in a way to make a vivid background for the period. Reinhardt, Stanislavsky, Meierhold, Copeau, Pirandello, Charlie Chaplin, each in his own way, represents the completion of an attitude toward the art of directing. But they are so few among so many. It would be easier in America to make our achievement fit our intention if there were more good directors today, more young men, for example, bringing to the playhouse what Belasco brought when he was young — a consuming love of the theatre, a capacity for infinite pains, a fearless but sympathetic command over both the human and the mechanical elements of production, a keen sense of his hour, and of the form of conflict that seemed most dramatic to the audience of that hour. Belasco's methods are outmoded; his means are the means of all great directors — faith and work.

The same play coming to the stage of the theatre through the
minds of different directors and designers often presents a very
different picture to the world. The photographs above show
the "*S. S. Tenacity*" of Charles Vildrac as Jacques Copeau
set it in the permanent frame of his naked stage at the Théâtre
du Vieux Colombier in Paris, and as Robert Edmond Jones set
it for Augustin Duncan's production in New York.

THE ART OF DIRECTING

By Stark Young]

In the course of stage history the director has borne
a varied name and a more varied relationship to the
theatre. He has sometimes been the owner of the play,
sometimes an actor from the company, sometimes the
regisseur, or director of the entire production in all its
parts, sometimes the producer or actor-manager. But
whatever the problem of the regisseur, or producer, or
actor-manager may be elsewhere, in our American
theatre at present the director is the man with the
script in his hand who stands behind the whole performance of the play, who to varying degrees prescribes
what the interpretation shall be, what the actors shall
do, and trains them to do it. He is the maestro, the
coach, the general behind the rehearsals.

The director is the artist who takes the drama as
it is put into his hands and labors to re-create it in
his own technical terms. And this drama when it
is re-created into these terms becomes theatre and
something that is different from what it was before.
Directing is an art or it is nothing.

There is no such thing as a play directed exactly as
it is written any more than there is a landscape painted

as it really is. In any art the material that goes to make up the work suffers a change before it becomes this work, and this change, this something added, derives from the artist working. In Corôt's "Ville D'Avray" the material was the landscape of trees, atmosphere, and light, the medium was the paint. In Houdon's "Voltaire" the material was a body and the character in that body, the medium the marble. The dramatist's material is men, life, experience; his medium the dramatic form. In the art of the director the drama itself is the material, and the actor in the midst of the audience and the designer's décor is his medium. It follows that when a drama emerges from the hands of the director it has undergone a restatement of itself, a translation into the terms of the theatre, and the importance of the thing added will measure the importance of the director.

At one extreme in directing is the virtuoso. He takes the play into his own hands and does with it what he chooses, twists it, makes it his own. He may go the limit in violating its quality, in forcing it to his own ends.

At the other extreme is the director whose aim is to carry out entirely the dramatist's idea. If the play is bombastic he makes his rendering of it bombastic, where it is cold he will be cold, where it is barren he keeps it barren, and so on; he covers nothing, he tries to discover and to restate in theatre terms the play's essential character and the style that expresses this character; to every element in the play he means to give its special quality and intention.

Both these types of directors are artists. If one

appears more sharply than the other to be an artist it is not because of his method but because what he creates is better or worse. It is a difference in degree, not in kind. We may prefer a performer who tries to play a concerto as closely as he can to what is written rather than one who sweeps it out of itself to his own mood and will. But in the end what finally decides the question as to whether or not either of the performers is an artist is the thing created. With Liszt, Schubert may become not only the material that Liszt interprets but also the material from which he creates something violently his own. The virtuoso director at his peril does what he wills in directing a play. He may be a good artist or a bad, according to the result that he creates, but he is an artist. The result must judge itself. The original drama may almost disappear before such a director has done with it, but conceivably at least we may be willing to forget it quite in order to possess the new creation, as we are willing to forget in El Greco the likeness of trees in order to achieve El Greco. In the theatre the trouble, however, with the virtuoso lies in the fact that there will always be few directors who have as much to give us as have the plays that they direct. The result so seldom justifies the means.

Great talents like Gordon Craig may do what they like with a play, and risk the outcome. Gordon Craig might take "Othello", for example, and change it into what as a whole it but slightly could be, or read into it something that it scarcely contains at all, and yet create for us a result magnificent in itself. Or he might lift one element in the play to an importance out of all proportion to the whole of it, and by doing so illumine and dilate forever the region that "Othello" can express. A dozen Gordon Craigs bringing to bear on Shakespeare's tragedy this radiant distortion and dilation in twelve different aspects might increase twelve times "Othello's" radiance and scope. But Gordon Craigs are rare. And we are apt to feel that anyone so determined to say what he has to say rather than what the dramatist intended should let the play alone and write another for himself.

The kind of director at the other extreme from the virtuoso would by some persons be rejected entirely as a creative artist, to use a phrase that is often heard but that makes no sense, since an artist is an artist only in so far as he is creative. To reply to that we may best abandon the comparison between the director and the play he uses and El Greco and the trees that go into his painting of a landscape. Shall we say rather a director and the play that he presents and an orchestra leader and his rendering of a Beethoven Symphony? In this case what comes to the artist is already established, as was not so with the landscape; something is already created. The score is ready to his hand. Into it the artist, working in his own terms, strives to imbue life and so create the symphony. If every instrument in the orchestra rendered exactly the score written for it we should still not have the symphony created. Not in nature, ideas, or art is there any truth that is ready and expressed and the same; it is restated in every man that experiences it and as significantly as the observer is significant. No director can give us a play as it is, however faithful his intention may be and however great his ability to carry out his intention.   His ideal may be a fine one; he strives to disappear and to leave the play exposed and expressed, to achieve a style that is an invisible medium, like a laboratory glass that reveals the delicate processes of an experiment. But he remains the artist by whose creation this style and revelation may arrive.

The relation among ideas, remarks, events, and emotions in a play, how they follow one another, how they dispose themselves together and so reveal the play, is expressed, so far as concerns their precise meanings and the definite things they have to say, in words and actions.   Beneath them all lies the main body of the play.   When in "Henry IV" we see Pirandello's hero daub paint on his face and put on the robes of Henry of Canossa, we know exactly what theme and disguise his plan has followed.   The exact observation that Hamlet has to make on his own failure in the power to act is expressed when he says —

> "Why, what an ass am I !   This is most brave
> That I, the son of a dear father murdered,
> Prompted to my revenge by heaven and hell,
> Must, like a whore, unpack my heart with words,
> And fall a-cursing like a very drab,
> A scullion !"

But these are more special and particularized elements of a drama.   In the whole of the play there is the emphasis of one part compared to another, the mass is stressed heavily here and lightly there according to its importance in the whole.   One speech leaps out from another, propelled by the inner conflict beneath them.

One speech is distant from those near it because it arises from meditation in the speaker or from his continuous habit of thought. One speech is ready in the speaker's heart before the thing it seems to answer has been said, its lips were on the other's lips ere they were born. The pulse or beat of a line or a speech or a scene is here quick, there slow; the emotion or thought exhilarates, it retards. All these are a matter of pure relationships. Beneath the particular situation, the particular thought, reactions, deeds, every play can be reduced to this abstract basis. Every play has this abstract pattern of values. On this side it is for the most part closely connected with the art of music. A director can best study the layout of a play as if it were a musical composition.

Music, as everyone knows, is of all arts, except architecture, perhaps, the most ideal. That is to say, music does not involve imitation or concrete instance or definite concept; its region is pure to itself. Music is the beautiful eternity, the idea, the essence, the general quality. In sum, to take an example, where Hamlet can only say to us,

"I have that within which passeth show"

music can put us into the very state itself out of which this poetry or our tears arise. In a production the matter of emphasis, themes, characters and events, the speed, the vocal tone rest all fundamentally and essentially on a base of music. So the height of a tower is a part of its idea. The quiet of the vowels and the contemplative measure in one of Virgil's pastoral verses is as much its truth as is the precise thing said in words, and to forget this is to forget the nature of art. To forget this is like saying that a madness to kill is expressed or conveyed in a remark stating "I am going to kill you" rather than in the eye and the onward rush of the murderer. The length, the beat, the duration of a speech in a play is a part of its idea. The time between two speeches is a part of their meaning. The tempo at which a cue is taken and the tone of the voice are as much — and often far more — the truth of a speech than the more exact and limiting words that are said. When Othello says:

> "Never Iago, like to the Pontic Sea
> Whose icy current and compulsive course
> Ne'er keeps retiring ebb, but keeps due on
> To the Propontic and the Hellespont;
> Even so my bloody thoughts, with violent pace
> Shall ne'er look back, ne'er ebb to humble love,
> Till that a capable and wide revenge
> Swallow them up",

the main truth of the outburst, even the sheer fact that it is an outburst, is conveyed by a tremendous current in the declamation, by the vocal tone and flood of sound rather than by the special concept in each and every phrase. And unless this outline and rhythm is established, the speech breaks down into something of forced images and elaborate if not false details.

When Marchbanks, with the poet's insight, says to Prossy, of the arid, hot heart and bitter, drab profession, that he can see nothing in Morell but words, pious resolutions, and asks if it is possible for a woman to love him, and Prossy, after trying to evade the question, says

117

"Yes," it is obvious that except for her mere acknowledgment of a fact, the whole moving truth must lie in the time she takes before she speaks and in the tone of her voice. In the case of individual actors it is their time sense, their sense of the exact moment for a cue, a speech, an answer, that does as much as anything else to engage the audience's attention with its constantly fresh vitality and surprise.

There is an element, of course, in the performance of a play that speaks entirely to our eyes. When the director begins to consider the expression of this aspect of a play he may wisely study every part of it as a set of pure relationships, a kind of visual music. He can study as he might a symphony what is the essential idea of a play and what groups, motions, positions, will most help in expressing through the eye what the other dramatic mediums are expressing through our other faculties or channels of perception. He can define those lines and masses on the stage, and then subordinate what is secondary and omit some of the confusion of empty or extraneous movements. He can study a scene for its last, fundamental idea or characteristic and try to find what line, what visual quality, will most express the essential idea of the scene, and can employ that line as something in itself expressive. And he can seek to establish, what is most important of all these, the visual continuity of the scene, its living rhythm in our eyes, from the time it begins till it ends.

Granted a clear or important idea for the play that he will present and the means and ability to carry it through, the director has still a problem like that of any artist, who for the prosperity of a work has to con-

sider what tact and judgment he will use to achieve the
right relationship between the work and the public.
There is a point beyond which if an artist carries his
idea he will lose the sympathy of his public and so
defeat his own end, which is to express his idea to them.
On the other hand, too much consideration of his public
may prevent the artist's going far enough to reach the
point at which his idea will get itself expressed. In
every art some concession is obviously unescapable;
music, for instance, has to be loud enough to be audible;
the musician must concede at least that much to his
public. But in general, as an artist you may choose to
trim your sails in order to arrive at your wished-for port,
or you may choose to miss the temporary destination
or success and instead to stretch the bounds of your
art, to chart new seas, to sight new forms, new possibilities for expression. You take your choice at your
peril and according to your own nature.

But the artist directing in the theatre has to remember that the theatre is essentially an impure medium.
It consists not only of what is on the stage but of the
audience in front. The director will have to make an
imaginative choice and proportionment of parts, so as
not to leave out the audience from his creation. However prophetic or illuminating the stage end of his creation may be, if the audience is not rightly involved in it,
the creation suffers, as might be the case with a pianist
who insisted on pouring water into the instrument for
the sake of some future aquatic scale but failed of any
sound or anything besides his strong idea or inspiration.
The director has to consider what effect he most seeks,
what is the truth that he would most express. When

this is found he must relate every detail to it, taking his choice as to how far he is creating for a complete present moment and how far for future innovation or extension. A thing admirably right in itself may, when the audience sees it, jump out of the frame and distort the whole picture. An unwelcome detail, however true in itself, may either wreck the truth of a whole scene or send it to a thrilling pitch. To say what has never been allowed said on the stage, what has been more or less banned as crass or outrageous, may swamp the play or may double its expressiveness. The director may take whatever chance he likes, but he has to work in all the elements of his art, the play, the actors, the audience.

When a play is new, hot from the author's forge, it may be taken as written for its own time, its idea as stated for the dramatist's own generation. The director's business is an interpretation of it in theatrical terms. But when there is a play to be revived, a few years or some centuries from its birth, the director's problem takes on another shift in restatement.

In so far as a play was ever a work of art it was a living thing. Within his dramatic form the dramatist arrested and found a right body for a section in the stream of life. Life may be said to rise and fill for a moment such a form. But the very essence of life as distinguished from the dead is this streaming, this ever-changing current of it. The living content, no longer wholly arrested in this form, goes on with its stream and is not to be distinguished from it. The form without the content is empty and dead. In the history of an art the process toward degeneration, and through and past that to a new summit of excellence, a new epoch, consists of two courses. First, there is the survival of the form with less and less of the sustaining life that once brought the form into being; this is the so-called decadence of an art. Second, there is the progress of a new quality of life needing its body and moving toward a form that will contain and express it.

In Euripides' "Bacchae", Dionysos, the god of ever-springing life and enthusiasm and ecstasy, could not be bound; prison bars, fetters, no obstacle had power to hold him fast. Only the forms of his own passion and of his own thought and his own motion could contain his divine life.

Pirandello, for the modern theatre, has dramatized this idea. The theme in Pirandello's work is the dualism between Life on one hand and Form on the other; on the one hand Life pouring in a stream, unknowable, obscure, unceasing; on the other hand forms, ideas, crystallizations, in which we try to embody and express this ceaseless stream of Life. Upon everything lies the burden of its form, which alone separates it from dust but which also interferes with the unceasing flood of Life in it. In "Henry IV" this man who has taken on a Form, a fixed mask in the midst of changing Life, remains in it until the moment when his passion and despair and violent impulse send him back into Life. But only for a moment: the impetuous violence of the Life in him expels him into his masquerade again: in his tragic struggle between Life and Form, Life is defeated, Form remains. To many a play, when it is revived, comes such a fate as this of Pirandello's hero. The life in the play is defeated, the ironic form remains.

The performance of a play at the director's hands is not a mere matter of the written text. Its truth can arise only from the combination of this text as it stands, plus the audience for whom it is given. In so far as a play is alive the living element in it is an impalpable, on-running, delicately perilous reality on which an illusion of permanence has been imposed by its form. The life in "Macbeth" seems to be permanently expressed by the play as we read it, and this might seem equally true for a performance of it. But this, in fact, is not the case. There are academic phases, obviously, that may be interesting in themselves. As history of literature, as poetry, as Shakespearean tragedy, it may, if you choose, possess an interest. But this is just the point at which we most need the director's imagination, the genius in him for re-creating the play in the necessary new terms. That side of "Macbeth" that is a living thing, that speaks to the life in us and arouses a response from it, and fecundates and increases the volume of that life, must be restated in every revival — and I may say indeed at every performance — of the play. The life in this play is not a fact, it is not a fixed and permanent statement, it is an ever-changing reality, unconfinable and in ceaseless flux, but real. The sixteenth-century "Macbeth" of Shakespeare derives from an earlier and more primitive base. It has beneath it such an element of shock and terror as is to be found nowhere else in drama. This primitive quality Shakespeare restated in terms of the morality and the complex style of his own Elizabethan age, and lo, we have his "Tragedy of Macbeth." And now in turn both this primitive quality and this Elizabethaness must be restated for us. Even if a director could discover every fact, every piece of business, exact reading, gesture, tone, of the first production of "Macbeth" and could reproduce them for us to the last jot, he would not necessarily convey to us the life in the play. He might give us only something beautifully curious, or antiquarian, or historic exhibitions in facsimile, but not "Macbeth" and its meaning to us. No, his business as an artist is to discover a rendering for "Macbeth" — which is his material — through his medium — which is first the actors and then the décor of his theatre — to discover a rendering of such a kind as will restate for the audience present the significance of the life of the play. There is no right way to produce "Macbeth." It would be a comfort to think there was, to have something to rest upon, just as some right way of living would be a comfort. But the essence of being alive is a constant, perilous choice, and a constant projection of imagination into living forms.

A part of the truth of a Greek play is its distance from us in time. To be alive it has to be restated for us somewhat as its original material had to be restated in it. For us a part of a Greek play's truth is its Greekness, with all that that may mean for us. In Restoration times a gentleman often carried a little bowl of gold or silver which he could take from his pocket and rest on the arm of his chair, and into which from time to time he might spit. Molière's gallants did a smart thing when they took a comb from their pockets and arranged their curls as they sat in a lady's salon. But the director who wished to give us the quality of gallant gentlemen in his revival of these social comedies could not show us such details; they would defeat his ends and give us not elegance but only ugliness. These are simple instances but they illustrate the case. What in these particular instances needs most to be conveyed is the living thing, the permanent idea in them to which we respond; in sum, their elegance. At whatever cost this must be created or the moment is empty.

The director's revival of a play, then, is a form of creation, and in so far as this is not so, the play lies dead on the stage, a mere fact, the empty shell where once there was an engaging life. All compromise, change or emphasis in a new production of an old play can have but this one end, which is in a way to keep it alive. The extent to which the director preserves closely the play in its original shape or violates or distorts it, re-creates its essentials in new terms, or even forces it so that we hardly recognize it for the same play, may affect the success of his enterprise, but it does not alter the principle involved. There are as many ways of doing "Macbeth" as there are generations of human life, and in its production the perpetual rediscovery of the body inseparable from its truth is the condition on which alone "Macbeth" is kept, not merely a matter of culture, but a thing that is alive in our experience.

When the director, as an orchestra leader might, has achieved through the actors under him the desired emphasis throughout the performance, the time values, the tone, and so on, he remains to be considered like any other artist making use of the means at hand. We may think of him as an artist in the use of his medium.

THE ART OF DIRECTING

Of late years there has arisen in the theatre a type of directing that proceeds on the basis of letting the actor alone. Up to the point of collision with the other players the actor can go his own way and almost unmolested in creating his rôle. The principle is to get good actors and let them go ahead. Up to a certain point this policy has worked. But it has been a limited and often fatal method. Provided you get good actors and in cases where only one or two actors carry the whole burden of the scene and can perhaps work it out between the two of them, you may succeed. But in general the scheme is almost as hopeless as turning a crew of sailors loose without an officer to run the ship. And, moreover, this method leads to a relaxation and laziness in the director himself.

The other extreme in directing is an older and more tried policy. In it the one hand controls everything and everyone involved in the play, and not only controls the actor but dominates his conception of a rôle and the entire playing of it. Such a director, at such an extreme, may even give the actor the tone, the gesture, the movement. He may, when he likes, make the actor an imitation of himself. Up to a certain point this method also has often worked. If we must choose, it is, on the whole, safer than the opposite extreme. Provided the director himself has ideas that are capable of making the play into something worthwhile and has the force or control to work the actors into his will, he may succeed. And the discouraging inferiority of the mass of actors seems to argue for such a tyranny. But it obviously throws away no little of the individual resonance of the actor. And it tends to mechanize actors and to make them stale. It gives them stage tricks where real invention is needed; it leads them toward a more or less passive exploitation of themselves.

The necessity of the second method, the one controlling head for the performance, is plain. The whole scale of the play finally depends on that. The good element in the first method, the hands-off and let-the-actor-do-it school of directing, consists in the fact that at its best it allows the actor freedom to create and the possibility of succeeding in himself, of happiness in his own soul. It leads him toward becoming a better and better medium in which the director may work. The ideal directing combines the two methods.

But of the actor as the medium there is more to say. As the medium in which the director works the actor may be thought of somewhat as paint is thought of for the painter or marble for the sculptor. In every work of art the artist takes his material from nature or experience and translates it into his medium, creating in it, as he works, something that was not there before. His creation is partly in terms of his material and partly in terms of the medium employed. Our consciousness of the medium is a part of our perception of a work of art and of our pleasure in it. One among the many reasons why Velasquez is a great painter lies in the distinction with which the paint itself is a part of his work, the texture, the brush, the density of the painting medium, and the color as well, are a part of the ideas that Velasquez's pictures present. In Shakespeare at his best, along with the dramatic emotion and the thought, we have always a sense of words being employed, of sheer phrasing and diction, as a part of our delight.   Something of the truth of an Egyptian statue is in the granite of it.

In the director's use of his actors it ought to be true that the more he can use the actor's own thing in his scheme of the play the better.   The different truths of a great sculpture in wood and a great sculpture in marble will consist partly in the difference between wood and marble.   It ought to be the fact that a certain deepening in the truth of an actor's contribution to a play will derive from the actor's getting his results in terms of himself, making up out of his own elements the result that he creates.   This will allow a better chance for those explosive accidents that we call inspiration, those moments when the actor is carried beyond his own plan or clear intention.   At such moments a certain unexpected contribution to the director's creation may come from the medium itself, which may contribute to his invention, give him an idea.   Many an architect has got a design, a motive, a form from some quality of texture, color, or weight of the stone that he is using. The limitations of marble may invite no little of the sculptor's pattern.   This might be called keeping the medium alive.   The director brings the actors' own truth to the creation of the larger truth that the director is after.

If, for example, then, you have, as in Lenormand's "Les Ratés", a scene in which a crude black man is brought suddenly to the discovery of a corpse and cries aloud, it ought to be true that the first thing to do is to let the man make the cry himself, express his own kind of emotion in his own kind of cry, and then to use all this so far as possible rather than to start by explaining the emotion and giving him a cry to imitate. If an actor, rehearsing for the storm scene in "King Lear", feels a certain way in the part, the director may use this feeling as far as he can toward the creation of the feeling that he himself wishes to express. He must believe that his actors are souls as well as bodies, and that the creation he seeks is composed of all our human elements. In sum, such a use of the actor medium by the director ought to be the means of keeping his performance alive in all its parts, as a good painter keeps the paint alive in every inch of his surface.

THE UNITY OF PRODUCTION

By Cloyd Head and Mary Gavin

THE search of the theatre is toward unity of production — toward an organic fusion of movement, light, sound, and stage decoration. These four factors, which together make up the theatre, are externally so unlike in expression that synthesis into a pure art-form presents difficulties which neither the old technique nor the new has thus far been able to surmount.

In the traditional method of producing serious drama the production is the resultant of two forces — the creative impulse, concentrated chiefly in the dramatist, and the interpretive impulse, concentrated in the producer and his assistants. While practically there is room for creative interpretation within the limits of any play, however closely woven, yet the play itself, relatively speaking, is complete before it reaches any of those who are to give it life in the theatre. Interpretation, inasmuch as by its nature it can merely approximate, must fall short of the author's design. It would seem, therefore, that unity between the written play and the interpretive production cannot ever be fully accomplished.

If we examine further into the method of the inter-

pretive theatre, we find another difficulty no less important to our purpose than this discrepancy between the
written play and the production, and the tendency
which the reflex interpretation of life via the written
play has to inhibit the creative impulse of the artists
in the theatre: the production employs a method structurally inorganic, based upon the addition of one
art-form to another. These art-forms have become in
expression antagonistic: acting, for example, is almost
invariably realism; stage decoration is conventionalized. Jointure, often primitive and accidental, sometimes subtle and well-nigh convincing, takes the place
of organic fusion.

These antagonisms are fully recognized by the theorists of the theatre; and it is proof at least of the difficulty of reconciling them that the greatest of the theorists are compelled to seek unity through elimination.
Jacques Copeau — who understands better than almost
anyone else the realistic tradition — finds it essential
to eliminate every medium except the actor and a permanent background. On the other hand the theorists
of the new movement, preoccupied with the development of light and of stage decoration, find themselves
in conflict with the actor. Gordon Craig looks to the
über-marionette (the highest conventionalization of
the actor) for a solution and a means of leading the
actor toward style. Others would revive masks; still
others turn toward the conventions of the Orient,
toward the Noh and the Javanese drama.

It is quite true that from any of these various expedi-
ents, and from others like them — such as the welding
by atmosphere of factors still unlike which is a phase

Francis Bruguière

"The Dybbuk", Ansky's Jewish folk drama, realized for the Neighborhood Playhouse the ideals of production and ensemble playing toward which they had worked for twelve years. Probably no company but one trained in singing and dancing as well as in acting, could have recreated for Alice Lewisohn, the director, this mystic drama with its awesome pageantry. Settings and costumes designed by Aline Bernstein.

of the technique of Adolph Appia — beauty may be derived; but the one tendency which they share in common is a certain evasiveness. A valid art of the theatre is not possible through the elimination or suppression of any resource which pertains to the theatre. The theatre, if it is to come through at all, must come through as a whole.

Historically the theatre is both the oldest and the youngest of the arts. It had its origin in movement as ritual. It followed the development of ritual, incorporating song into movement; from song was born antiphony, and out of antiphony came characterization. Thenceforward drama became ever more and more concrete, ever more and more dependent rather upon words than upon movement. At the last it became essentially an art of representation between actors. So music and the dance and choral expression, which had been an integral part of the theatre, were no longer necessary to it. Instead drama developed. No artist can regret this development. It reduced the theatre, however, to a place of representation for the written play.

In the course of time drama, for its representation, recalled these various arts. But they returned, not as an integral part of the theatre. In their long dissociation they had abandoned their theatrical development. They were subsidiary arts. "Theatrical" had become a synonym for "tawdry," for the insincere: "drama" alone — and apart from the theatre — had retained its dignity.

The Wagnerian music-drama will probably mark the turning-point from which a new understanding of the theatre began. Wagner saw the necessity of, and to a large degree understood, the structural synthesis of art-forms in a free association. But, just as without him the new movement might have been long retarded, so his work preceded those technical resources in equipment by which synthesis in the modern theatre can alone be made possible. He inherited the realistic technique of stage decoration to which, without greatly modifying it, he gave an imaginative significance. This in itself forecast a new *mise en scène*. It becomes therefore significant that Adolph Appia, who first evolved and utilized a modern system of lighting, based his experiments — and his experiments also in decoration — upon the Wagnerian music-drama. When it is said that the theatre is both the oldest and the youngest of the arts, what one implies is this : that at its origin the theatre was a synthesis from a central inspiration ; but the technical equipment by which the modern theatre can hope to express, even after it has found, organic unity is scarcely older than a single generation.

There is a thread of continuity between the ritualistic theatre and the new movement in the persistence of certain phases of the lyric drama. As long as the drama remains lyric — as in the Orient, where lyricism is traditional — the break with these origins can fortunately never be quite complete. These origins, although the theatre cannot turn back, nor find any vitality save as a revelation of life now, are deeply suggestive. It is true that in our own time we have no ritual sufficiently dynamic to compel expression through art. But what does exist for us is the spiritual content of life, the sources which are the creative motives of life always. Presumably these inmost sources are changeless; and it is the business of art, unless one is mistaken, to create in conformity with them. The nearer the theatre approaches this conformity, the more vital it will become.

So we return with more than a technical reason to the most important of our inferences: namely, that unity cannot be derived by the artificial addition of one art-form to another. A valid art of the theatre can be sought only through an underlying principle which will govern and control all factors which contribute to theatrical expression. And inasmuch as synthesis has but one purpose, an authentic revelation of life, the principle from which organic unity is to be derived must be consonant with life-sources. This principle, the only source common alike to all art-forms, is rhythm. It is the focus where they meet, the source of the stream which finds its channel through stage decoration, through sound and through movement — as through life itself.

Taking rhythm as the basis of theatrical technique, it becomes apparent that some revaluation of drama in its relationship to the theatre is essential. Such a revaluation is not without precedent. Dramatic technique has always been conditioned by the theatre. What distinguishes the present from the majority of former revaluations is that the new theatre will condition not only external technique but substance as well. The inspiration out of which the play is born is the fundamental rhythm of the production. This inspiration needs, or it does not need, a theatre. If it demands a theatre for expression, then it is theatrical; if it does not demand a theatre, then — no matter how skillfully it conforms to any other definition whatsoever — it is not theatrical and should have no place in a theatrical art of which the ideal is unity.

When it is insisted that a piece to be played in the theatre must be in this meaning intrinsically theatrical, the development starts at the exact moment when the inspiration begins to seek form, at the moment from which alone unity of production becomes possible. It is a long road from the inception of the idea to the finished production. Throughout this development — expression by the most diverse media — there can be no break in the continuity of the rhythm. The evolution through the various channels must be creative always, each of the media unfolding and expanding the rhythm until it is complete and the play exists as a whole from which no factor or element can be withdrawn. Then only will a play become inextricably interwoven with the theatre and the theatre itself become a valid art-form.

Every man of the theatre would know the practical difficulty of such a program, which involves the personal as well as the æsthetic equation. Indeed it could scarcely be accomplished without a change in the viewpoint of the artist. Attempts have thus far been something of a compromise. The more skilled craftsmen are modifying their technique rather to conform with new ideas in their own crafts than with any new conception of the theatre as a whole. They are working to that extent blindly — and they must so continue to work until the theatre formulates its own individual

technique.   Then doubtless a new generation of artists
will arise, trained to a broader understanding.   Such a
training will not be exclusively in their own work, but
will in many respects be alike for all of them — a training in the method of perception as well as in the execution of what they perceive.

The resources of the modern theatre, which, though
infinitely more complex, are at the present time no
less definite than the resources of any other art-form,
can be utilized only by artists working in group organization.   The relationship between the four major factors — stage decoration, light, sound, and movement —
is so sensitive, the adjustment between them so delicate,
that independent effort (independence of work, not of
thought) becomes almost impossible.   The play must
grow in the theatre itself — and the basis of a theatre
group is in this matter of training chiefly.   In Europe
one finds that the great theatres demand a formal
apprenticeship — not in the art as an art only but in
the method of the particular organization of which later
the artists are to become a part.   This apprenticeship,
however, unless one is mistaken, confines itself solely
to the actors.   In the older technique this doubtless
is sufficient; but in the theatre where unity of the entire
production is the technical *desideratum*, this apprenticeship should be shared by all artists of the organization.

Theoretically, conceiving the production as a central
rhythm flowing into expression through these various
channels, the basis of ensemble production is the clear-
ing of these channels and the resultant inter-relation
between them into group feeling.   This cannot ad-
versely affect the individuality of the artist; for the

more clearly he makes himself a channel the more nearly unhindered will be the expression of his individuality. On the other hand, clearness of perception will tend to eliminate the reliance upon personality, the personal, which is a hindrance to artistic integrity, to the creative development of the artist singly and in group organization — and is indeed perhaps the largest contributing cause to the undeniable inferiority of theatrical art. Although complete impersonality, complete clearness of perception, is beyond the reach of any artist, there is dynamic power even in the recognition of it as an ideal.

The actor, as already has been suggested, is the crux of the problem of organic unity; and it is not flattering to the present status of theatre technique that his very presence requires justification. The other media have by their form a kind of artificial protection against the personal; but the actor, who is the direct expression of life, has become — perhaps because of that very fact — the chief channel of the personal. Now while it is true that the older technique stressed the actor to the comparative exclusion of the other media, nevertheless the reason for this emphasis, that he is the direct expression of life, is too fundamental to be rejected. The relationship between the actor and the audience is instinctive. The actor therefore is indispensable.

This depersonalization of the actor expands, without diminishing, his function and vitality in the theatre, altering only the method by which that function may be made clearer and more direct. Words primarily, beneath their objective purpose, are rhythm finding form through sound, just as action is rhythm finding form through movement. The words that the actor speaks and the movement visualized by him are both carried on the same rhythm that creates the light and the stage decoration.

In the personal technique only the greatest actor — who it may be instinctively feels this — can make a pause at all more dynamic than an interruption. The continuity of his performance is a continuity only of characterization. In the new technique it will perhaps become possible for the actor, by making himself a channel through which the rhythm of the production as well as the continuity of his characterization flows, to become more truly creative and to unite with the other media instead of being isolated from, and so in conflict with them.

The understanding of the laws of rhythm alone has power to release in the actor a creative vitality consonant with the other media of the theatre. And this, like the technique of all art-forms, is not to be acquired without training.

The training of the actor is a training in *rhythmic* expression. Of known methods this seems to be the one which can best be adapted to his purpose. He must first clear himself of all that is personal, of those obstructions of will and conscious effort by which the channel of his inspiration is inhibited. These must definitely be broken down. Almost he must seek his inspiration beneath the conscious self in that depth which is called the subconscious and which, for our purpose, may be said to approach the universal where greater rhythms play what music they will. He must be trained by letting moods sweep through a self made wholly receptive and creating their own expression. This, as every creative artist knows, would be but a liberation, a formal approach toward those sources from which expression rises. If he trust this, disintegrating first his artificial coördination in order that he may regain a truer coördination, he will emerge an artist equipped to the uttermost of his power in the control of this medium.

As such training applies to the actor, so too it applies to those artists whose inspiration will be expressed through lighting, for example, through music, and through stage decoration. Moreover, rhythm is the basis of group feeling, the release not only of the individual artist, but the coördination of one artist with another. A group must unify before it can separate. Through rhythm the actor, and therefore his action, has the same sensitive relationship to the *mise en scène* and the *mise en scène* the same relationship to him that the actors have to each other. This sensitization permits of that endless modification of rhythm through the influence of one artist upon another by which the entire structure of the production may be expanded harmoniously without interruption of the continuity.

In this the actor, by virtue of the fact that he is the "living presence", whose relationship both to the audience and to the other factors is instinctive, becomes no longer the crux of a difficult problem, but the strategic center of all that is vital in the art of the theatre. For with intimacy and directness of appeal is included also that power of greater revelation which the other artists may utilize in finding their own expression.

SCENE DESIGN

SCENE DESIGN

IT is not much more than a dozen years since the curtain at Wallack's Theatre went up on Granville-Barker's production of "The Man Who Married a Dumb Wife", with designs by Robert Edmond Jones. Before that, the designer, as one of the first-rank artists of the theatre, was unknown in America. The impulse to use his talents came, obviously, from abroad — came straight, in fact, from Gordon Craig. But the need for him here was so keen that, once given an opportunity, he took his place immediately. Probably the most distinctively creative contribution yet made by any American group to the American theatre is that made by the group of artist designers working largely in New York during the last ten years — Robert Edmond Jones and Norman Bel Geddes, Lee Simonson, Herman Rosse, Aline Bernstein, and others. A record of production made during these years shows these designers not only creating the visual aspect of the production, but influencing happily the selection and even the writing of plays, the development of lighting, and experiments of all kinds in the synthesis of production. Robert Edmond Jones once said that the setting for a play should be "the wind that quickens the action." This might well be paraphrased to make it the place which the designer has taken in the theatre. Because stage design can be most easily recorded pictorially, there has grown up a very good record of the designer's accomplishment and the part it has played in theatre progress in such books as Hiram K. Moderwell's "The Theatre of Today", Sheldon Cheney's "The Art Theatre", Kenneth Macgowan's "The Theatre of Tomorrow" and "Continental Stagecraft", Robert Edmond Jones' "Drawings for the Theatre", and Norman Bel Geddes' "Project for the Presentation of the Divine Comedy." Two new books on Stage Decoration, one by Sam Hume, the other by Sheldon Cheney, amplify and complete this record.

Drawings for the Theatre

"The Man Who Married a Dumb Wife", by Anatole France, is not so small a comedy as its length indicates. It is a big comedy in miniature. Perhaps that is why Granville-Barker included it with "Midsummer Night's Dream" and "Androcles and the Lion" in his American season in 1915, and why it remains so long in the memory. Or, perhaps it is because, when the curtain went up on this first setting by Robert Edmond Jones, a new era began in the American theatre, with a new theatre artist — the artist designer — added to the playwright, the actor, and the producer.

THE LIVING SCENE

By Kenneth Macgowan

SCENERY is not a very easy thing to make up one's mind about. Scenery *per se*. It is trivial. If Inigo Jones had made backgrounds for Shakespeare's plays instead of Ben Jonson's masques, we would value Jones more, but not Shakespeare less. Scenery is at the mercy of the actor. If Irving had played Macbeth in the expressionistic production of Arthur Hopkins and Robert Edmond Jones, the setting would have had a chance to do its work, it would have achieved praise instead of boot kicks, and it would be comfortably forgotten when Irving was still remembered by those inevitable partners, the octogenarian and the antiquarian. Scenery may also be vital — even deadly. "The Miracle" without Geddes would have been distinctly less; "Arabesque" without Geddes might have been a little more. To be sure, it is only the inferior play that lives or dies by scenery; yet think how far the attempts to cut up Shakespeare to fit scenery have held back his fine racing dramaturgy. Scenery is limited in what it can do, and yet it has played a large and dramatic part in the refertilization of the stage during the past thirty years. We have overestimated the importance of scenery as scenery, and we find it hard to separate it properly from the other ingredients in this most synthetic of arts, and to judge its part properly.

To discuss the æsthetic principles of the scenic art is by no means easy, because it is hard to set limits to scenery. Canvas and paint cannot live without light. They cannot be shifted without some kind of machinery. Good scenery is essentially a part of the actor, and the actor a part of it. For the moment, I think we can drop any technical discussion of lighting equipment, and we can throw machinery clear out of the door — on the distinct understanding that without a physical technique of lights and machines no production is likely to get very far.

More than that, the mere physical shape and aspect of a stage setting is very difficult to talk about without wandering off into the whole modern movement in stage direction. The new scenery affected the directors, and through them the actors and even the playwrights. The ideas of Appia and Craig played upon Reinhardt, Meierhold, and Stanislavsky. These directors brought new scenic forces into the theatre. And men like O'Neill, Dymow, Molnar, and Dunsany reacted to the whole new movement, and made new demands upon it.

Finally, scenery has not been content to act upon the director, the actor, and the playwright alone. It has shocked the physical playhouse into the beginnings of a new form. If we do not limit our talk about scenery very closely we shall find ourselves talking about circus theatres, architectural stages, and stages without prosceniums. And we will have to end up our discussion by considering theatres without any scenery at all.

There seem to be a few definite basic principles. Scenery must serve the actor and serve the play. It must provide points of vantage for the actor — entrances and exits, places of advantage, and promontories of proper display — all in utter subservience to the action and the mood of the play. But the final test of scenery is simply this : Does it make the performance more appropriately dramatic, does it dramatize the mood of each scene ?

Before we can think about the means by which the designer dramatizes the mood of a play and capitalizes its actors, it may be well to clear away a certain haze. This is the conflict and the union between the scenery of a century and more ago and the scenery of today, and it is also the conflict and the union between the realistic and the imaginative scenery of the new movement.

Modern scenery began as an alliance of the realist and the poet against the shallow and ugly and unillusive artificiality of the scenery that ruled the stage until the first decade of the twentieth century. This was a scenery full of false perspective, badly rendered, overloaded with hideous ornament and detail, the whole thing offensive and distracting to the eye. Two types of artists hated this. One was the realist, like David Belasco, who wanted the stage to look like a real room, solid, plausible. The other was the man of imagination, like Gordon Craig, who wanted beauty and, at the least, "a noble artificiality." There was a little of each in the many Continental directors who spurred the new movement on — men like Max Reinhardt. The pioneers began by banning the mechanism of the old stage. There could be no false perspective and shallow pretence.

This was a natural reaction. All about them, Appia and Craig saw a stage filled with flat and banal artificiality. There was neither beauty nor truth to life in the jaundiced meadows and mildewed mountains and splayed rooms which the hack scene-painters spread over back drops and wings in very, very false perspective. The thing was a palpable fraud, and also a hideous one. The meadows, the mountains, and the rooms were obviously not the real thing, and neither were they beautiful or vigorous or expressive. They were just an ugly cheat.

The realistic and the imaginative artists had to hate them equally. Craig and Appia might have accepted the stage conventions of the older theatre — the simple flats and back drops — and awakened them into new life, as the Russians did. Instead, they fought them, and fought them on the one legitimate issue on which they could be fought by both realist and poet. Paintings in two dimensions do not and cannot harmonize with three-dimensional actors. So away with false perspective and its painted shadows! Make room for solid plastic, for rocks and walls against which the actors may live and move and have their being, and over which lights may play!

The first result was the triumph of realism and the invention of a great many machines for shifting heavy settings quickly. Machines ultimately refined themselves to the point where one of them could throw a background of colored light on a cyclorama. And so in the new movement we must find room for an interior heavy enough to need a sliding stage or an elevator to manage it, and an atmosphere that hangs in living light around the actor. Both extremes fall easily within the limits of this art. Even the old-fashioned back drop of the opera house has its place if only it is painted with the dramatic vigor and the expressive color of Bakst or Roerich. We even find the imaginative artist drawn back to the elder theatre that he once attacked, drawn back forcibly because he finds in its inevitable pretence a way towards frank theatricality.

All this should only reinforce the truth that nothing matters in background except significance. The medium and method do not count. If the artist can create an effect upon the stage that is characteristic of the play and its emotion, then he has done the work expected of him. It will be his right to name the means.

The first means to scenic drama is color, backed by design. With these, a realistic or an imaginative scene can be made to reinforce and heighten action. One of the simplest and best examples that I have ever seen was Robert Edmond Jones' design for a cheap hotel room in "The Devil's Garden", a play produced some years ago by Arthur Hopkins. The action of the scene showed a husband learning of the infidelity of his wife and the villainy of his employer. Its dramatic ingredients were passion, hatred, and the thought of murder. Jones painted an ordinary, cheap, real room. He got the emotional effect of the scene from the color of the wall paper — a deep, terrible red, made the more sinister by an over-pattern of straggling black. This was not a room for French farce, domestic comedy, or poetic drama.

Beyond color and design lies light. Unobtrusively or obviously, it is playing its part in every fine piece of scenery placed on the stage today. Even when the pattern is realistic, light may illuminate it with creative meaning, and fit it closer to the meaning of the playwright. There is nothing so very unrealistic in Appia's setting for the death of Tristan, yet what a drama the twilight plays as it creeps up the ailing body, lights the face for a moment with renewing strength, and then leaves Tristan in the shadow while it stabs the door through which Mark approaches.

The means that the designers have found for making scenery dramatic appear in their clearest outlines when the play becomes more imaginative. Then we strike the triple theory of the thing — simplification, suggestion, and synthesis.

First, simplification. The stage must not be cluttered up with detail. Detail distracts the spectator from the actor and the action. Detail tends to make significance and beauty more difficult. The setting for the cathedral scene in "Faust", which Joseph Urban designed several years ago, is ever an admirable example. Here all the elaborate structure of a Gothic edifice is boiled down to a single column and three minor details. The stage is free for Marguerite and drama.

The same setting illustrates the second vital principle — suggestion. The artist reduces the setting to its essentials. Then he makes these essentials suggest a great deal more than they can literally present. He sets the imagination of the spectator to work. In this case, the shape of the pillar dates the period of the play, the size of its base makes us realize how tall it must be, and how high the church must tower over us. After a glance at this one object we have built the whole physical and spiritual structure of the church that looms above the cowering Marguerite.

As for synthesis, that is a hard thing to separate out from the rest of the process. Indeed it must not be separated out. Its essence is fusion of color, design, and light into a single atmosphere appropriate to the moment. And here the designer reaches out a hand to touch music, movement, the spoken word, all the parts of the theatrical whole.

I think a description of two settings will help to re-emphasize what the designer can accomplish to aid actors and authors. One is Lee Simonson's scene for the embankment episode in "Liliom" where the two roughnecks wait to rob a messenger of the payroll which he carries. Simonson provides the railroad embankment which the author requires, but he raises it high in air, partly to eliminate the necessity for many physical details such as rails and sleepers, partly to provide a dramatic stance for Liliom when he is shot, but largely in order to provide room for a passage or culvert underneath it. Through this culvert we see in the distance the village from which the messenger is to come. It provides a most dramatic means of bringing the man upon the scene. He must pass through its darkness and in this shadow he will be robbed. There is a threat in such a culvert. The mere sight of it arouses memories of the terrors of childhood when your way lay through just such a haunt of robbers. When the curtain goes up on this scene, the stage is literally set for violence. Color and light, of course, play their proper and helpful part.

The second setting is far less realistic, and easily the most effective I have ever seen in the theatre. It is Isaac Grünewald's arrangement of the prison scene in "Samson and Delilah" at the Royal Opera House in Stockholm. Instead of painted prison walls, there is only darkness, suspended amid black hangings. The millstone to which Samson is fettered becomes some strange old primitive thing that revolves on its edge as the man chained to it presses against a pole in its center, and pushes it around. The millstone symbolizes and dramatizes imprisonment and torturing labor. A single shaft of light falls on the stone. At one moment it makes a gleaming crescent of the edge. This grows larger as the stone turns, and then suddenly it flashes into a great silver disk, and Samson stands silhouetted in this spot to sing his aria. Then the procession of the moon begins again, and the torture goes on.

The business of design — the visual dramatization of a scene — is not so very simple even when genius resides in the designer. If an act is not all of a piece, then the task is extraordinarily difficult. Suppose "The Devil's Garden" had had a tender episode between the wife and a child just before the return of the husband; could Jones have managed it by asking the director to keep the mother and the girl in a spot of brilliant light from a side window, and then blot out the sunlight with a cloudy sky when the child had left? The possibility of injecting lighter notes into the scenes in "Liliom" and "Samson and Delilah" is far harder. Yet sometimes such a task must be met.

Back of these means and principles lie certain ma-

Francis Bruguière

Lee Simonson's designs for "Liliom" undoubtedly added to the success of the play as produced by the Theatre Guild. Above is the setting for the railway embankment, as imaginative as it is simple, which made a fine use of an arch as a means of suggesting distance and darkness. The players are Joseph Schildkraut as Liliom and Dudley Digges as the Sparrow.

terials and devices which the designer has found to make his task easier and the results surer or more varied. Of such is the elaborate new technique of applying color which the scenic studios have perfected. Credit goes, first of all, to Joseph Urban for his importation of *pointilage* and a studio of Continental craftsmen who could apply it, and, second and more permanently, to Robert Bergman for the most subtle and elaborate of new processes for spreading living, vibrant color in place of flat, dead tones. Craig, and a host after him, have found draperies and screens a way to escape realism and expense and to come closer, willy-nilly, to an abstract and theatrical stage. Too little can be said here of the use that has been made of changing light — arbitrary and vibrant and too often startling — to accompany and explain the drama as the action progresses. At first it had the faults of most experimentation. Now it is beginning to be used with a sure hand.

The designer has served the actor best perhaps in breaking away from a level stage floor. Scene-shifting devices made this possible in the beginning. Without such machinery, realistic plays could rejoice in different stage levels only if the whole evening passed in a single spot. Thus in "He Who Gets Slapped", aided by the circus locale, Lee Simonson was able to provide a complex of steps, ramps, and platforms, all of which seemed natural and proper, and all of which proved extraordinarily useful in handling a large number of people and in keeping their relations clear and simple. The audience saw them all. Each could talk across to the other.

From machinery and realism, the stage of many levels passed across to formalized productions of Shakespeare. There Jessner introduced a permanent arrangement of steps or platforms for "Othello", "Richard III", and many another drama. These displayed the actors in three dimensions and permitted a dramatic sort of symbolism in the relations of characters in height and position. The success of such use of levels, coupled with the movement toward frank theatricality, has resulted in the Russian constructivist movement fathered by the parent of the "theatre theatrical", the director, Meierhold. In constructivist settings — we have seen some in New York in "Loudspeaker", "Pinwheel", and "God Loves Us" — a high, permanent, and usually very complex arrangement of steps, levels, run-ways, chutes, and platforms tries to reflect something of the mechanical, skyscraper quality of life about us, and tries also to combine with this means for theatrical entrances and exits, a continuous flow of action without a pause for the ordinary changes of scene.

The designer and his work cross many æsthetic theories, old and new. None has fitted in so well with the essence of his trade as expressionism. A good deal of bad scenery has been put on the stage in its name. We have had far too many cock-eyed and lopsided flats reflecting or expressing the same degenerating qualities in modern playwrights and their work. But the basic theory of true expressionism is the same as the basic theory of scene design, and all good scene design, realistic or abstract, has to follow its line whether consciously or unconsciously.

The expressionist in modern art is more interested in the expression of his emotions than in the representation of any object in nature. Thus he may paint a wheatfield in such a way that it will create a feeling of fear in the spectator; and it doesn't matter in the least whether the artist ever felt fear in looking at a field of wheat — as he might have when a child. It doesn't matter whether the painting looks at all like a field of wheat; the artist may distort the stalks into spears and he may paint the field a terrible and nauseous yellow-green. For the matter of that, he may just as well express the emotion of fear through an arrangement of green and yellow planes and lines that have no relation whatever to any real object. The emotion is the important thing, and the artist's ability to summon that emotion in the spectator. That is expressionism in art, and it applies to the stage setting with singular aptness.

After all, even the most conventional and realistic stage setting has two jobs to do. It tries to look like a convenient place for the action of the drama, a place provided with walls or doors or whatnot. And it tries to give you some emotion that the acted drama will convey. When the designer is working with a realistic setting he may still be an expressionist — in fact, he *must* be an expressionist. He must convey an emotion not to be found in the generality of walls and doors. It is not, of course, an irresponsible emotion rising only within his being. He is merely the medium through which it is translated from the text of the playwright. The designer who is working on an imaginative play believes that the emotion is far more important than any resemblance or plausibility in the place represented. Hence he is ready to give up even doors and walls if he can get more emotion — and the right emotion — without them. In the end he is apt to discover that he has also got more *theatre* — that he has got closer to the artificial play-acting essence of the stage.

Thus from theory to theory — through practice — the scene designer is pursued. He serves many of them as he goes tumultuously on his way. Some of the theories are his and some are not. He finds himself closely allied with the ideas of a non-representational theatre inherent in Meierhold and other radicals. He takes up old-fashioned scenic methods to get a fresh joke across, or to achieve a naïve quality of fancy or extravagance. He rediscovers the proscenium portals of pre-Victorian days, notes that they serve well for Shakespeare, and discovers that very soon he is likely to be designing a playhouse to use them. Soon he finds himself imagining a kind of theatre quite outside our own. He is embarked on creating or re-creating a playhouse that has no place for scenery. The scene designer ends by calling for his own abolition.

THE PAINTER IN THE THEATRE

BY SHELDON CHENEY

IT is not very long since the painter in the theatre was still a newcomer and a novelty — and therefore subject to all the misunderstanding and attack on one side and all the unconsidered praise on the other which fall to the lot of any innovator in the arts. With the first burst of new decorative activity, marked by such events as Norman Geddes' début with the Los Angeles Little Theatre, the initiation of Sam Hume's work at the Arts and Crafts Theatre in Detroit, and Lee Simonson's flaming introduction of color with the Washington Square Players in New York, there was considerable talk in studios, little theatres, and dramatic publications to the effect that "at last the artist has come into the theatre."

Much paint has flowed under or over the stage bridge since then. It is a rare critic who has not perceptibly changed his attitude on the question of the painter in the theatre. The most remarkable change has developed among those who did most to open the doors of the theatre to the decorators. They have curiously tempered their enthusiasm, and they are particularly shy about the word "painter." They remember a bit uneasily that in that earlier day they looked on the setting and the method of staging the play as the key problem of the new theatre; that they touted lustily any painter who stepped into the playhouse, as if he thereby automatically became the artist of the theatre; that they wholly overlooked certain correlative facts about acting, playwriting, and stage architecture. What they are coming to recognize now is this: we can go forward only by developing a new drama, a new stage, a new standard of acting, and a new stagecraft concurrently. They are realizing, moreover, that practically all the useful accomplishment of the painters on our stages so far has merely served to round out a passing phase of art, has been fitted to a drama and a stage that close up an old era instead of opening a new one.

It is just as well to understand at once that the painter in the theatre is justified only from the time when he ceases to be the easel artist, only when he becomes characteristically the theatre artist, thinking in terms of the theatre, of light, color, sound, movement, projection of emotion into an auditorium from a stage.

There should be no need to emphasize the point. But at least one artist who has "done" an opera for the Metropolitan has boasted in public prints that he considers and will continue to consider his backgrounds as primarily pictures, let the play and players fit in as they may. Not altogether irrelevantly there comes into my head a snatch of the old song: "And they fit all day, and they fit all night." There have been enough such instances to justify the suspicion still lurking in some quarters that the painter wants the stage for just that sort of selfish exploitation of his talents.

THE PAINTER IN THE THEATRE

It is easy, indeed, for all of us to remember plays that were all but buried under "scenery", and as a variant there have been plays bad in themselves, but helped along to something like success by the compelling beauty of the settings.

Of course the new theatre will have nothing to do with the bad play, and we might safely leave the matter there — were it not for the Russians. While the rest of the world was developing a simplified, plastic type of setting to take the place of the painted back drops, cut-outs, and borders of our Wooden-Indian period, a group of Russian painters kept on building up and refining the good old stuff until it reached a splendor that blinded most critics to the fact that it is, on final analysis, still the good old stuff. Anisfeld, Roerich, Golovin, Bakst — mountains of color, soaring line, gay pattern, overwhelming sensuous atmosphere — but painted perspective, painted shadows, two-dimensional pretense of three-dimensional magnificence. This is not the art of the theatre — neither of the future nor of the present. It is a dressing up of the past in colors that the past had missed, and has found too late. In opera, already torn between two other arts, this third, picture-making, may be safely added. No unity to lose, no sense of the plastic human figure moving on a plastic stage — therefore let the painters join in the fun by doing their bit from their own standpoint, willy-nilly.

It would be foolish to try to dismiss this very talented group of Russians and the subject of painted perspective thus in a single paragraph, without at least adding these reservations: these painters *do* sometimes work plastically; there is perhaps a legitimate place for their sublimated canvases in a certain type of unreal-realistic ballet, with a purely sensuous appeal of movement, music, and color, without dramatic unity; and painted perspective doubtless can be used to advantage in settings of the newer theatre, when conventionalized (fantastically, as in Jones' "Til Eulenspiegel", or naïvely as in Derain's "La Boutique Fantasque"). But these *are* exceptions. Pictures beautiful for their own sake, not designed to be integral to a dramatic scheme, do not belong to the stage. The artists who make them should be politely but firmly asked to go back to their north-lighted studios.

Here ends the first part, which has to do with the painter as painter.

Regarding the painter who has become thoroughly and primarily the theatre artist, who thinks in terms of the plastic stage and the action on it, the first question is fairly enough this: what is the æsthetic justification for calling him in at all, for trying to transplant him from one art to another? We *can* transplant him, of course, even some of the best of him, because of the doubtful estate of the easel picture in a changing world, and because the architects have lost themselves in a maze of tradition, academicism, and business, and have no place in their buildings for mural decoration with the breath of modern life in it. But why does the stage need him? The answer can be worded out of Gordon Craig, who rediscovered that the theatre is by exact definition first of all "a place for *seeing*"; who has re-affirmed on a thousand occasions the fundamental importance of what can be understood by the spectator

The Russian Ballet and the work of Leon Bakst gave a fresh
life to the tradition of the painter in the modern theatre.
Bakst who treated his back drops like glorified canvases and
spread his colors with a bold hand, was typical of the newer
painter-artist-designer.   Discarding   photographic   methods
he injected a new vitality into an old medium by treating it
as an artist's domain, open to bold interpretative uses and
freed from conventional bondage.   When, after the Russian
Revolution, the Ballet went to France, under the direction of
Serge Diaghilev, it soon attracted to itself such distinguished
French painters as André Derain, Marie Laurencin, and
Pablo Picasso, who painted this curtain for "The Three-
Cornered Hat" (*Le Tricorne*).   Also in the wake of the revolution, many Russian painter-designers came to America,
among whom are Nicholas Roerich, Boris Anisfeld, Soudeikine
and Remisoff, all of whom have made contributions in which
their native Russian quality is strongly marked.

through the eye — "the art of the theatre has sprung from action — movement — dance"; and who, in emphasizing the importance of the visual element, added the memorable note: ". . . not a word about it being a place for hearing 30,000 words babbled out in two hours."

It is generally agreed that this rediscovery of Craig's marks a turning-point in the history of the modern theatre. Only by a complete understanding of the multiple nature of theatre art, and its dependence upon movement and visual design as an integral part of its "form", can anyone gauge truly the importance of the modern movement. Before Craig (and there are only too many of our theatres still existing in the pre-Craig milieu) stage art was made up of play-texts, acting, and something ordered in from the scenic studios. The best play-texts (the Greeks and Shakespeare) had nothing to say about movement and scene; it was only the rarest of actors who conceived of the action or movement beyond his own little physical orbit; and the scenic studios "supplied the art" in accordance with tradition, and in diluted imitation of the grand manner of a century or two earlier — without the faintest notion of harmony of play and setting, of rhythm, of unity of impression, of creative use of line, mass, and color.

If the actor, the playwright, the business-manager, and the purveyor of "scenery" could not bring the new attitude to the stagings of plays, to whom could the theatre turn if not to the painter? Once the visual viewpoint was restored, after centuries of specialization in appreciation of playwriting and acting, the only thing to do was to call in that artist who alone had been trained to create through the eyes. Certainly the painter had better than any other contemporary crafts-man some understanding of the meaning of unity as applied to the arts; he understood the visual effective-ness of design, statically if not dynamically; and he had some glimmering of the spiritual value of color. Even some of the most obvious principles of his own art were immediately applicable — and new — to the current stage: pictorial composition, chiaroscuro, and something vague called style. So he came in, by right of gifts needed by the theatre.

The painters who have come to understand the stage, and then taken the theatre as they found it — picture-frame stage, fourth-wall convention, realistic or roman-tic plays, movie-minded audience—have immeasurably bettered the current of drama. They have perfected the means of staging until a new beauty has come into the playhouse, a satisfaction of the visual senses that makes complete the multiple appeal of the theatre. To the romantic play and romantic acting they have added a fullness of lighting, coloring, and general *décor*. The realistic drama they have rescued from a too-studied literalness on the one hand and the flapping-canvas absurdity on the other. Where the painter has not been called upon in the person of one of the recognized group the commercial studios have been put to it to copy their methods, to the general betterment (if sometimes unintelligent betterment) of production in the mass.

When the painter came in, he had at the end of his tongue that word "unity" — so inapplicable to ninety-nine hundredths of the productions then filling the stages; and beyond his own contribution of lighting and setting that "fitted" the play, he has been able to pound into many a producer some understanding of the importance of unity as applied roundly to acting, tempo of staging, and the score of other matters that go to make up production. In his own contribution he gradually forced into acceptance the principle that more is to be gained by simplicity and suggestion than by photographic exactitude and elaboration, a principle valid enough anywhere, but thrice golden when applied to backgrounds on a stage — at least when one is dealing with the passive drama of to-day. He dressed this drama appropriately, richly, honestly, to bring out its own best points.

I credit him, too, with the larger share in the next step forward, the reach after synthesis. Synthetic production, as generally understood by the student and critic of the theatre, is, I believe, one jump beyond unified production. Where unity might suggest merely a harmony achieved by passive means, a holding together by avoidance of overemphasis on any one part, synthesis suggests a building-up with an eye to full exploitation of every available element, a more architectonic and dynamic method of production. Most of us who were talking much about synthetic production ten years ago were finding our material in a coördinate study of painting, acting, and drama-writing. Certainly the painters (or men who had studied painting on top of long acting experience, like Craig) brought much to the discussion of that phase of the "new movement", and did even more by their part in actual production.

What the painter finally arrived at was stylization, and stylization is his greatest gift to the theatre as it exists today. Stylization, I suppose, may be defined as the creative quality that an artist puts into a production as a revelation of his own individual vision: the manner of producing, distinctive, all-pervading, lifting the *performance* to the true estate of dramatic art. It does not necessarily rise out of the painter's contribution to the production; it may be conceived out of a feeling for vocal rhythm, or a sudden divination of a motive of life, or a theory of acting, the other elements being stylized as visualized from this point of departure. But the fact remains that since the painter came into the theatre, there are more really important productions conditioned first from the visual viewpoint. Producers now are more apt to *see* the drama moving before their eyes before they even begin to choose their actors; and it is the painter in them that makes them see.

Thus in the drift toward unity, the seeking for synthesis, and latterly the achievement of stylization, it is the theatre artist with painter's background who has led the way. He has developed to something near perfection the methods of producing current plays. He has achieved a pictorial rhythm that goes far toward "holding together" each performance. He has given professional flare to mounting, where previously there were only professional writing and professional acting against any nameless sort of background.

Having said all that — trying to keep in mind that to do so much is an achievement well meriting praise — still I find the question constantly knocking at my mind: how much *does* this rounding-out of nineteenth century drama mean? How much would it mean if the painter single-handed had developed the realistic-romantic formulas to utter perfection, if he had taken the picture-frame stage and put in it realistic or romantic pictures so fine in their field that no one can hope ever to surpass them?

Well, frankly, to go no further would mean to me that he had failed in his biggest duty as theatre-artist. If he fails to break through the picture frame, if he fails to demand and help create a new type of stage, a new philosophy of production and a new drama, he has betrayed his trust. If he is content to dress up, over and over again, the current realistic and romantic plays, if he lets even the best things that our playwrights are doing limit his vision and his practice, I for one am ready to let him out of the theatre by the same door he came in. For the salvaging of realism and romanticism seems to me to have precious little to do with the making of the future theatre.

I wish that I might say more of what I think that future theatre may be — a theatre utterly non-representational, expressing not a realistic but a microcosmic and theatrical vision of life, presented on a stage that is frankly a platform for acting — but that is a subject inviting an essay all to itself.

The painter has been feeling toward this new thing, often blunderingly, often timidly, but more fruitfully than any other experimenter. If he has shown us that he alone cannot make the new theatre, that in a sense must be credited to him too. Perhaps his greatest service at the present juncture is in proving that the first pivotal man in the playhouse *is* the dramatist, and that we can get only a small part of the way toward a new unified theatre until a new group of playwrights catches up with this little band of visual visionaries.

ART AND ARITHMETIC

By Claude Bragdon

THE art of music is all compounded of mathematical relationships: it is, in a sense, arithmetic made audible; but the mathematics of the arts of space, though quite as basic, are more obscure. Jay Hambidge, in "Dynamic Symmetry", dealt with one aspect of this subject, "The Beautiful Necessity" opens other vistas, and here I shall endeavor to present still another view — the possibility of deriving fresh ornamental motifs from the so-called "magical" arrangements of numbers. For obvious reasons the subject is here related to the new art of the theatre, but the idea involved is applicable to any of the arts of space, and particularly to that *art of light* — of mobile form and color — of which the theatre is likely to be the matrix, because there, more than anywhere, the attention of the artist is acutely fixed on light, its reactions upon consciousness can be observed, and opportunities abound for exploration and experiment.

As a practicing architect I was long ago impressed with the need of a form-language: a style, a manner, a medium — call it by whatever name — which should express our modernity; that is, our habits, tastes, beliefs (if we have any beliefs), in the same sense that Greek architecture and sculpture expressed the habits, tastes, and beliefs of the Athenian of the age of Pericles.

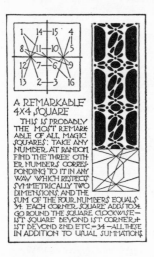

A REMARKABLE 4X4 SQUARE

THIS IS PROBABLY THE MOST REMARK- ABLE OF ALL MAGIC SQUARES: TAKE ANY NUMBER AT RANDOM FIND THE THREE OTH- ER NUMBERS CORRES- PONDING TO IT IN ANY WAY WHICH RESPECTS SYMMETRICALLY TWO DIMENSIONS, AND THE SUM OF THE FOUR NUMBERS EQUALS 34. EACH CORNER SQUARE ADDS TO 34. GO ROUND THE SQUARE CLOCKWISE— 1ST SQUARE BEYOND 1ST CORNER,+ 1ST BEYOND 2ND ETC.=34 —ALL THESE IN ADDITION TO USUAL SUMMATIONS

A style is never the conscious creation of an individual, but the product of many minds: it emerges gradually from the depths of the racial or national consciousness, as a coral island emerges from the depths of the sea. Therefore I narrowed my attention and endeavor to a single phase — ornament, a field wherein we are unabashed pensioners of the past, fed from "Meyer's Handbook of Ornament", or some equally stale trough, filled with the garbage of dead styles. I determined to find, if possible, food more energizing and appropriate, even though less delicate to the taste.

Keats' famous phrase — "Beauty is truth, truth beauty" — gave me the necessary clue. But what is truth? Philip Henry Wynne once told me that mathematical truth alone could be completely demonstrated, and I remembered Arago's answer to Madame Daguerre, when she complained that people were saying that her husband was crazy because he was trying to make permanent the image in a mirror: "He who, *outside of pure mathematics*, declares a thing to be impossible, speaks without reason." This was only another way of saying that mathematical truth is not relative, but absolute. *Seek therefore in number and geometry*, prompted the inner voice.

One of the most amazing revelations of the properties of numbers — of mathematical truth — is to be found in *magic squares*. A magic square is a numerical acrostic: a square of numbers so arranged that all vertical, all horizontal, and the two long diagonal lines yield the same sum. But by what process can this "mathematical truth" be revealed to the eye, as well as to the mind — how translate it into visible beauty? Fortunately there is a workable method. Most

47	10	23	64	49	2	59	6
22	63	48	9	60	5	50	3
11	46	61	24	1	52	7	58
62	21	12	45	8	57	4	51
19	36	25	40	13	44	53	30
26	39	20	33	56	29	14	43
35	18	37	28	41	16	31	54
38	27	34	17	32	55	42	15

MAGIC SQUARE

MAGIC LINES IN 2 KNIGHT'S-MOVE MAGIC SQUARES SHOWING INTRINSIC INTEREST AND BEAUTY OF THE "WEB" ITSELF, ALL UNADORNED

magic squares, because the numbers which compose them are *consecutive*, contain what is known as a *magic line*, discovered by tracing the numbers in their natural order from square to square. This process creates a pattern in space, a "web", always full of interest, sometimes beautiful. This beauty may be brought out and enhanced by accenting intersections, stopping out certain interspaces, by making the web a scaffolding, as it were, for *notan* — light and dark — and color composition; in short, by dealing with it in any way in which the æsthetic intuition may direct. It will give that intuition something to work with, a firm foundation — "beautiful bones" for any garment of flesh.

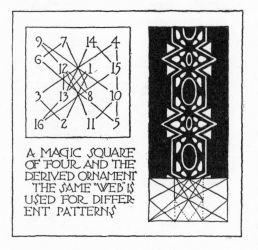

A MAGIC SQUARE OF FOUR AND THE DERIVED ORNAMENT THE SAME "WEB" IS USED FOR DIFFERENT PATTERNS

One peculiarity of the ornamental patterns derived from this source and developed by these methods is that they are free of associations with anything other than themselves. They may superficially resemble Moorish, Chinese, or Hindu ornament, by reason of the fact that the common source of them all is geometry and number; or, treated in a certain way, they may suggest Celtic interlaces, but nevertheless here is something distinctly *sui generis*. Now, by reason of this quality of *unrelatedness*, these patterns might prove extremely useful to the artist in the theatre, called upon to realize to the imagination some environment or locale which no eye has ever seen — heaven, fairyland, the kingdom of dreams, the fourth dimension. In problems of this sort he now has difficulty in avoiding some betrayal of the mind through the memory, some blurring of the desired impression brought about through the intrusion of forms or details associated with some one of the historic styles, bringing the imagination suddenly to earth, like a bullet through a balloon.

There is a scene in "The Light of Asia", for example — Buddha in heaven before his incarnation — which would be robbed of certain terrors for the artist who had at his command an ornamental mode almost as abstract as mathematics itself, and it might be resorted to in the setting of Dunsany's one-act play, "The

PLANE PROJECTION OF HEXADEKAHED-ROID (A 4 DIMENSION AL FIGURE). MOTIF FOR THE JAZZ CUR-TAINS IN FIRST ACT

THE MAGIC SQUARE OF THREE AND MAGIC LINE YIELDING MOTIF FOR LAMBREQUIN AND CURTAIN IN THE FIRST ACT SCENE "OH LADY, LADY!"

Glittering Gate." For that gate must impress the audience, as it does the two sorry cracksmen, as being the very door of heaven itself. As such, it might appropriately be inlaid "with patines of bright gold", but these must inevitably form a pattern, and one not derived from any of the so-called historic styles. De-nied this source, where shall the artist turn for inspira-tion? To the deepest well-spring of his being, or, if that yields nothing but dryness, to these diagrams and to the pages of "Projective Ornament", where the application of mathematics to art is made plain.

This style of ornamentation would lend itself with an especial grace, also, to the setting and costuming of the vaudeville act, the revue, the musical comedy, because these things, though essentially of the modern world, are yet divorced from the realities of every-day life, being an avenue of escape from them. The literal, the realistic, therefore, is the last thing that is wanted. I once ex-perimented in this field with a stock production of "Oh Lady, Lady!" — a comedy of no par-ticular distinction, and of a now al-

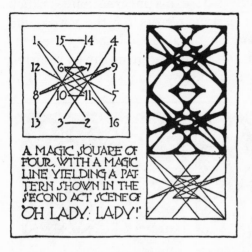

A MAGIC SQUARE OF FOUR, WITH A MAGIC LINE YIELDING A PAT-TERN SHOWN IN THE SECOND ACT SCENE OF OH LADY, LADY!

ready outmoded *genre*, but with music by Jerome Kern of a surpassing loveliness and charm. The two scenes — "a hall in the wealthy Mrs. Farrington's place on Long Island" and "a Greenwich Village private roof garden" — lent themselves with an especial grace to just the sort of fanciful treatment the whole impos-sible, ridiculous, delightful thing seemed to demand — wherein the ladies and gentlemen of the ensemble tripped in and out for no particular reason, and every-one, at any provocation or under any pretense, burst into song or into dance. My only aim was to make the settings likewise musical and rhythmic, so the first scene was dominated by great jazz curtains extending from floor to ceiling, and the second by colored geo-metric shades and lanterns. The result proved highly pleasing to the audiences, which greeted the rise of every curtain with spontaneous applause.

I commend all this to the attention of other designers in the hope that they, with more art, may better my instruction, for why should we forever revolve within the circle of the historic styles, striving to express our newness in dead languages learned by rote? There are doubtless other and better approaches to the solution of this pressing problem

EULER'S KNIGHT'S-MOVE MAGIC SQUARE OF FIVE CONTAINING MAGICALLY DEVELOPED LINE—THE NUMBERS IN NATURAL ORDER—MAKING A 'WEB' FROM WHICH COMES THIS PATTERN USED FOR THE GLITTERING GATE

of an ornamental mode which is our own, than the one here so cursorily sketched. The point I wish to enforce is the necessity of attempting something other than mere copyism of the past.[1]

[1] Those who desire to pursue this subject further are referred to Mr. Bragdon's " *Projective Ornament, Architecture and Democracy* " and an essay entitled " *Ornament from Magic Squares* ", published in the December, 1926, *Architectural Record*.

SHAKESPEARE, THE DESIGNER'S TOUCHSTONE

By John Mason Brown

To achieve immortality is one thing, to survive it another, and Shakespeare is one of the few playwrights who have succeeded at both. For the fate of playwrights is as a rule limited to the life of the theatres for which they write. They are almost inevitably the contemporaries of the architects who have built their playhouses for them, and thus conditioned their work. And the nearer they are to the theatre of their own days, the more inextricably they become immersed in its limitations as well as its conventions. When the conventions are discarded and the limitations are outgrown, the average playwright has perished from the stage. If he survives at all, it is in the classroom, or in special revivals, which either capitalize the quaintness of his craftsmanship or coddle it with the meticulous devotion of pedants. But in the theatre, where he can alone claim life, he is dead and forgotten. Usually, too, as he grows into a legendary Titan, his readers decrease until they are limited to specialists, and even his supposed admirers content themselves with reverent and indefinite mutterings of his name alone.

The fate of Shakespeare is, therefore, all the more

extraordinary. Hailed by Robert Greene in 1592 as an "upstart Crow" he has lasted as the only "Shake-scene," when his predecessors, as well as his contemporaries and successors, have slipped into immortality and died. He has outlasted his playhouses, survived his many adapters, and even lived down his admirers for some three hundred years, during which, from Burbage to Barrymore, the long procession of English-speaking players have been identified with his characters, and actors in every country have felt their reputations secure only when they have tested their talents in his plays.

If Shakespeare lived as the actor's playwright for some three hundred years, his stage history has taken a decisive turn during the last thirty. He is no longer the actor's testing ground alone. He is now the producer's challenge and the designer's release, as is proven by the fact that, in almost all of the notable experimental productions which the last thirty years and the New Movement have revealed, the play has been Shake-speare's. He has been the only dramatist the more advanced directors could count upon to keep pace with the ever-increasing facilities of the back-stage. Though maintaining his own integrity as a playwright, he has allowed the scene painter to assert himself as the scenic artist by granting him material for independent interpretative work of his own. Accordingly, from Moscow to Manhattan, contemporary directors have waged their most important warfare against the cluttered realism of the older stages under the Shakespearean banner. In short, he has become the dramatist of the New Movement, if not its champion.

In "the good old days", which in the theatre, as in all things, can be defined as the days that are dimmed in remembrance or safe from recall, the emphasis went almost exclusively upon the player. It was Booth's "Hamlet", Salvini's "Othello", Forrest's "King Lear", or Garrick's "Richard III", much more than it was Shakespeare's. And Shakespeare himself was kept alive as a vehicle rather than as a playwright. From Betterton down, each succeeding generation in the English and American theatre centered its major interest on the star instead of the play. Accordingly it was Booth's performance which lasted as a memory and not the play that Shakespeare wrote. The very audiences that took the plays for granted apparently never tired of watching each new performer with a jealous and alert interest as he made his "points." They came to the theatre much as the Greeks had come, except that where the Greeks focussed their attention upon a dramatist as he made his "points" by the retelling of a popular legend, these older English-speaking audiences riveted theirs upon an actor as he made his "points" on a popular but mythical Shakespeare. Certainly, their interest could not have centered on the production they sat before, because, with the exception of the star, the stage was peopled with supernumeraries. Certainly, for almost two hundred years the settings could have attracted but little notice, for actor-managers lavished their money on spectacles and pantomimes, and with almost one accord skimped on Shakespeare. And surely, too, the individual stamp of the director was of no importance, because the actor managed his own "business", and, needless to say,

managed it to his own advantage, so that the performance became an exhibitionist's paradise. The actor
was glorified and the play, in a garbled and emasculated
form, was not "produced" at all as we know production today.

With the New Movement, however, the emphasis
has changed. The director and the designer have
stepped into an unheard-of prominence, and, where
once a performance was known only by its player, it is
now just as apt to be identified by its designer or its
director. The more closely in touch with the theatre
of Europe and America a person is, the more apt he is
to speak of Craig's "Hamlet", Jessner's "Othello",
Granville-Barker's "A Midsummer Night's Dream",
Reinhardt's "King Lear", Jones' "Macbeth", or
Copeau's "Twelfth Night." And this new emphasis
indicates as well as anything else the current trend in
Shakespearean production, though it omits the idea
which prompted the shift and the change it has made
possible. For the stressing of the designer and the
director in the New Movement is important to Shakespeare only in so far as it has freed him as a dramatist
and placed the final emphasis on his plays.

It is not to be thought that Shakespeare has always
survived immortality unaided, or that Garrick, Kemble,
or Macready, standard-bearers of the "great tradition,"
used Shakespeare's texts alone. As Professor Odell
has made clear in "Shakespeare from Betterton to
Irving" he was victimized for nearly a hundred years
by endless adapters, who, sharing the enthusiasm of
Davenant, felt they "loved Shakespeare so much they
could not leave him alone." The result was that from

the Restoration well into the nineteenth century he was target for a host of minor play-doctors, who, though they sang his praises in their prefaces as the world's greatest dramatist, did not hesitate to rewrite him in their playing versions. He was treated by Davenant, Shadwell, Dryden, and Tate as a brilliant barbarian who had to be rewritten before he could please the cultivated audiences of the Restoration, with their love of the Unities and the frigid exaltations of "Heroic Tragedy." The whole attitude was summed up by Tate, who admitted in his preface to "King Lear" in 1681 that he had found it "a Heap of Jewels unstrung and unpolish'd; yet so dazzling in their disorder that I soon perceiv'd I had seiz'd a Treasure."

Some years before Tate retouched "King Lear", "Romeo and Juliet" had been revived at Lincoln's Inn Fields, as "wrote by Mr. Shakespear." Soon after the production, however, it was made "into a Tragi-comedy" and tested for a while in both forms "so that when the Tragedy was Reviv'd again, 'twas Play'd Alternately, Tragical one Day and Tragi-comical another; for several Days together." The "tragical" version was assuredly one of the last versions of this or any other of the plays to reach the stage as "wrote by Mr. Shakespear" for many a year. And the habit of improving upon him did not stop with the Restoration. In 1700 Colley Cibber remade "Richard III" into a composite picture of the "Histories" that still persists, but Cibber's text was at least compiled rather than composed by him. The untampered texts sank into such a deep obscurity that it was quite natural of Quin to be perplexed when he saw that Garrick was going to revive "Macbeth" "as written by Shakespeare." In despairing ignorance Quin asked "What does he mean? Don't I play 'Macbeth' as written by Shakespeare?" But, as a matter of fact, neither did Garrick, who omitted the drunken porter from "Macbeth" as a violation of the Unities, and wrote a lengthy speech for "Macbeth" to deliver just before his death to insure the "deep damnation of his taking off." And this same Garrick, as the leading Shakespearean actor of his day, if not of all time, played "King Lear" with a Pollyanna ending that found Lear and Cordelia happily in charge of their kingdom once more. It was this same Garrick, too, who omitted the grave-diggers and Ophelia's burial from "Hamlet", and improved "Romeo and Juliet" by reviving Juliet in the tomb so that the lovers could have one more last and truly powerful farewell. But Garrick's sins were slim compared to the crimes committed in the name of Shakespeare on the English stage of Garrick's day. It was not until 1823 that Elliston and Kean resurrected the last act of "Lear" and the original contributions of actor-managers began to disappear from Shakespeare. Though Macready, Phelps, and Kean read unadulterated lines, the sins now shifted to those of omission, but what was far more important than the omission of single speeches was the omission of Shakespeare's own dramatic structure. As the settings, approaching the realistic ideals of Irving and Tree, became more and more solid during the nineteenth century, they became more and more difficult to move, and the true scene sequence of Shakespeare, which most characterizes his craftsmanship, became increasingly impossible to preserve. For the convenience of the stage manager, several garden or interior scenes were lumped together in order to "cut down changes." In this matter Shakespeare's own text was not consulted, because, judging from the popularity of the practice, almost any stage manager was supposed to know more about Shakespeare's own job than Shakespeare did himself. His scenes were combined into acts, and, groaning under a realism he had never desired, Shakespeare emerged as a playwright using a technical form not completely divorced from that of Henry Arthur Jones. In other words, though his lines had earned the right to be heard, his plays were still refashioned into "well-made" plays, just as if he himself had been entirely innocent of the art of playmaking when he dashed off successes for the Globe Theatre.

To the traditionalists the innovations of the New Movement have seemed sacrilege, but the simple truth of the whole matter is that there are no authentic Shakespearean traditions. They died, it must be repeated, with his contemporaries, and were buried by Sir William Davenant, the chief connecting link between the theatre of Shakespeare and that of the Restoration, who took pains to rewrite the plays in order to fit them to the needs of new playhouses and new audiences. What we have been brought up on as our Shakespearean tradition, with its archæological costumes and settings, goes no further back than the cradle songs of Queen Victoria. For a full two hundred years before the archæologists of the latter half of the nineteenth century busied themselves in the theatre, Shakespeare had been played in "modern dress," whether the time

Fleischman

Max Reinhardt is keenly interested in new experiments and never hampered by tradition. "King Lear", as he gave it in Vienna with Ernest de Weerth as his designer, was defined by no time or place. "O, ye are men of stones" was taken as the key to the play. De Weerth dressed his characters in rubber, which under the proper lights gave them a statuesque aloofness, as in this costume of Helena Thimig's Cordelia.

was the Restoration or the reigns of the four Georges, as the contemporary prints show all too clearly. With the exception of Richard III, Henry VIII, and Falstaff, Elizabethan costumes disappeared from the stage, to be replaced by "modern dress" in a slightly exaggerated form. Thus Mrs. Pope dressed Cleopatra in the hoop-skirt and powdered wig of her day; Mrs. Abington's Rosalind appeared in a strange combination of the latest style in large hats and the most common costume of the men who crowded to see her; Mrs. Yates encircled her Lady Macbeth in skirts wide enough to hide all her crimes, and Garrick dressed Hamlet in a contemporary French costume, King Lear in the regal robes of the Georges, and Macbeth as a nobleman fresh from court. Even Kemble, who prided himself on his attention to details of costume and setting, wore the uniform of a dragoon when he appeared as Hotspur. When the costumes were not contemporaneous, they were mildly allegorical, and distinctly theatrical. Thus tragic heroes, even as played by Garrick, were often topped with feathers, because plumage was as surely a symbol of tragedy as were the green baize carpets that covered the stages of Drury Lane and Covent Garden when a tragedy was to be played. And warriors, for the torrential passions of the "classic" plays, were inclined to dress à la Romaine. It was only natural, therefore, that, when the first of the archæologists entered the theatre, and tried to do away with the venerable tradition of Shakespeare in modern dress, which had lasted nearly two hundred years, they should have met with disapproval. When they set about placing "Hamlet" in an authentic Denmark,

SCENE DESIGN

and "Antony and Cleopatra" in a British Museum
Egypt, they came as innovators, discarding the practice of Betterton, Cibber, Garrick, and Kemble. It
was Macklin, the same Macklin who had revolutionized
the playing of Shylock by making him into the tragic
figure we know today, that broke with tradition in 1773
by dressing Macbeth in Scottish costume. And the
plaid bonnet on his veteran brow was the signal for one
of those riots which were so common in London theatres of the time. Macklin had thrown his hat into
the ring, and, little by little, the plaid bonnet conquered. Mrs. Siddons introduced long and statuesque
lines, because . . . because of her fondness for statues,
and before anyone really knew what was happening or
why, the archæologists were in the theatre. And poor
Shakespeare, concerned only with the living qualities
in character, and not caring a fig for history except as
a factory for his plots, poor Shakespeare, with his
"small Latin and less Greek", was the cause for exact
reproductions of forums and palaces, regardless of
whether they possessed playing values or not. With
them, too, came costumes, aiming at exactitude, but
on the whole as historically inaccurate as Shakespeare's
own texts, crammed as they were with anachronisms,
and peopled as they were with Englishmen regardless
of their locale. And the whole matter of pseudo-
Gothic trappings and stained-glass window costumes
took possession of the stage, devoting little or no
attention to what the playwright had said, or to the
inner meaning of the plays. Yet overnight again, the
origins of this tradition became dimmed, and what was
only a new tradition was venerated as an old one, and

has come down to us supposedly inviolate because it is supposedly Shakespearean.

Though critics without end could have called for the final restoration of the text, and directors without number could have desired to produce the plays as "wrote by Mr. Shakespear", the original number and order of his scenes could not be revived until the designer had cleared the way. In the whole sweep of the English stage as traced by Professor Odell, there is not a single mention of a scene-painter who went to Shakespeare for his inspiration instead of going to actor-managers. From Streeter through Stanfield and J. Selby Hall these decorators seem to have been content to paint only the scenes they ordered. Apparently it had not occurred to them that the salvation of the Shakespearean text was, in its last analysis, the designer's own very special problem as well as one of his finest opportunities. For when all is said and done, Shakespeare, like every practising playwright who is worth his salt and earns it, wrote with the playhouse of his own day in mind. But because the playhouse that he knew and worked in had disappeared as a theatre form, quite without justification, producing managers assumed for a great many years that Shakespeare's own dramatic structure had likewise become obsolete. Until recently, and unfortunately even now in some cases, they have treated it as an accidental part of his art as a dramatist, instead of holding it the groundwork of his dramatic effects. Accordingly they have taken on themselves the task of refashioning his plays and casting his own structure to the winds.

Nor was it in England or America, where Shakespeare

has been taken for granted as a literary legacy, that the first experiménts were introduced which made the playing of the whole text possible. Instead it was Germany, ever active in the theatre, that first faced the length and the form of Shakespeare's plays as a theatre problem. It was Goethe who, as director of the Court Theatre at Weimar, devised one of the earliest "unit settings" to meet Shakespeare's dramaturgic demands. This fact alone, were it not for many later and additional contributions, would almost be enough to justify the Germans in calling Shakespeare "unser Shakespeare." What Goethe started, Immermann carried even further in planning a stage with proscenium doors, a back-stage, and a fore-stage, which thus facilitated the continuous and unadulterated playing of the Shakespearean texts and established a precedent for many of the most modern radicals.

It is in just this way, and because he has been in actual command of the back-stage, that the designer has been able to be of service. His genius as well as his ingenuity has had much to do with making the use of Shakespeare's scene sequence possible. He has differed from the older scene-painters in that he has been willing to make his stage fit Shakespeare, rather than make Shakespeare fit his stage. Occasionally, in such interesting experiments as John Corbin's production of "The Tempest" at the Century Theatre in 1916, or Forbes-Robertson's farewell performance of "Hamlet" at Harvard, Shakespeare has been seen in reconstructions of Elizabethan playhouses, where his craftsmanship has been unimpeded on the stage for which it was intended. But the modern designer has not been contented with research and reconstruction alone. He has wanted to face the more difficult problem of translating Shakespeare into terms of the modern theatre. To do this he has summoned all the devices at his command. He has used screens or curtains, worked as a painter or a builder, employed revolving, wagon, or elevator stages, planned unit settings, or even contrived adjustable constructions. All of these have been only means to the designer's own approach, which in the New Movement, for the first time, has been that of an interpretative artist. Knowing that Shakespeare was, in a sense, his own designer, the modern designer has rebelled against the realistic régime which cluttered the stage at the end of the nineteenth century. He has rebelled because its heavy and archæologically correct settings not only doubled on the scenic passages in Shakespeare but also undid them by representing realistically what their poetry had suggested abstractly. In other words, the modern designer has realized that Shakespeare was a poet as well as a playwright and has begun to seek for the best way in which to present him as both.

Moreover he has abandoned the old-fashioned habit of treating each individual scene as an isolated problem. Instead he has treated the play as a whole, culling from it a general and abstract idea which he could apply to the entire production. He has seen that a Shakespearean play was not necessarily the affair of any one character, or even of a group of characters in conflict. It could as well have a cosmic meaning. The supernatural forces of " Macbeth ", for example, its ghosts and its witches, to live afresh for an incredulous age, could shake off their fish-net trappings and take on a new and fatalistic meaning by emerging as the forces enslaving Man. Accordingly, the more radical designer has aimed at more than backing beauty with beauty. He has hoped his settings could serve as symbols, abstractly suggested so as to prod and not confine the imagination of his audience.

He has not always been fortunate in his choice of means nor has he always succeeded in realizing his intention. Frequently he has revelled only in a scenemakers' holiday, at the expense of both the play and performance, and he has been, at times, even more self-centered in his interests than the old actor-manager. But from Gordon Craig to Robert Edmond Jones, when he has sensed his function aright, he has brought not only a new talent into the theatre, but a fresh loveliness and power to Shakespeare.

At best, however, the designer has been only a contributor. Though he has cleared the stage for Shakespeare, and placed the plays before settings as quickening in their suggestion as the texts themselves, his work has been only a contribution to the entire production of which the director is in charge. From this moment, too, Shakespeare has become the playwright of the director, and his fate, as well as that of the actor, and the designer, is in the director's hands. The director of the New Movement is an autocrat, a final interpreter, who orchestrates the entire performance. He is seldom a player and never an "actor-manager." He has not, therefore, been tempted, as the old actor-managers were, to omit or cut scenes in which he did not appear, or add effective "bits" for his own ag-

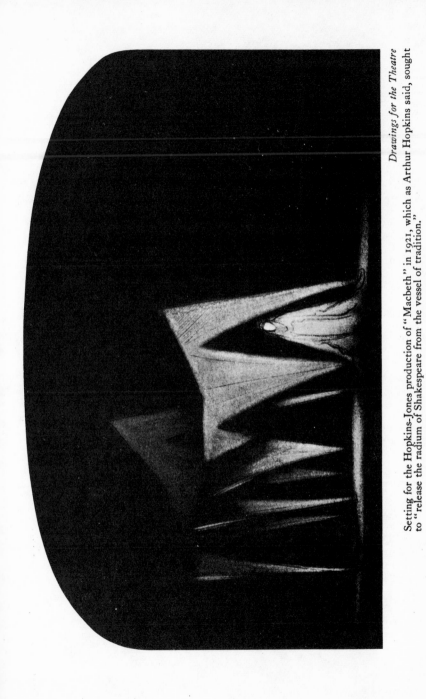

Setting for the Hopkins-Jones production of "Macbeth," in 1921, which as Arthur Hopkins said, sought to "release the radium of Shakespeare from the vessel of tradition."

grandizement. Nor has he wanted to surround himself with supernumeraries to make the comparison throw his own playing into a more favorable light. He has, in short, been able to see the production as a whole and work disinterestedly for the coördination of its parts.

Like the designer, he has faced the problem of translating the plays into the most living terms of the contemporary theatre. And, like the designer, and often hand in hand with him, he has sought to emphasize their cosmic significance. He, too, has worked in abstractions, but where the designer has been able to work in the pliant materials of his own medium, the director has faced actors with their all too solid flesh. He has had to train them to the stylization he has wanted, blending their actions into the backgrounds his scenic artist has provided. In his charge, too, has been the pacing of their scenes, the manipulation of crowds, the complete intensification and patterning of the performance.

This modern director of Shakespeare, with his superhuman responsibilities, is a virtuoso figure, as yet unknown in America, and known to England chiefly in Granville-Barker. He has been found in Paris at the Vieux Colombier, where Copeau, working on a permanent stage, has almost substituted properties for scenery, and relied on his actors, thus unfettered, to liberate the play. He exists in Budapest with Hevesi, who in one season offered some fifteen Shakespearean plays to his public, and in Prague with Kvapil and Hilar, who at rival theatres have found Shakespeare their most popular playwright. But it is in Germany

that this virtuoso director thrives most, with Reinhardt, Jessner, and Weichert heading a long list of
directors who have placed the stamp of their own per-
sonalities on their productions. And it was, by the
way, from this same Germany, too, that the Saxe-
Meiningen Company came to London in 1881 and
introduced a new ideal in production by the perfection
of its ensemble and the grouping of its crowds.

He is not infallible, this director of the New Movement. He fumbles often, but even in his failures he
permits a Shakespearean play to reach the stage as a
play instead of as a vehicle. And above all his virtues
is the fact that he is not ashamed of treating it as
theatrical property, living only in the theatre.

LIGHTING

By Irving Pichel

THE problem of stage lighting is curiously unlike the other æsthetic problems of the theatre. The possibilities of expressiveness in acting, for example, are definitely limited by an instrument, the capacities of which, however great, are known and have been, in more than one instance, extended to their utmost. While there is an everlasting refreshment of experiment, technical study, and approach to some sort of formal perfection in acting, it may well be — due simply to the mortality of actors and audiences — that the past has seen as great acting as the future shall ever know.

It seems to us much the same with the stage and its scenery. The stages of the Greeks, the Globe, the Vieux Colombier, set form above machine. Sandwiched between these stages those of Inigo Jones or the Bibienas, of Linnebach, Haseit, Strnad, or Norman Geddes, with their mechanical ingenuity, make architecture evanescent, or, at least, ductile. Both kinds of stages, most ancient or most modern, aim at a certain goal which has been as clearly apprehended in the past as it is likely to be hereafter, save as machinery is more perfect in the future.

Above all, as the actor has a body with just so many limbs and one familiarly featured face, the theatre has one body — auditorium and stage; their relations may apparently alter, but the one must always, somehow, be opposite the other.

Light in the theatre is exempt from this kind of limitation, for the means of its production have just begun to develop. In the imagination, in the great and lesser lights of the universe, we have caught a glimpse of a goal. The pathway is, however, just beginning to open, and means for travelling it are unlimited in possibility.

The art of stage lighting, unlike those of acting, architecture (theatre), stage mechanics, scene design and painting, costume, has almost no history. Such history as it has, until the past two decades, is simply the history of artificial illuminants. And it may be noted that in the history of illumination the point when new chapters came to be written in the theatre was the moment when each and every source of light did not need to be hand tended.

It is very little more than three hundred years ago that illumination and the theatre had their first meeting. The Greeks played by the light of the sun. So did Shakespeare and his fellows. A torch on the stage of the Globe or the Swan indicated night, but did not illumine it. And it may be worth considering that light, in these ancient theatres — the light of the sun — did not reinforce the "mood" of play or scene, but mitigated it. Œdipus, his eyes streaming blood; or the wholesale slaughters of Elizabethan tragedies, must have seemed happily less terrible to an audience seated in the sun.

LIGHTING

It is true that before the theatre moved indoors, once and for all, plays were performed by artificial light — at court, in schools, in Renaissance gardens lighted by flares and pyrotechnics. Even a cursory reading of the stage directions of the masques of Ben Jonson or James Shirley indicates frequent spectacular illumination. The methods of these elder technicians will some day be investigated and described.

Generally, however, dependence was upon the same means by which the audience chamber was lighted — candles hung in chandeliers. The lights above the stage might be lowered and those above the audience raised into a well, so that, during the action of the play, a differentiation between audience and stage might be effected. So, with slight modification, things remained for a century and a half. A row of candles along the edge of the stage, the first footlights, made the actors' faces a little brighter. The supplanting of the wax or tallow candle by an oil lamp gave a brighter light less in need of frequent tending, but did not change the emphasis from simple illumination to effect.

The introduction of gas, with its numerous burners placed along a feed pipe for borders and footlights, did more than make available for stage use a brighter, more easily handled light. It introduced as well the possibility of controlling the intensity of the light. The gasman became an important member of the stage crew. With the invention of the lime-light for spotting and flooding, and the use of color which the lime made possible, the present-day situation sprang into being. The substitution of electricity for gas has done little to change the aims of stage lighting, though it has made available brighter and more flexibly controlled illuminant. The new instrument, however, added to the old, simple problem of illumination one new aim which we may term generically "effect."

"Effect" aimed at the reproduction, through the control of light intensity and color, of the effect of the lights of nature. Illumination, by the use of more or less scientifically constructed border reflectors, improved. Color circuits enabled the operator to flood the stage with light of any hue. Added to this general illumination, we have today a variety of lights which can be directed to a given area — floods, spot lights, large and small strip lights.

Still, by and large, the lighting of the stage generally aims at the illusion of something other than a stage and the lights are made to give, as far as they can, the effect of a light source of wholly different physical properties. To a very slight degree, indeed, have the optics of the instrument now in hand been studied and the lighting machine used with reference to its inherent capacities. It should be possible, with a little ingenuity, to devise a machine far better adapted to the imitation of natural light, if that is to be the aim of stage lighting. The discarded Fortuny system and some of its modifications do, in fact, approach the illusion-ideal far more successfully than our border-flood-spot system. Every producer recognizes the uselessness of the machinery we have as an illusion machine. Accordingly, we find any fair-sized production making almost no use of the stage switchboard or equipment, but carrying its own switchboard, dimmer box, specially constructed borders, and junction boxes. Big travelling shows which depend upon scenic effect, like the various " Follies ", use nothing belonging to the theatre in which they play except the electric current.

On the other hand, where sheer illusion is not the aim, the devices we have are being found capable of almost any demand that can be made of them, and, moreover, invention proceeds at a vastly more rapid stride when the artist or inventor seeks to apply the laws governing optic machinery and not to imitate the sun by means of light sources and lenses governed by different physical principles. As witness, we have had added to the resources of the stage X-ray type reflectors, parabolic reflector spots and, above all, the Clavilux of Thomas Wilfred, which is almost unexplored in its potentialities.

Lights, as used in the theatre, whether for illusion "effects" or for more arbitrary ends, fall into two classes, diffused and directed. In the first class are all border lights and footlights, strips, floods. In the second belong the various types of spots, which, by the use of lenses or reflectors, aim to bring the light rays toward parallel.

For a modern equipment, border lights are almost an anachronism, unless they are divided, not only into color circuits, but into sections so that the stage may be lighted sectionally. Even then the only border light that has any general usefulness is the first border, sometimes called the concert border. It is from this unit, or a corresponding location, that the main light in an interior scene using a ceiling must come. And most carefully lighted modern productions substitute for the first border of the theatre a pipe batten, from which are hung various units — spots and floods — directed to the particular areas of the stage at which light is desired. The further advantage of this arrangement is that each light may be colored at will and a far subtler variety of hue as well as intensity achieved than if the stage is lighted solidly with one color from an evenly diffusing unit.

It is the arrangement and organization of the control system — the switchboard and dimmers — that constitute the heart of the lighting problem, rather than the sort of equipment to be used. Some grouping of lights, by sizes, locations, or colors, is necessary and there are certain obvious places on the stage where lights may most advantageously be placed — the front edge of the stage for footlights, when they are used, a bridge crossing the stage behind and above the proscenium arch, a tower at each side of the stage directly behind the proscenium, stand lights right and left at the front, middle, and back of the stage, and overhead lights at the center and back of the stage for lighting interior scenes, and a certain number of specified sources in the auditorium.

Each of these locations should be provided with adequate pockets to provide current for the maximum number of lights to be used there. Each location should be represented on the switchboard by a main switch, and each outlet at the location by a subsidiary switch. Each circuit coming from an outlet should have a dimmer. With the interlocking mechanism the particular grouping of dimmers is more or less

Robert Edmond Jones and Kenneth Macgowan made a trip
through Europe some years ago to sketch the productions
which represented the best and most distinguishing features
of the European designer's and producer's art. The result
of their work was published in a book which they called "Continental Stagecraft." Isaac Grünewald's setting for the millstone scene in "Samson and Delilah" (above) at the Royal
Opera in Stockholm, Macgowan calls "easily the most effective I have ever seen in the theatre. The millstone symbolizes
and dramatizes imprisonment and torturing labor." This
sketch was made from the production by Mr. Jones.

immaterial, so long as the sequence in which they are placed has some logical reference to the lights they control. This type of installation implies a new starting point when we come actually to light the scene. With a definite system of fixed lights, one turns on the lights and then modifies them according to his judgment of the requirements, pictorial or emotional, of the given scene.

With equipment to be set as needed, the starting point is not full light, but darkness. The scene that is designed for its own sake must be illuminated for its own sake. Light modified in intensity, color, and direction is a concomitant of the picture.

With the stage or scene designed for the player, and the player only, this is not so. It is without meaning when the actor is absent from it. And so, without the actor, it needs no visibility. It is not a scene to draw an admiring gasp from an audience when the curtain rises upon it, whether the stage stands empty or not.

With such a scene — and it is the only sort of scene we care to consider for the time, as the painters and picture makers can offer all the guidance needed where the other sort is to be used — with this scene the light enters with the actor. If he is to be "discovered", he is discovered in light. If he enters, he enters with light, unless the dramatist brings him from darkness. It needs much study, however, to be certain whether the living part of the production, the actor, should ever enter into an empty light. In the type of scene we consider, wherein our lights are used according to their own capacities, and not as simulacra of the sun, the scene (visible only when there is light) is dead when the human being is absent. The only light, perhaps, into which an actor should enter from darkness is a light occupied by another player or group of players.

Does not this begin to reveal an entire technique for the lighting of the scene? The light shall be where people are.

And where are the people? Placed in groups or attitudes which convey a sense of their emotional relationships. Grouping is never merely pictorial composition. It is a sort of geometry, outlining the patterns established by the relations of the characters of the play. They are the points of the diagram. The lines connecting the points image the lines of force drawn from person to person, some strong, some weak. Visualized in terms of light, these points and these lines indicate to us the position of light sources, the directions of the beams and their intensities. Some indication of their color we may find, too, in the degree to which we are sensitive to the relation between color and emotion.

The lights should move, too. Not with the violent swing of the musical comedy front spot (though this has its uses, at times) but fading away or becoming dim in the area the player leaves and brightening before him.

Now, this is an abstract statement, and so, bare and incomplete, as abstractions are. But the director can carry the doctrine further. There are times when the background counts, as environment to shape character or action, and it must be visible to the degree in which it has significance. But always this significance is given the environment by the people who have been in it or are to come into it. The form of the mountain is interesting (dramatically) when a man looks at it, climbs it, is crushed by it. It may be personalized, and to the degree in which it is it enters into the scheme of lighting.

This brings us, in the long run, to naturalistic lighting and the naturalistic background. As far as the picture has human connotations, it asks a loving light to reveal the place of man in nature. Farther than this, it is not necessary to go. The imitation of the appearance of the world at large is for painters.

If light is gauged by the players, their numbers, the extent and rapidity of their movements, the patterns their relative positions and their movements trace, there is no danger either of overlighting or underlighting the scene. It is not necessary or particularly expressive to imitate the color of sunlight or moonlight, as such. The important matter today, as in the first theatres, is that the players shall be visible. Our advantage over the ancients, who had only the sun, is that we can reveal the player and eliminate anything that does not pertain to him in the scene he dominates.

COSTUMES

COSTUMES

A costume is obviously a part of any stage design in which it figures. To be successfully conceived, it must be in the same spirit as the setting, as well as in harmony with the line and color. But it must be more than that; every successful costume must have its own completion in terms of its own material and of the period and personality it represents. And even given all of this, a costume does not achieve its life until it is worn by an actor and takes on the living character which he assumes. Certain actors have a way of imbuing their costumes with life and making them a part of the life of the play. So Haidee Wright as Queen Elizabeth, and Katherine Cornell as Mary Fitton in Norman-Bel Geddes' costumes for Clemence Dane's "Will Shakespeare", so Doris Keane in "Starlight", and Ethel Barrymore with the gleaming robe that Helen Dryden gave her in "Clair de Lune." So Albert Carroll as the Prince of Wales in the Grand Street Follies and the Buddhist Monk in "The Little Clay Cart" at the Neighborhood Playhouse. The designer's relation to the problem of costume is explained in Aline Bernstein's essay "Designing for Actors"; the actor's part is developed in Stark Young's "On Wearing Costumes."

ON WEARING COSTUMES

By Stark Young

If the ability to see the point appears anywhere in the theatre, it appears in the wearing of a costume. A costume ideally designed and ideally worn is a visual description of what the speeches and movements express in words and actions. And seeing the point with regard to the costume consists of first discerning its characteristic quality and then knowing how to translate this quality into the actor's own body, by which the costume is carried and through which it is animated, through which it comes to life and is itself, or else remains thwarted and is dead.

Costumes become the art of the theatre when clothes are translated into something which they were not before and have added to them something that was not there before. This something added derives from the play, from the scene, the lights, the dramatic mood and idea, the whole theatrical occasion of which the costumes make a part. A costume when it has become the art of the theatre is not a mere duplicate; it has the same relation to the original garment that a costume in a portrait of Velasquez has when it becomes the art of painting. To the original clothes Velasquez has

Whether she wears the stiff regalities of "The Czarina" (above) or the undulating hoops of "Romance", or the bulging bustles of "Starlight", Doris Keane is unerring in her knowledge of how to use her body so that each fold of her costume becomes dramatic.

added something that was not there before and they have become painting. And if a designer doing an historical costume takes it from a Velasquez canvas, he does not slavishly reproduce it; he does with that painted costume what the painter did with the original clothes: he translates it into theatrical terms exactly as Velasquez translated them into painting terms.

Costumes created in terms of the art of the theatre are designed either to interpret and create a dramatic mood or to add to this intention the element of period or epoch or locality. In one case there is a mood to be expressed. It may be radiance, realistic exactitude or rapture, or mystery or magnificence, or romance or any of the infinite moods that the theatre can present. Beginning with actuality, with clothes as they exist for any observer, the artist designer does what the artist in every case must do, which is to establish and create the relation of his own inner world to the world outside of him. He uses the literal costume with which he begins as the means through which he can express what he has to say. He will extend a line here or heighten a quality there, he will intensify a tone, he will eliminate and underscore, he will do whatever is necessary to force the costume to say the dramatic thing that is necessary to the moment. Sometimes for his designing he is entirely free. He has no clothes that he must follow or resemble, he can use fabric, color, and line purely in themselves to express what he likes. His final problem, however, is the same as it is when he uses actual and recognizable clothes for a starting point: the expression of an idea in stage garments.

The designer when he comes to period costumes has

to deal with an actuality that is in all cases whatsoever already established. That is to say, he deals with costumes that are already expressive; the quality of an epoch adds another element to the problem of the dramatic mood and is to be converted into that mood.

A costume truly expressive of its epoch catches exactly the characteristic quality from the civilization out of which it arises, the social ideas, canons of taste, the point of view with regard to life and art. The Spain of Philip the Fourth finds its provincialism and remoteness from the rest of Europe, its magnificence and courtly suavity, its power and wealth, and self-assurance and elegance, expressed in those costumes that we see in Velasquez' pictures. The periwig that we see at the court of France and spreading from there throughout the fashions of Europe never got to Spain at all, the natural hair worn long persisted — together with the stiff-starched collar — for two generations after the rest of the world had abandoned it. The fanaticism and pride, the wealth and decorum and austere magnificence show in the fabric and in the cut and design of the gowns of those Infantas and the court suits of Velasquez' admirals and kings and princes. The costumes of Ghirlandaio have all the severity and distinction of the Florence of his day. The figures of Lisa Tornabuoni and those ladies and cavaliers and scholars with her in the chapel frescoes of Santa Maria Novella stand firmly without being dull, they are alive and stiff at the same time, they are angular and elegant, decorous and intense at the same moment. They have a grand austere thinness and a kind of poignant chic. The textiles they employ are severe and rich, intricate and strangely puritanical, and the design and flow of the lines and masses of their garments are both harsh and wistful. In the costumes of the Byzantium of later Greek days, the moody splendor of the East, the decaying exoticism of Hellenic civilization, the eclectic culture, the relaxation and excess of the barbaric, all appear. These qualities in historic costumes — or in costumes from foreign lands whose separation from us in space amounts to one in time — the designer recreates in the terms of the art of the theatre. The actor wearing the costumes has for his necessity the problem of how he shall bring to them their characteristic quality, and, in so far as he is an artist in this one respect of wearing costumes, how he can recreate them in terms of himself and express himself in terms of them, adding even to the costume, as the designer artist has created it, something that up to the moment when the actor artist puts it on was not there before.

I remember once watching the performance of a young actress in the part of Mrs. Candour in "The School for Scandal." At one moment in the play, when she was about to leave the drawing-room, she linked arms with two of the gentlemen and left the room hanging on them, laughing merrily and archly. What the player should have had, in order to fill and carry this costume of hers, what lustre of voice and movement, was everywhere about her to be learned. She should have known from the powder in her hair if from nothing else, or from the height of her heels, or the flounces and hoops of her costume, that such a manner as she displayed was not possible. She might have known this from the very furniture of the room itself. That chair of the late eighteenth century sits lightly on its legs and shows an exquisite damask in its covering, but it sits nevertheless secure, its design is poised and secure, its utility certain. It has an elaborate and chaste finish, a highly veneered and highly civilized frailty, and polish and reserve. That fan on the table, "chicken skin, delicate" as the Pompadour's which hides nothing and hides all; the clear, suave panels of the wall; to these too, as well as the chair, she might have gone to school, just as she might have got the proper manner from the study of her lines, from the very style of the writing itself, whose high finish, whose artifice, whose suave design and whose removal from the direct prose of everyday show no relation to a society of guffaw and rollicking about. To walk so in such a gown meant that this young actress did not wear her eighteenth century costume at all. She had no idea what her clothes expressed, and walked in them, just as they in their turn hung on her, without connection and without point.

If an actor in a Sophoclean tragedy is given a costume and wants to learn to wear it, he can study the nature of the period and the essential quality that underlies Sophocles' conceptions. Character, events, emotional reactions, are seen by him in large and typical outlines, universal and stately, and are never particularized into individual detail or realistic and subjective minutiæ. The reading of the verse exhibits the stately and simplified scale of recitation suited to such a drama. The movements of the actor's body, of his hands and arms and head, his stride and his carriage, have the general and nobly chosen and simplified style that the whole conception of the play requires. Having discerned these qualities in the play and achieved them in the acting, the actor must recognize that they are inherent in the costumes as well, and are to be carried into the wearing of them. Let him think of the Greek marbles, of that land with its sure, final outlines. Let him think of the music that the Athenian playgoer heard as he watched those garments moving under that clear light and with the sea wind blowing on them; a music of harmonious lines, the voice of the flute, of pipes single and pure above the murmuring and more solid texture of strings. He must keep clear like that the lines of his costume, lines flowing singly or in complex rhythms upon the mass of it. A quick movement or a nervous carriage, a sudden and individual impetuosity of gesture, deny the very character of the costume and through that begins the loss of the dramatic effect.

If you take a Venetian brooch from the time of Veronese, with its mixture of jewels, its enamels, its complex design and elaborate finish, it will seem perhaps elaborate to excess. But if you put it on a piece of brocade of the same period, with its rich design and complex detail, the brooch will seem perfect and right. If an actor in an Elizabethan costume, with its numberless details, its rich stuff, its gems, gold lace, and complex and ornate design, will fill it with its characteristic quality rather than try to evade or soften this quality, he will find that certain highly Elizabethan speeches, ornate, rich, complex to the utmost, will take their place more easily and achieve their right scale of beauty.

In such cases the costume is a kind of décor that can give to speeches their right placement and scale.

The wearing of a costume may be either witty or poetic. If an actor's costumes are an Eastern Magian's, flowing and rich, or a common hobo's or a dandy's of our day, he may put into the wearing of each the full of inspiration, may enlarge their scope, creating an image, beyond them even, of radiant significance, as the poet does with his experience. In that robe this Magian may so move that it says "this is the line of my soul, this wide shadow is my mystery, this trailing flow is my dignity and prophetic progress and quietness." The muted and thwarted soul, or careless nights under hedges, or bitterness or droll gallantries, whatever impulses toward life the poet wills, may be created in the hobo clothes; and in the dandy costume ironical poignancy or cursed triviality. Or the wearing of costumes may be a shine or crackle of comment on them and on the characters they clothe. Through this witty carriage of costumes, epigrams become a part of their texture. Mirabell's shoes may be worn so that the very heels speak. They are the heels of their day of fashion, but the actor's standing in them and reflecting upon them delights us with its comment on these heels, just as his swish of the wide-skirted coat is both this modish eighteenth-century garment and a dash of observation upon it. If we saw an actress in the costume of Mistress Millamant, with its full skirts and its close bodice, its damask and aristocratic flare, we should know how much she senses the smart sweetness and perfection of Millamant, who is the poetry of wit, by her first movement on the stage, by how much she has of "that brave vibration each way free" and "how sweetly flows the liquefaction of her clothes."

The same poetic imagination or witty comment may be achieved by playing against the costumes, by wearing them as contrasts through which a reverse idea is expressed, sodden clothes on a regal character, for example, grand modes on comic housemaids, girlish frocks on somewhat elderly exponents. This is only another way of wearing costumes, keeping them alive. Behind its effect the same principle works as in the familiar theme of Pierrot, for example, the wistful heart beneath the clowning mask; or in Falstaff, the frisking animation set absurdly against his bulk, and the grandiose and fraudulent pretense set against this absurdity, or in Hauptmann's Hannele, the radiant vision and exaltation within those sordid rags.

Just as the actor's being fills his body, which in turn expresses it, so the actor, himself, body and being, fills his costume, which expresses him or what, during the time he has it on, he must be. This that he must be while he has on the costume derives from his translation of it into his own mood; from this translation derives the idea that the costume provides a body for, and through the idea within it this costume body is alive.

"It is easy," Kingsley's good fairy says to the child, "to make a thing; the great feat is to make a thing make itself."

DESIGNING FOR ACTORS

By Aline Bernstein

WHEN an actor comes upon the stage his clothing is not his own, but that of the character he is playing. Upon this principle costume design is built. No matter how beautiful a costume may be in form and color, if it has not an underlying rightness of characterization it will count for nothing in the theatre. To understand his problem, the costume designer must, at the outset, establish his relationship to the dramatist and actors. Unfortunately his difficulties are sometimes multiplied because two people are employed to design a production, and settings and costumes are placed in different hands. As no two people see or think alike, or ever are of the same quality, it is almost impossible to make a fine unity of composition under such circumstances. Even when the costumer works alone, he faces hard problems, since costume is not a thing in itself but is only another aid for the actor, giving point and truth to his work and to the dramatist's intention. A costume must be felt as right not only in the beginning, but throughout the play.

When the play has been carefully studied, and the general line of each character determined, then the play of characters upon each other and their movement throughout the play must be traced. As the action of a play develops, the characters move on a stage that varies in lighting, color, and setting, and this constant sequence of fusion and transition the costume designer must meet in his own work. One of the most important things for the designer is to have as nearly as possible a perfect understanding with the actor. Even before the designing has begun, it is worth a great deal to take plenty of time to understand each actor's idea of his own part. Many actors resent the designer's plans for them, and often with good cause. The actor thinks of himself as a unit, and not always as part of a whole production. Yet it is unfair to impose upon him a suit of clothing at variance with his own idea of the part, and to make him wait for a fitting at the costumer's before he sees the design. Often an actor has valuable suggestions to make, which no designer should be too proud to accept. A costume can be made beautiful or ugly, regardless of its design, by the one who wears it. It is worth all the tact and patience in the world to make the actor happy and at home in his clothing when the final dress rehearsal comes. The dramatic person can make a rectangle of linen into a thrilling essential of life. By walking across the stage, Isadora Duncan could make her simple garment hang and flow and come alive, always in perfect accord with her intention. Yvette Guilbert could invest a pocket handkerchief with all the loveliness of a beautiful young woman. It is not alone the inky cloak of Hamlet, it is the blackness of his soul that colors his garments. I do not wish to minimize the importance of design; I only want to point out the power of the actor within the costume.

That clothing itself has character is another fundamental of design. Somehow or other a generous man cannot be dressed in exactly the same clothes as would seem suitable for a mean man. His temperament will shape his taste as well as his behavior. There is bound to be difference of appearance, usually greater than the casual observer would imagine. People think that, through lack of money or time, they are unable to express their real selves in their clothing. This is true to a certain extent. But to an eye keen to read signs, there is invariably something of an intensely personal choice in color or line or ornament. To the designer falls the work of taking these little things and making them tell in characterization by exaggeration in one direction or another. A slight rake of line, the over or under starching of a collar, the set of a sleeve at the shoulder, and a thousand other seeming trifles make for fine distinctions in character.

There are times when one is justified in the extreme of exaggeration for theatrical purposes, — a much easier task in period design than in modern dress, for there is always the decided form of the period represented, upon which the changes can be based.

As to the actual designing of period costume, the material at hand is endless. The designer is wise who goes to the painting and sculpture or to the lesser arts of the period he is creating, for information, rather than to costume books. All costume books have been made from these sources, and it is easy to understand how much fresher the material will be at its source,

Francis Bruguière

A photographic play, such, for example, as "The Rise of Silas Lapham", demands a representative echo in the designer's setting and costumes. To achieve this and still add enough imagination to heighten the quality of life into the quality of art is a difficult feat which Lee Simonson accomplished with rare skill. One of the counts against the purely realistic playwright is that he so often dulls the imagination of his coöperating artists — actor, director, and designer.

than when it has passed through other minds and hands. Besides, the pleasures of research are tremendous, losing oneself in another time, going behind its scene, choosing just the right things from its store. It is sometimes hard to remember that all of what we call period costume was once everyday dress. There was a time when people wore farthingales not only to sit for their portraits and perform ballets, but to do all sorts of things that we ourselves do, taking walks, going to funerals, sitting round the fire at home. One must watch carefully to find what are the essential lines of a period, and build the characterization on that frame. The line of the actor, the line of the character, and the line of the period must be perfectly combined. Once this is clear and defined and the essential features of the costume are determined, then these elements must be transmuted into terms of the theatre, because a real dress of the period, perfect in each detail, would never be as effective on the stage as one in which the idea had been heightened and dramatized. Make the small waist smaller, the full skirt fuller, the straight line straighter, — or less straight. There must be meaning in every part, and the complete idea must be expressed with material and scissors.

An intention of beauty must always be in the idea. But that beauty must not belong alone to the design on paper, for costumes come to life only when they are worn. There must be beauty and fitness in choice of material, in cut, in fit, and in workmanship. Everything must count, and whatever does not aid the design will weaken it and must be eliminated. Realizing this, the designer must face the fact that costume is not static. It changes constantly with movement. The variety of combinations in any set of costumes is limitless.

All of this is equally true in the costuming of a modern play, although the heightening of modern costume is a very subtle matter. Though it is not always realized, there is every reason why just as much actual designing should be done for a modern as for a period play. Dollars are often lavished with a prodigal hand, the best dressmakers are employed to get a gown becoming to an actress, without any regard to character or place. I have seen a leading lady step out of a tent in the desert in a flowered chiffon gown, exquisitely finished and unwrinkled, got from heaven knows where, and surely heaven could only understand why.

It would be interesting to trace certain vagaries of dress to necessity, and in many instances this is possible. One wonders, however, why at certain times sleeves suddenly became bulbous at the top, what caused the eighteenth-century extension of the skirt at the hips, or the Victorian bustle. There seems to be a never-ending desire to make clothes approach and depart at certain points from the line of the human form. Climate has had in the past much to do with the choice of materials, but with our different mode of life and facilities for heating, materials are used as much for their decorative value as for anything else. For example, fur is now used as trimming, regardless of its use for warmth.

It is just as well that it is often impossible to buy expensive stuffs for use on the stage, for in makeshift lies a limitless field for the ingenuity of the designer.

"The Dancing Cobbler", a costume designed by Jean Berain
(1638–1711), who was in his day the oracle of taste, and who
designed both settings and costumes for the lavish theatrical
productions of the court of Louis XIV.

COSTUMES

With the aid of that magic curtain arising between the audience and the stage the designer can make his translation of materials. The most gorgeous brocade can be retold in terms of satine and velveteen and a little judiciously applied paint. Things on the stage must be more like themselves than reality, stripped of all but the most telling qualities; and stuffs so used will have a value more theatric than the original. Every material has a texture, a quality, and a weight peculiar to itself, and all of this can be made to serve the designer after he has learned and mastered their ways. Our machine-made cheap silks, for example, have none of the interesting surface of the hand-woven silks of the past, and to represent these fine materials some way must be found of recapturing their beauty with paint and brains and clever fingers. If a designer feels that he can represent a fourteenth-century wood-carving by dressing his actor in oilcloth, let him do it. No matter how many people have used oilcloth, his feeling will carry something new into his interpretation.

It is difficult to say what is the most important feature in the construction of a costume, one thing depending so much upon another. Color and applied pattern are certainly important but are often unduly stressed. In the cut, which is a matter of making the flat surface conform to the round, we have what I consider the greatest essential of style and character. With perfect cut, a finer effect can be gained with white muslin than with an ill-cut garment of the loveliest color in the world. The cut of the costume has the mental quality, and the color the sensuous. But the most important thing about a costume is the acting that goes on inside of it.

THE DANCE

Arnold Genthe

Isadora Duncan, who began a new period in American dance history, dancing The Marseillaise.

THE DANCE

ONLY in a modern book on the theatre could there be any apology for including the dance as one of the theatre's essential arts — the dance, out of which the theatre sprang, and which was for centuries its basic art. In the theatre of the East, the tradition still remains which conceived of the actor as equally a dancer and a singer, and nobody goes from our Western theatre to China or Japan or India without realizing how much the theatre gains from such association of ideas. It is an interesting accent on the theory we are trying to develop — that the distinguishing mark of to-day's theatre in America is its tendency towards a correlation of all the arts — that during the last generation the art of the dance has had so great a revival, — through Isadora Duncan, in the dramatic ballet (coming to us out of Russia) and in the hoofers of our revues and vaudeville. The final importance of the Neighborhood Playhouse to our dramatic history will probably lie in what it did to revive among us, not only in theory but in practice, the idea of the advantages to a theatre of the actor-singer-dancer. Moreover, at a time when we are beginning to think of a native American theatre in terms of its sources and of its tributaries, it is distinctly interesting to note the increasing attention that is centering, still half unconsciously, on the ritual dances of the American Indians, and the primitive steps of the Negro for what they can teach our theatre of what Mary Austin calls " The American Rhythm."

THE INDEPENDENT ART OF THE DANCE

By Ruth St. Denis

DANCING is the irradiation of the human personality in terms of geometric movement. These movements should have as their basis the laws of geometry, as rigidly adhered to as are the laws of mathematics in music. There are laws of causation that govern movement that we have not even begun to study, much less put into practice. The man who has done most to formulate these laws and their correspondents was François Delsarte. He was not so much an inventor of a system as a true discoverer of the basic impulses of gesture and movement. If, as real students and not mere imitative pupils of the dance, we start with the spiritual or fundamental elements of movement, we shall find ourselves in the company of this great pioneer, seeking to discover and release, rather than to invent and arrange. The inspired dancer should move after an inner law, an inner ideal: when he has in this way attained to a complete and comprehensive art form he can truly be said to be a great dancer.

But only here and there an occasional individual is consciously striving to raise the physical technique of the dance to a point where its ascending spiritual life may be revealed in terms of art; for the dance is now in its infancy, in its purely physical plane of expression. Dancing has suffered from a sort of arrested development. It has been such a charming toy in its infantile stages, so easy and delightful to watch and to perform, that scarcely any of its higher altitudes have been reached. We have endless repetitions and endless rearrangements of old gestures, but very little pushing forward into unknown fields of expression. Holding us back is our utter dependence upon music, upon external and audible rhythm and harmony to give life and animation to the body. This easy correlation of movement to music is the instinctive experience of the childish or primitive being. As that being develops it should depend more and more upon its own ideas, volition, and expression. Dancing should be enjoyed and recognized and discussed with the same consideration that is accorded the other arts. But we cannot command the attention of the intellect until we dance from the intellect. We cannot appeal to the depths and the heights of man's spiritual being until we move also in the spiritual plane. In my efforts to attain this goal I have been at work for many years on the principle that the dance is an independent art; that it can and should exist independently of music.

When I deplore this dependence upon music, I am not of course referring to coöperation with music. Such coöperation is another story. By dependence I mean precisely what the word implies since therein is the reason for the arrested state of the dance, as compared with other arts. Music has allied itself with poetry and drama and our songs and our opera are the result of the combining of these arts. But it has concerned itself very little with the dance in its higher aspects. It is not relevant to refer to the many well-known scores of dances and ballets, for it is in these very compositions that music betrays its weakness in relation to the dance. The moment that the simplest of rhythms is obtained, to which almost any child can dance, the composer generally feels that he has reached the end of dance music. This is what one might term the doggerel of the dance and such music is abundantly provided. But of the prose of the dance and of its higher altitudes of poetry, there is as yet very little, and this great dance music will not be written until the dance itself has developed independently, so that composers will have a great art to ally themselves to, as they already have in poetry for song and in drama for opera.

Dancing is essentially a visual art. Its appeal is primarily to the eye. No true judgment of its higher manifestations can be made until the consciousness of the spectator is allowed to focus on its essential and adequate means of expression, the human body. Movements of the beautiful human body are as satisfying and complete as the full tones of a voice or the music of a stringed instrument.

As an independent art, the dance will finally evolve a technique that will be different from the familiar schools of the present day. The foundation of this technique will be based on the natural movements of the human being, as his personality has developed up to now — his reactions to the objective world on the physical side, his natural gestures that arise from his emotional

states, and finally a freer and more beautiful speech
of gesture that will reveal the faith and wonder of his
soul.

At present our teaching begins with an imposed
technique. The uses of primitive and concrete rhythms
are obviously necessary and delightful. All of us
instinctively delight in the sensuous reaction to an
African drum beat on which so much of our music is
founded. But in the art of dancing this teaching of
gesture by this means alone is a binding and limiting
thing. It denies and stultifies the imagination and
effaces the individuality. In this method the great
consideration is that every child should move exactly
like every other child, every pirouette and every arabesque being like every other pirouette and arabesque.
If such movements are looked upon as merely the words
of the body, that should be spoken correctly and alike
by all dancers, this is quite as it should be, in the same
way as all poets need a certain elementary grammatical
training. But as the acquiring of a perfect grammatical
technique has never yet made a poet, so neither can it
make a dancer. For this reason I feel that in general
too much emphasis is laid upon the conforming and
technical side of dancing and too little on the inspirational. One reason is that dancing is largely taught
from an ensemble basis, both financial considerations
and tradition having determined this course. While
to deny altogether the value of training in a dancer's
equipment would be as foolish as to claim that a dancer
need only to hire a symphony orchestra to express her
soul, still I feel that the new system of training should
begin with the study of the spiritual life of the dancer

and from that basis proceed to the opening up of newer and truer forms of technique and expression.

We so often forget that, before technique was, man had something to say and it was in his efforts to say this something that he evolved a means of speaking, whether through poetry, painting, dancing, or sculpture. So the principal thing, now, as it was thousands of years ago, is to have something to say and then to find a way to say it. The dancer should be poet, artist, philosopher, and scientist. In the education of the dancer, there should run parallel with the mere physical training of the body the training and enlarging of the consciousness. Nothing is ever so effective, dramatic, and novel as a real vision of greater and deeper truth. No striving of young dancers for a mere external trick of costume or gesture or lighting effect will take the place of hours of research, of the willingness to meet life in its homely and commonplace phases honestly and industriously and above all of longing to know more of God and the universe. The body is not a mere geometrical toy that it is amusing to watch in its antics and gyrations. (Although this is still largely the popular conception of the dance.) The body of man is the veritable temple of the living God. It has great and infinite possibilities of revealing the strength and beauty of the divine consciousness as reflected in the mind of man. It is this revelation that we should expect from the dancer of the future.

THE SPIRIT OF THE CLASSIC DANCE

By André Levinson

Nothing is more difficult than to reduce the essential æsthetic realities of the dance to verbal formulas. Our ordinary methods of analysis are of very little use in dealing with this art, which is primarily a discipline of movement. The dancer in motion is a harmony of living forms, masses, and outlines, whose relations to each other are continually varied by that "motion which causes the lines to flow." We are exceedingly ill equipped for the study of things in flux — even for considering motion itself as such. We cling to things at rest as though they were landmarks in a turbulent chaos. A modern engineer, for example, who wishes to study the mechanism of a revolving screw, would doubtless begin his studies by stopping the motor and taking it apart, in order to understand clearly the technical methods employed by the designer. The dancer has a fairly wide technical vocabulary, but it is one that is useful only to himself. Even the most expert spectator can decipher its hieroglyphics only with great difficulty — not because of ignorance or unintelligence on his part, but because these technical terms invoke no corresponding muscular association

in the layman's consciousness. It is because the art
of the dance is so peculiarly inarticulate that it has
never possessed a proper æsthetic philosophy. Choreo-
graphic thought — and here we fall straightway into
the use of an improper and misleading term — has
always been condemned to expression through para-
phrases — high-sounding but inaccurate. It has had
to content itself with the shifting, uncertain expedient
of the analogy, which is, according to Nietzsche, the
surest way of falling into error. We approach the
dance by aid of analogous hypotheses and the habits
of thought employed in our consideration of other arts
with the inevitable result that we substitute the obvious
facts of a static art for the elusive dynamics of the dance.

The great Noverre, called the "Shakespeare of the
dance" by Garrick and "Prometheus" by Voltaire —
who is still the most vital and thorough theoretician
who has written on the subject, desired above every-

la Riuerenza, & due Seguiti innanzi..

Fatto quefto, faranno vn'altro Tempo della Sciolta.

thing to incorporate the dance into the group of "imitative arts." Carlo Blasis — the same incidentally
who established the theory of classic instruction —
struggled manfully to evolve some plausible connection
between the spectacle of the dance and the poetry of
the spoken drama. Others have conceived the dance

as strictly limited to the expression of definite ideas —
thereby sacrificing it to and confusing it with pantomime. It seems as though everyone had piled upon
this art mistaken attributes or supplementary burdens
in his efforts to redeem — even if only in a small way
— the actual movements of the dance.

I cannot think of anyone who has devoted himself
to those characteristics which belong exclusively to
dancing, or who has endeavored to formulate specifi-
cally the laws of this art on its own ground. Those
famous dance historians whose names I have mentioned have listed, described, and analyzed a certain
number of fundamental dance movements and set
down the empirical laws which rule the execution of
their elements. The grammar of Zorn is complete in
its descriptive matter and the recent treatise of Cec-
chetti is invaluable as a method of instruction. But
no one has ever tried to portray the intrinsic beauty of
a dance step, its innate quality, its æsthetic reason for
being. This beauty is referred to the smile of the
dancer, to the picturesque quality of his costume, to
the general atmosphere surrounding him, to the syn-
chronizing of his bodily rhythm with the beat of the
music or again to the emotional appeal of the dramatic
libretto of the ballet; but never is it shown to lie in the
contours of the movement itself, in the constructive
values of an attitude, or in the thrilling dynamics of a
leap in the air. All the other arts are foisted on the
dance as instructors. Blasis even insisted that a
dancer should, at any given moment, be a suitable
model for the sculptor Canova. But a statue is motion
captured and congealed, the eternal prison of one spe-

cific form. And while it is true that every movement does break up into moments of action and moments of rest, it is only these moments of rest, of stable equilibrium, and not the complete movement of the dance that can be said to find an analogy in sculpture.

I am sure that an artilleryman, thoroughly familiar with the motion of projectiles, able to calculate accurately the trajectory of a shell, the force of the explosion that sets it in motion and the range of the missile released, could much more easily discover the principle of a dancer's leap than some loose-thinking poet, however magnificent his style. For the gunner operates with a knowledge of dynamics. Doubtless his aim is wholly material — destruction, pure and simple — while it is the desire of the dancer to create beauty which causes him to make use of his knowledge of mechanics and that finally dominates this knowledge. He subjects his muscles to a rigid discipline; through arduous practice he bends and adapts his body to the exigencies of an abstract and perfect form. In the end he brings the physiological factors — muscle contraction and relaxation — completely under the domination of the sovereign rhythm of the dance. This is what makes it so difficult to separate the gymnastic elements of the dance from its ideal essence. The technique of a dancer is not like the mechanical workings of a jointed doll; it is physical effort constantly informed by beauty. This technique is no supplementary reënforcement to his art, nor is it a mere device, designed to gain easy applause, like (according to Stendhal) the art of the versifier. It is the very soul of the dance; it *is* the dance itself.

SPIRIT OF CLASSIC DANCE

Of all the various techniques it is that of the so-called classic dance — a term designating the style of dancing that is based on the traditional ballet technique — which has prevailed in the Western world. It seems to be in complete accord not only with the anatomical structure of the European but with his intellectual aspirations as well. We find this technique in all those countries where man is fashioned like us and where he thinks in our way. The little definite knowledge we have concerning the system of gymnastics of the ancient Greeks warrants our identifying certain of their "modes" with those of the contemporary dance. Today the universality of the classic style is disputed only by the oriental dance, that finds in the Cambodgian ballet its highest and most complete expression. The superb efflorescence of the dance in Spain is in itself a vestige of an oriental civilization, repelled but not annihilated.

Opponents of the classic dance technique pretend to consider it an academic code, imposed on the dance arbitrarily by pedants and long since obsolete. It is true that it does recapitulate the experience of centuries, for we find that certain of its fundamental ideas were accepted by the dancing masters of the Italian Renaissance. It was they who first broke away from the so-called "horizontal" conception of the dance, based on outlines and figures marked by the feet of the dancer on the floor — what you might call his itinerary. The outlines of the choreographs of the seventeenth century, reproducing on paper the curving path drawn on the ground by the feet of the dancer, are the last vestiges of this "horizontal" idea, which was gradually

227

displaced by the vertical conception of dancing — the configuration of motion in space. This important process, so fruitful in its developments, lasted throughout two centuries and strangely enough has never been even

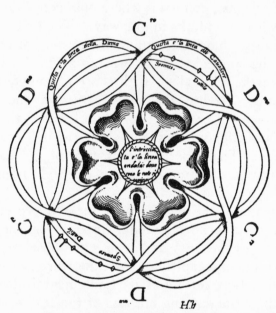

The choreograph of an early court dance devised in honor of Signora Cornelia Orsina Cesi, Duchess of Ceri, in which the path of the dancers' feet traces out the pattern of a rose upon the floor.

touched upon by any of those many chroniclers of the dance, who, as I have said before, invariably prefer to approach the subject as writers, musicians, or historians of folkways and manners. Inasmuch as the verbal formulas that serve to designate dance movements and attitudes have remained practically unchanged all this time, the superficial observer is apt to overlook this development.

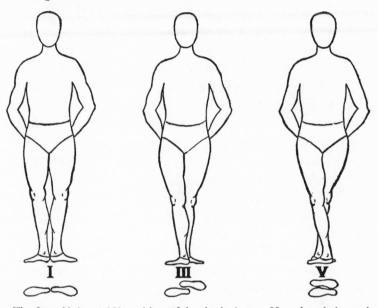

The first, third and fifth positions of the classic dance. Note the relative positions of the feet — in the same straight line at the first position and in parallel lines in the other positions.

As a matter of fact there is no question but that the meaning of these formulas changes with each generation. The five fundamental positions, which are the ABC of the dance, may seem to be the same for Feuillet, the choreographer of the "grand Siècle", and for Mademoiselle Zambelli — to mention one of the fairest flowers of contemporary classic dance. But this is not actually so. In the outlines of Feuillet that have come down to us the feet, in the first position, make an obtuse angle. In the modern they are in the same straight line in the first position, and in the other positions in parallel lines. This may seem to be a trifling detail of growth and change, when one thinks of Isadora Duncan dancing a Beethoven symphony. But this almost imperceptible difference, this slight shift of a geometrical line, these feet pivoting at an angle of so many degrees, represents an enormously important acquisition, capable of infinite combinations and variety. This trifling detail is actually a realization of that essential principle and point of departure of classic choreography which took two centuries to prevail — that of turning the body — and more particularly the legs of the dancer — outward from its center.

I find myself at times looking at the history of the modern dance as though it were some charming but infinitely obscure romance that needed a key to unlock its mysteries. This key is an understanding of what a dancer means when he speaks of turning out the body. The movement of the oriental dance is concentric. The knees almost instinctively come together and bend, the curved arms embrace the body. Everything is pulled together. Everything converges. The movement of the classic dance, on the other hand, is ex-centric — the arms and the legs stretch out, freeing themselves from the torso, expanding the chest. The whole region of the dancer's being, body and soul, is dilated. The actual manifestation of this can be readily seen or even better felt in the trained body of a classical ballet dancer. The dancer spreads the hips and rotates both legs, in their entire length from the waist down, away from each other, outward from the body's center, so that they are both in profile to the

The short, light spread of the ballet skirt has evolved from the
need of the dancer to have a costume that would leave her
body completely free. This sketch of Pavlova by John
Copley, which Cecil Sharp and A. P. Oppé included in "The
Dance" illustrates the practicality of the traditional costume.

audience although turned in opposite directions. The so-called five fundamental positions are merely derivations or variations of this outward turning posture, differentiated by the manner in which the two feet fit in, cross, or by the distance that separates them. In the fifth position, where the two feet are completely crossed, toes to heels, you have the very incarnation of this principle of turning outward — that is to say, of the spirit of classic dancing. The fifth position is Taglioni; the third was Carmargo. A whole century of experimentation and of slow, arduous assimilation lies between the two. The orthopedic machines, true instruments of torture, that were used to turn pupils out in the days of Noverre would not be tolerated today. But it does take several years of daily exercise, beginning at the ages of eight or nine years, to give a dancer the ability to perform this mechanical feat easily.

At this point, the reader may demand precisely what is gained by this hard-won victory over nature. Just this — the body of the dancer is freed from the usual limitations upon human motion. Instead of being restricted to a simple backward and forward motion — the only directions in which the human body, operating normally, can move with ease and grace, this turning outward of the legs permits free motion in any direction without loss of equilibrium; forward, backwards, sideways, obliquely, or rotating. The actual extent of motion possible is considerably augmented, and since the feet are thus made to move on lines parallel to each other there is no interference and many motions otherwise impossible are thereby facilitated. As a good example of this, I might cite the *entrechat* — that exhilarating movement where the dancer leaps high in the air and crosses his legs several times while off the ground. This effective "braiding" movement necessitates the turning outward of the body — otherwise the dancer's legs would block each other.

What a tiresome recital, you may be saying, and all of this in trying to talk about so elusive and illusive a thing as the dance! But I assure you it is justified, for the very illusion of this enchanting art — which seems to ignore all natural laws — depends on an intelligent ordering of physical effort. The dancer then is a body moving in space according to any desired rhythm. We have seen how the turning outward of the body increases this space to an extraordinary degree, pushing back the invisible walls of that cylinder of air in the center of which the dancer moves, giving him that extraordinary extension of body which is totally lacking in oriental dancing and multiplying to an infinite degree the direction of the movement as well as its various conformations. It surrounds the vertical of the body's equilibrium by a vortex of curves, segments of circles, arcs; it projects the body of the dancer into magnificent parabolas, curves it into a living spiral; it creates a whole world of animated forms that awake in us a throng of active sensations, that our usual mode of life has atrophied.

I have not tried to explain clearly more than one of the salient and decisive characteristics of the classic technique. The rich development of the dance that increases its sway from generation to generation corresponds to the gradual elaboration of this principle of turning outward.

If at the beginning of the classic period the dance served merely to give law and style to the carriage and deportment of the perfect courtier, or if at the time of the "*fêtes galantes*" it was still skipping and mincing, it has gradually become exalted and transfigured until it is now called upon to express the loftiest emotions of the human soul.

When once the enthusiasm of the romantic period had created the idea of the dance of elevation, it was only one step further to make the dancer rise up on his toes. It would be interesting to know at exactly what moment this second decisive factor entered in. The historians of the dance, unfortunately, are not concerned with telling us. It is, however, evident that this reform was at least a half century in preparation. The heel of the shoe raised up, the instep arched, the toe reached down — the plant no longer was rooted to the soil. What happened was that the foot simply refused to remain flat any longer. It strove to lengthen out the vertical lines of its structure. It gave up its natural method of functioning to further an æsthetic end. And thus it is that when a dancer rises on her points, she breaks away from the exigencies of everyday life, and enters into an enchanted country — that she may thereby lose herself in the ideal.

To discipline the body to this ideal function, to make a dancer of a graceful child, it is necessary to begin by dehumanizing him, or rather by overcoming the habits of ordinary life. His muscles learn to bend, his legs are trained to turn outward from the waist, in order to increase the resources of his equilibrium. His torso becomes a completely plastic body. His limbs stir only as a part of an ensemble movement. His entire outline takes on an abstract and symmetrical quality. The accomplished dancer is an artificial being, an instrument of precision, and he is forced to undergo rigorous daily exercise to avoid lapsing into his original purely human state.

His whole being becomes imbued with that same unity, that same conformity with its ultimate aim that constitutes the arresting beauty of a finished airplane, where every detail, as well as the general effect, expresses one supreme object — that of speed. But where the airplane is conceived in a utilitarian sense — the idea of beauty happening to superimpose itself upon it, the constant transfiguration, as you might call it, of the classic dancer from the ordinary to the ideal is the result of a disinterested will for perfection, an unquenchable thirst to surpass himself. Thus it is that an exalted aim transforms his mechanical efforts into an æsthetic phenomenon. You may ask whether I am suggesting that the dancer is a machine? But most certainly! — a machine for manufacturing beauty — if it is in any way possible to conceive a machine that in itself is a living, breathing thing, susceptible of the most exquisite emotions.

An interesting comment on the instruments of an early dance orchestra from Della Nobilta di Dame, a 17th Century manual of court ballets by Fabritio Caroso.

THE NEGRO DANCE

Under European Eyes

By ANDRÉ LEVINSON

NEGRO music, having conquered the public, is now, more and more, occupying the attention of the theorists. In France, André Coeuroy has devoted a volume in his collection, "Modern Music", to Jazz. This book as well as the ingratiating account of Émile Vuillermoz and the excellent critical essays of Darius Milhaud treat Negro ragtime as worthy of the most serious consideration and give it a definite place in musical history. Jazz is henceforth admitted into the hierarchy of the arts, and although it is only a little while since it was the butt of press and public alike, the time is doubtless at hand when it will provide a worthy subject for a doctor's thesis at the Sorbonne. It is therefore high time that we should look a little more closely into the subject of Negro dancing, which is the saltatory complement of ragtime and which can be called at once the cradle and the prototype of Jazz.

Negro dancing may suggest at once any one of a variety of quite separate problems. The student of æsthetics may be interested in defining the indigenous principles of the dance and of judging its intrinsic artistic value. The moralist, on the other hand, in his search for an explanation of our times, may be more concerned with the effect of this black virus upon European civilization. The ethnologist, comparing the aborigines of the Ivory Coast and the cotton pickers of the plantations of Louisiana, may find the Negro dance of primary importance as an organic phenomenon. While, as it is found in our present-day dance halls, it may appear as a symptom of an epidemic contagion of society which should concern the pathologist. It is, therefore, necessary to set down in the beginning that this article is merely attempting to present a European interpretation of the Negro dance as it has lately been demonstrated by the colored artists of the "Revue Nègre" at the Champs Elysées.

Just as we might gain a clearer understanding of the peculiar composition of a jazz band by contrasting it with the more familiar symphonic orchestra, in the same way we may obtain a better idea of the Negro "steps" if we compare them to the dancing of the classic school which has been developed in the West through centuries of elaboration and selection. Such a contrast of black and white will, I believe, serve to emphasize the essential characteristics of the Negro dance.

The classic ballet is not only a silent art but completely imperceptible to the ear. The harmony between the movement of the body and the rhythm of the music is constant but tacit. An anecdote often told of Philippe Taglioni, the father of the famous dancer Marie Taglioni, makes him say that he had never heard the step of his daughter; should such a thing have happened, he would have cursed her. These words of the irascible old ballet master, although perhaps exaggerated, bear out the traditional rule for the good dancer of the classic school that, without in any way stressing the phrase of the music, he should be able to make the onlooker sense it. This type of dancing is like a visual projection of the rhythm realized in the musical accompaniment; sight and sound, movement and acoustics, are completely disassociated. Every so-called "temps" of the classic dance, as the term itself indicates, is equivalent to a musical phrase, but is perceptible to the eye alone. To arrange a *pas de ballet* is to establish a fixed and exact relation between a succession of musical sonorities and a series of muscular tensions and relaxations. Thus the classic dance and the music that accompanies it express the rhythm that is implicit in both, in two different but analogous ways. This is a fundamental principle in all Western choreography.

Primitive dancing, on the other hand, being a spontaneous phenomenon, ignores any such differentiation and confounds these two categories of sight and sound. Almost all folk-dancing, from the Russian hopak to the bourrée of Auvergne, from the Scotch reel to the tarantella or the jota of Aragon — and most conspicuously of all, the Negro "step" — is based upon a direct and audible expression of the rhythm. Each one of these dances is primarily a staccato of feet, scanning the music — all the more striking because of its rapidity and clear articulation.

The savage or folk dancer is essentially an instrument of percussion. When Vicente Escudero, the famous Flamenco dancer, performed the Farruca, he made the floor of the stage resound like a powerful sounding board. It almost seemed as though huge drum sticks were beating upon a gigantic drum. The timbre of this harsh music changed according to whether the *Bailarin* beat the floor with the sole of his foot or with his heel. He was a living xylophone and had at his command a complete scale of gradations. He, himself, was his own musical instrument. The castanets and twanging guitars, the hand-clapping with which the *Quadro* added to the sound, were mere auxiliary equipment to the staccato of the solo dancer's feet. The string pluckers followed the dance improvisations of Escudero. Between the Spaniard and Jimmy Huggins, the black clown of the "Revue Nègre", there is no difference excepting in the dance routine and in the general deportment of the dancer — none in the fundamental method of expression. Whether he is shod in the brodequins of Andalusia or the iron-rimmed boots of the Cossack, the primitive dancer stresses with a vigor, gay or savage, the heavy accents of a monotonous but striking rhythm.

When the ballet dancer rises up lightly and silently falls back as though upon a delicately resilient spring, we refer to her "ballon" as though she were indeed a floating thing of air, without weight and equally without sound. The peasant leaps high and falls back with all his weight, so as to shake the earth. The ballet dancer wears the softest satin slippers with flexible soles, for "why should one put shoes on the wings of a bird?" as the madrigal poets were wont to ask, — while Harland Dixon, record holder of the Charleston, wears the most formidable patent leather shoes, regular varnished dreadnaughts, that have succeeded the red heels of yesterday. Pavlova glides, Dixon taps; this, not to be technical, is the difference between the *pas de ballet* and the Afro-American dance step. In "La Sylphide", Marie Taglioni delighted her audiences by appearing to run over a field of grain without bending the stalks. The mere effort to achieve such an optical illusion serves to define a style in the dance. The Negro stepper, who pounds the platform with unremitting vigor, producing an infernal racket, is a no less sincere expression of another type.

The Negro dancer is not content with the noise of his feet alone, but has constant recourse to every accessory that may reinforce the resonance of his battery. In the sand dance, for instance, his feet grind through sand that is scattered over the stage, while clappers and sounding boards exaggerate the effect. The first aim of any dance of this kind is an intense and penetrating reproduction of some rhythmic formula, although, for the sake of contrast, it sometimes introduces the most pearly of pianissimos. The primitive, human instinct is violently affected by such rhythmic insistence. The monotony of this measured tramping, the symmetry of its pattern, has the effect of a narcotic, while its gradual acceleration brings about a sense of exhilaration amounting to a positive ecstasy. The drummer, who is the soul of any genuine Jazz band, is essentially a dancer.

Negro ragtime itself contributes enormously to these performances. This music, with its bewildering syncopation and rubato, its rhythmic *tours de force*, executed with such unimaginable dexterity, positively dazzled European audiences. This dancing, with its automaton-like quality, its marvellous flexibility and rhythmic fantasy, is as impossible for us to reproduce as it is astounding to us to watch. Here we recognize ourselves to be in the presence of an innate gift, not a conscious art — a gift that has become more or less atrophied in the cultivated human being. Such is the ransom we pay to civilization. With us, extreme sensitiveness to rhythm comes rather as the result of a high degree of musical cultivation. We produce it, as it were, in a hothouse, and rhythm itself becomes a reasoned and artificial discipline — almost a philosophy, sometimes even a fetich. With the mulattos and quadroons of the "Revue Nègre", who took Paris by storm in 1925, this sense of rhythm was more of a physiological — I am almost tempted to say glandular — phenomenon, allied to their excessive hysteria and their unbelievably high animal spirits. It is a fruit of savagery that we may well envy. It encroaches in no way upon that "candeur de l'antique animal" that Baudelaire admired so much. In other words, the undeniable rhythmic superiority of these Negro dancers is nothing less than an adjunct of their irrepressible animality. The tom-tom of the cannibal may be termed the apotheosis of brute rhythm.

We should not, however, jump to the conclusion that because of this extraordinary rhythmic gift alone the Negro dancer or musician should be taken seriously as an artist. Rhythm is not, after all, an art in itself. Its beat is indispensable to the melodic and harmonic elements of music and provides a basis for the plastic variations of the dancer, but when rhythm becomes completely free and dominates any realm of art the result is inevitably rudimentary and inferior. A picture that is entirely subservient to rhythm is no more than a decoration. Rhythm is a force of nature that must be transposed and reabsorbed before it can become an æsthetic entity. By itself, it is a form without content; a motor revolving in the void; a function and not a substance.

The savage is overflowing with this formless and purely instinctive motor energy and so, as the basis of the Negro dance today, we find an elementary and blind release of this rhythmic instinct — shock of bare feet on the ground — clatter of heels — a first trace of form. The metre directs the flow of a formless emotion. The beating out of the measure gives articulation to the headlong tumult of the senses. The movement of the dancer is no more than a function of this musical continuity, like the drive and recoil of a piston under pressure.

Eventually this rhythmic movement tends to free itself and becomes an end in itself. In the interval between two accents the dancer may begin a diversely figured ornamentation and through such elaborations virtuosity is born, as well as imagination. The English sailor crosses and recrosses his feet; the legs of the crouching Cossack dart out alternately. When he lifts himself he gives a cabriole in which his legs swing away from the center of gravity to fall back into equilibrium. The dancer's effort to accomplish more and more difficult feats leads him on and is stimulated by rivalry with other performers, until, as in the case of Oriental fakirs and jugglers, a truly amazing proficiency is achieved.

This vast repertory of steps, crossing and leaping from the rudimentary to the complex, tends to fall into certain definite classifications, culminating in those steps which possess an intrinsic beauty. The Negro frenzy, although it is completely devoid of any nobility and almost "pre-human", if not actually bestial, can attain to a positive grandeur. Josephine Baker, who was responsible for the Charleston rage in Paris, is an extraordinary creature of simian suppleness — a sinuous idol that enslaves and incites mankind. Thanks to her carnal magnificence and her impulsive vehemence, her unashamed exhibition comes close to pathos. As I wrote, when she first appeared at the Champs Elysées, there seemed to emanate from her violently shuddering body, her bold dislocations, her springing movements, a gushing stream of rhythm. It was she who led the spellbound drummer and the fascinated saxophonist in the harsh rhythm of the "blues." It was as though the jazz, catching on the wing the vibrations of this mad body, were interpreting, word by word, its fantastic monologue. This music is born from the dance, and what a dance! The gyrations of this cynical yet merry mountebank, the good-natured grin on her large mouth, suddenly give way to visions from which good humor is entirely absent. In the short *pas de deux* of the savages, which came as the finale of the "Revue Nègre", there was a wild splendor and magnificent animality. Certain of Miss Baker's poses, back arched, haunches protruding, arms entwined and uplifted in a phallic symbol, had the compelling potency of the finest examples of Negro sculpture. The plastic sense of a race of sculptors

When Josephine Baker, Florence Mills, and other colored
dancers from America took Paris by storm in 1925, even so
eminent a European critic as André Levinson admitted that
their new steps and their sense of rhythm were a serious contribution to the dance. "The plastic sense of a race of sculptors came to life and the frenzy of the African Eros swept over
the audience. It was no grotesque dancing girl that stood
before them, but the black Venus that haunted Baudelaire,"
he wrote of Josephine Baker in the " Revue Nègre."

came to life and the frenzy of the African Eros swept over the audience. It was no longer a grotesque dancing girl that stood before them, but the black Venus that haunted Baudelaire. The dancer's personality had transcended the character of her dance.

Dainty Florence Mills gives a sweetened travesty of this type of dancing. There is not the slightest trace of the wild thing in this rococo Creole. She was a suitable interlude for "Paul and Virginia." The excellent performance of the clowns and Negro steppers that supported these two dancers in the Champs Elysées revues tied them up once more to the primitive cycle. Their extravagant technique would put the virtuosity of an acrobat to shame. If their dances are often mere exhibitions of skill, without further aim, their variety is astounding — entrances accompanied with pirouettes worthy of an Arab jumper; crouching, kicking steps, the glory of the Cossack; leaps into the air on one foot, body swaying backwards, while the free leg serves as a counterweight; breathless races, never moving from the spot, and finally halted by an imaginary tornado; hobbling steps, with one leg dragging behind as though paralyzed; and so on without end. In all these antics the obsession of the rhythm is dilated by humor. The dances of Douglas and Huggins — "Mutt and Jeff", for instance — gain their best effects through a pretended awkwardness and a voluntary burlesquing of the movement.

The road is long indeed from the valley of the Niger to the lights of Broadway; from the primeval forest to Upton Sinclair's jungle in Chicago. The savage has turned into a city rowdy. The ceremonial, sacred

THE DANCE

character of the dance ritual has entirely evaporated from what has become a mere divertissement, offered to the white idlers of the world's capitals. The grandeur of those ancient observances dedicated to Priape and Hecate, pure rhythmic orgies induced by a panic terror of the demons who inhabit the night; those symbolic ceremonies with dancers dressed in stags' antlers or flamingos' claws, are only the symbols of a gay and remunerative extravaganza.

Although Josephine Baker, by her extraordinary and disturbing genius, is able with one bound to join her savage forefathers and with another to go back to our common animal ancestors, the Negro dancers of today are no longer beings possessed by devils, but merely professionals. The really devil-ridden today are those European idlers who passively give themselves up to an enjoyment of the Negro dance without setting up any barriers to its atavistic, demoralizing appeal. But we are not concerned with a study of morals. One curious fact, however, must be mentioned. Ironically enough, while their white admirers tend to retrograde towards the primitive, the Negroes themselves seem to progress, as we understand the term. Many of the Negro steppers, such as the eccentrics Mutt and Jeff, who are so much admired at the moment in Paris, no longer expend their greatest efforts in beating out the measure as noisily as possible, but have developed a sort of rhythmic shuffle that is faint, almost to the vanishing point. They alternate their feet quietly, in an almost complete silence. They play with the stress of the rhythm and subtilize the accent. A little more and they will give complete satisfaction to Taglioni, *père*.

THE NEGRO DANCE

As the technical process becomes so radically modified, and as the action of these dance routines becomes more and more subtle and dissimulated, so does the whole character of the dance become more refined and its morale more elevated. The mad arabesques of the incomparable Josephine can give us an almost shocking insight into our own more somber depths, but Florence Mills, for instance, is developing towards an almost precious elegance. It is no longer the tigress before us but the marquise, who has rubbed burnt cork on her cheeks, instead of her customary rouge, before dancing a Court Charleston "ad usum Delphini."

THE DANCE OF THE SPROUTING CORN

By D. H. Lawrence

PALE, dry, baked earth, that blows into dust of fine sand. Low hills of baked pale earth, sinking heavily, and speckled sparsely with dark dots of cedar bushes. A river on the plain of drought, just a cleft of dark, reddish-brown water, almost a flood. And over all, the blue, uneasy, alkaline sky.

A pale, uneven, parched world, where a motor-car rocks and lurches and churns in sand. A world pallid with dryness, inhuman with a faint taste of alkali. Like driving in the bed of a great sea that dried up unthinkable ages ago, and now is drier than any other dryness, yet still reminiscent of the bottom of the sea, sandhills sinking, and straight, cracked mesas, like cracks in the dry-mud bottom of the sea.

So, the mud church standing discreetly outside, just outside the pueblo, not to see too much. And on its façade of mud, under the timbered mud-eaves, two speckled horses rampant, painted by the Indians, a red piebald and a black one.

Swish! Over the logs of the ditch-bridge, where brown water is flowing full. There below is the pueblo, dried mud like mud-pie houses, all squatting in a jumble, prepared to crumble into dust and be invisible, dust to dust returning, earth to earth.

That they don't crumble is the mystery. That these little squarish mud-heaps endure for centuries after centuries, while Greek marble tumbles asunder, and cathedrals totter, is the wonder. But then, the naked human hand with a bit of new soft mud is quicker than time, and defies the centuries.

Roughly the low, square, mud-pie houses make a wide street where all is naked earth save a doorway or a window with a pale-blue sash. At the end of the street, turn again into a parallel wide, dry street. And there, in the dry, oblong aridity, tosses a small forest that is alive; and thud-thud-thud goes the drum, and the deep sound of men singing is like the deep soughing of the wind, in the depths of a wood.

You realize that you had heard the drum from the distance, also the deep, distant roar and boom of the singing, but that you had not heeded, as you don't heed the wind.

It all tosses like young, agile trees in a wind. This is the dance of the sprouting corn, and everybody holds a little, beating branch of green pine. Thud-thud-thud-thud-thud! goes the drum, heavily the men hop and hop and hop, sway, sway, sway, sway go the little branches of green pine. It tosses like a little forest, and the deep sound of men's singing is like the booming and tearing of a wind deep inside a forest. They are dancing the Spring Corn Dance.

This is the Wednesday after Easter, after Christ Risen and the corn germinated. They dance on Monday and on Tuesday. Wednesday is the third and last dance of this green resurrection.

You realize the long lines of dancers, and a solid cluster of men singing near the drum. You realize the intermittent black-and-white fantasy of the hopping Koshare, the jesters, the Delight-Makers. You become aware of the ripple of bells on the knee-garters of the dancers, a continual pulsing ripple of little bells; and of the sudden wild, whooping yells from near the drum. Then you become aware of the seed-like shudder of the gourd-rattles, as the dance changes, and the swaying of the tufts of green pine-twigs stuck behind the arms of all the dancing men, in the broad green arm-bands.

Gradually comes through to you the black, stable solidity of the dancing women, who poise like solid shadow, one woman behind each rippling, leaping male. The long, silky, black hair of the women, streaming down their backs, and the equally long, streaming, gleaming hair of the males, loose over broad, naked, orange-brown shoulders.

Then the faces, the impassive, rather fat, golden-brown faces of the women, with eyes cast down, crowned above with the green tableta, like a flat tiara. Something strange and noble about the impassive, barefoot women in the short black cassocks, as they subtly tread the dance, scarcely moving, and yet edging rhythmically along, swaying from each hand the green spray of pine-twig out-out-out-out, to the thud of the drum, immediately behind the leaping fox-skin of the men dancers. And all the emerald-green, painted tabletas, the flat wooden tiaras shaped like a castle gateway, rise steady and noble from the soft, slightly bowed heads of the women, held by a band under the

The dances of the Pueblo Indians are many and varied. Hopi, Zuni, and Keres borrow from one another the ceremonials, the gods, heroes, and masks with which they honor their dead ancestors and the powers of the heavens, and attempt to bring down their blessing in rain and crops. Among the dancers are certain clowns — the Koyemshi of the Zuni, the Koshare of the Rio Grande Pueblos — who are both holy and ribald, and always vital and vivid. This is a drawing of one of the Koshare by a native artist.

chin. All the tabletas down the line, emerald green, almost steady, while the bright black heads of the men leap softly up and down, between.

Bit by bit you take it in. You cannot get a whole impression, save of some sort of wood tossing, a little forest of trees in motion, with gleaming black hair and gold-ruddy breasts that somehow do not destroy the illusion of forest.

When you look at the women, you forget the men. The bare-armed, bare-legged, barefoot women with streaming hair and lofty green tiaras, impassive, downward-looking faces, twigs swaying outwards from subtle, rhythmic wrists; women clad in the black, pre-historic short gown fastened over one shoulder, leaving the other shoulder bare, and showing at the arm-place a bit of pink or white under-shirt; belted also round the waist with a woven woolen sash, scarlet and green on the handwoven black cassock. The noble, slightly submissive bending of the tiara-ed head. The subtle measure of the bare, breathing, bird-like feet, that are flat, and seem to cleave to earth softly, and softly lift away. The continuous outward swaying of the pine-sprays!

But when you look at the men, you forget the women. The men are naked to the waist, and ruddy-golden, and in the rhythmic, hopping leap of the dance their breasts shake downwards, as the strong, heavy body comes down, down, down, down, in the downward-plunge of the dance. The black hair streams loose and living down their backs, the black brows are level, the black eyes look out unchanging from under the silky lashes. They are handsome, and absorbed with a deep rhythmic absorption, which still leaves them awake and aware. Down, down, down they drop, on the heavy, ceaseless leap of the dance, and the great necklaces of shell-cores spring on the naked breasts, the neck-shell flaps up and down, the short white kilt of woven stuff, with the heavy woolen embroidery, green and red and black, opens and shuts slightly to the strong lifting of the knees: the heavy whitish cords that hang from the kilt-band at the side sway and coil forever down the side of the right leg, down to the ankle, the bells on the red-woven garters under the knees ripple without end and the feet in buckskin boots, furred round the ankle with a beautiful band of skunk fur, black with a white tip, come down with a lovely, heavy, soft precision, first one, then the other, dropping always plumb to earth. Slightly bending forward, a black gourd rattle in the right hand, a small green bough in the left, the dancer dances the eternal dropping leap, that brings his life down, down, down, down from the mind, down from the broad, beautiful, shaking breast, down to the powerful pivot of the knees, then to the ankles, and plunges deep from the ball of the foot into the earth, towards the earth's red center, where these men belong, as is signified by the red earth with which they are smeared.

And meanwhile, the shell-cores from the Pacific sway up and down, ceaseless, on their breasts.

Mindless, without effort, under the hot sun, unceasing, yet never perspiring nor even breathing heavily, they dance on and on. Mindless, yet still listening, observing. They hear the deep, surging singing of the bunch of old men, like a great wind soughing. They hear the cries and yells of the man waving his bough by the drum. They catch the word of the song, and at a moment, shudder the black rattles, wheel, and the line breaks, women from men, they thread across to a new formation. And as the men wheel round, their black hair gleams and shakes, and the long fox-skin sways, like a tail.

And always, when they form into line again, it is a beautiful long straight line, flexible as life, but straight as rain.

The men round the drum are old, or elderly. They are all in a bunch, and they wear day dress, loose cotton drawers, pink or white cotton shirts, hair tied up behind with the red cords, and banded round the head with a strip of pink rag, or white rag, or blue. There they are, solid like a cluster of bees, their black heads with the pink rag circles all close together, swaying their pine-twigs with rhythmic, wind-swept hands, dancing slightly, mostly on the right foot, ceaselessly, and singing, their black bright eyes absorbed, their dark lips pushed out, while the deep strong sound rushes like wind, and the unknown words form themselves in the dark.

Suddenly the solitary man pounding the drum swings his drum round, and begins to pound on the other end, on a higher note, pang-pang-pang! instead of the previous brumm! brumm! brumm! of the bass note. The watchful man next the drummer yells and waves lightly, dancing on bird-feet. The Koshare make strange, eloquent gestures to the sky.

And again the gleaming bronze-and-dark men dancing in the rows shudder their rattles, break the rhythm, change into a queer, beautiful two-step, the long lines suddenly curl into rings, four rings of dancers, the leaping, gleaming-seeming men between the solid, subtle, submissive blackness of the women who are crowned with emerald green tiaras, all going subtly round in rings. Then slowly they change again, and form a star. Then again, unmingling, they come back into rows.

And all the while, all the while the naked Koshare are threading about. Of bronze-and-dark men dancers there are some forty-two, each with a dark, crowned woman attending him like a shadow. The old men, the bunch of singers in shirts and tied-up black hair, are about sixty in number, or sixty-four. The Koshare are about twenty-four.

They are slim and naked, daubed with black-and-white earth, their hair daubed white and gathered upwards to a great knot on top of the head, whence springs a tuft of corn-husks, dry corn-leaves. Though they wear nothing but a little black square cloth, front and back, at their middle, they do not seem naked, for some are white with black spots, like a leopard, and some have broad black lines or zigzags on their smeared bodies, and all their faces are blackened with triangles or lines till they look like weird masks. Meanwhile their hair, gathered straight up and daubed white and sticking up from the top of the head with corn husks, completes the fantasy. They are anything but natural. Like blackened ghosts of a dead corn cob, tufted at the top.

And all the time, running like queer spotted dogs they **weave** nakedly through the unheeding dance, comical, weird, dancing the dance-step naked and fine, prancing through the lines, up and down the lines, and making fine gestures with their flexible hands, calling something down from the sky, calling something up from the earth, and dancing forward all the time. Suddenly as they catch a word from the singers, name of a star, of a wind, a name for the sun, for a cloud, their hands soar up and gather in the air, soar down with a slow motion. And again, as they catch a word that means earth, earth deeps, water within the earth, or red-earth-quickening, the hands flutter softly down, and draw up the water, draw up the earth-quickening, earth to sky, sky to earth, influences above to influences below, to meet in the germ-quick of corn, where life is.

And as they dance, the Koshare watch the dancing men. And if a fox-skin is coming loose at the belt, they fasten it as the man dances, or they stoop and tie another man's shoe. For the dancer must not hesitate to the end.

And then after some forty minutes, the drum stops. Slowly the dancers file into one line, woman behind man, and move away, threading towards their kiva, with no sound but the tinkle of knee-bells in the silence.

But at the same moment, the thud of an unseen drum, from beyond, the soughing of deep song approaching from the unseen. It is the other half, the other half of the tribe coming to continue the dance. They appear round the kiva — one Koshare and one dancer leading the rows, the old men all abreast, singing already in a great strong burst.

So, from ten o'clock in the morning till about four in the afternoon, first one half, then the other. Till at last, as the day wanes, the two halves meet, and the two singings like two great winds surge one past the other, and the thicket of the dance becomes a real forest. It is the close of the third day.

Afterwards, the men and women crowd on the low, round towers of the kivas, and take off their ceremonial dress, while the Koshare run round jesting and miming, and taking big offerings from the women, loaves of bread and cakes of blue-maize meal. Women come carrying big baskets of bread and guayava, on two hands, an offering.

And the mystery of germination — not procreation, but *putting forth*, resurrection, life springing within the seed, is accomplished. The sky has its fire, its waters, its stars, its wandering electricity, its winds, its fingers of cold. The earth has its reddened body, its invisible hot heart, its inner waters and many juices and unaccountable stuffs. Between them all, the little seed: and also man, like a seed that is busy and aware. And from the heights and from the depths man, the caller, calls: man, the knower, brings down the influences and brings up the influences, with his knowledge: man, so vulnerable, so subject, and yet, even in his vulnerability and subjection, a master, commands the invisible influences, and is obeyed. Commands in that song, in that rhythmic energy of dance, in that still-submissive mockery of the Koshare. And he accomplishes his end, as master. He partakes in the springing of the corn, in the rising and budding and earing of the corn. And when he eats his bread, at last, he recovers all he once sent forth, and partakes again of the energies he called to the corn, from out of the wide universe.

ARCHITECTURE

ARCHITECTURE

THE building in which a theatre is housed is in a way the face that it turns to the world. To be an honest face, it should reflect the spirit of the theatre within just as the theatre itself should represent the life without. Probably no kind of building is farther away from the life of which it is a part than the modern American theatre building, the direct descendant of French courts and Italian operas. Yet this is not perhaps altogether a carelessness of mind. Perhaps these romantic buildings with their exaggerated decoration, their crimson and gold hangings, aristocratic boxes, and heightened ornament are not only a repetition of the past, but a reflection of the romantic tendency hidden under our mechanistic exterior; an eagerness to revive, in our level democracy, at least the semblance of aristocratic pleasures; another expression of our desire to forget reality in the theatre. Even from that point of view, however, they are generally unsuccessful because they are too ugly, too cramped and sordid to be evocative. In some of the newer city theatres, and especially in the community playhouses, like The Pasadena Community Theatre, The Cleveland Playhouse, the Lobero Theatre of Santa Barbara, the theatre at Yale University, there is a reflection of our intention to set our theatre free of its business surroundings and at the same time to make it a building more related to its time.

THE THEATRE IN THE MACHINE AGE

By Sheldon Cheney

ALTHOUGH I am aware of the dangers lying in the path of him who attempts either creation or criticism with reference to a theory, I have found some interest recently in exploring the by-paths of contemporary theatre architecture impelled by the largely theoretic idea that we are coming to a typical "machine-age" playhouse. That is, without any set of demonstrable facts, with little proof in actual buildings, I think I can find indications that the present decorative theatre building is almost as dead as the artificial court life of which it is spiritually a relic; and that in its place, before long, stage artists and engineers will be constructing theatres in the spirit of the uses of today, with the truth and directness of the machine inherent in every line.

How profoundly the machine has changed human life — so that in the Western world it is proper to speak of this as the machine age — few of us pause to consider. More than changing political institutions, more than the crumbling of the religions of faith, and more than the spread of the scientific spirit, the conquest of mechanics has changed the conditions under which the individual lives, and has affected the course of so-called civilization. The enormous increase in the ease of transportation and inter-communication, the despatch and neatness with which our ordinary physical tasks are accomplished, the extraordinarily enlarged productiveness under machine-industry, the day-by-day living with machines — telephones, automobiles, plumbing, vacuum cleaners, etc. — these things have changed not only the outward circumstances of man's life but his thinking and his emotional responsiveness; and a new art must grow out of this new life, if we are not to die spiritually, an art expressive of a new set of truths and understandable to the machine-age mind and emotions.

What are the qualities that may conceivably be correlated in the two fields? Without answering directly — for the relation between physical life and æsthetics offers little solid ground for argument — one may suggest that they have to do with directness of expression, clarity, freedom from ornament, precision, intensity. To many who have never bothered about reasons, I think the older modes of art have become distasteful. The authority of other times, lingering in the art galleries and theatres long after it was forced out of legislative halls, fostered the idea that art was a refuge from everyday current life. For a time the conception of court art, of display art, of a decorated haven, persisted. But removed from living human activity, it led inevitably to sterility and decay. The stuffy court architecture, lavishly but weakly ornamental, became faintly disturbing and distasteful, although it served even up to twenty years ago as model for most of the important buildings in every Western country.

ARCHITECTURE

The theatre particularly, and even later, reeked of the atmosphere of the regal love-nest, was the repository for pretty gimcracks and exuded a soft voluptuousness.

But the idea that art is a refuge from, rather than an intensification of, life is fast losing ground; the falsity of the transfer of the frills of one era to answer the æsthetic hunger of another is being recognized; and even the theatre emerges seeking a new decorative mode and contact with contemporary living. Itself a highly organized machine, we are slowly learning the truth that it can be appropriately and inspiringly clothed only in the austere and frill-less but beautifully proportioned modes of the industrial era.

Although, as I have said, there is no example I can show with the words "Here is a machine-age theatre", there are other fields of architectural practice in which the modernist accomplishment is sure, complete, and stirring; and one can argue with some certainty from that analogy. Long ago industrial building began to throw off current architectural dishonesty, the attempt to ornament it into something it was not, and sporadically appeared with an engineer's directness of purpose and fitness to use. Frank Lloyd Wright carried the new truth into domestic building and created a style that is today detectable in "advanced" building in half a dozen European countries. But chiefly in the skyscraper — the business building of congested cities — the new problem created by great height brought a new ingenuity that outran the architect's attempts to disguise what was unfamiliar to him under familiar forms; and, thanks to the engineers and a few heretic-architects nurtured on Wright and Louis Sullivan, a new style of building, structurally true and at least not falsely ornamented, pierces the sky in many an American city.

The relationship of this architecture to the modern machine embraces more than a likeness of materials — steel in the honeycomb frame, metal doors and window-frames, and bronze or brass elevator grilles and cages. If the architect has not caught from the mechanical engineer's designing something of mass-proportioning, of glorying in the clean line, in simplification and smoothing of surface, in precision, he has missed the most obvious contemporary source of stimulation to his imagination. I dare say there has been more essential architecture — creative building to satisfy æsthetic need — during the last thirty years in our ocean liners, our flying ships, and our automobiles than there has been in set buildings. In these things the problem of building has been linked with a machine-problem, and the mechanical "feel" has determined the decorative expression. Do you get half the æsthetic thrill from the house you live in that you do from the motor car you ride in ? Powerful, fleet, with power and fleetness confessed in every line, absolutely without applied ornament, expressive of its purpose and the machine it carries, bespeaking the integrity of mind and love of craftsmanship of its designer, how often can you find its counterpart in architect's designs ? And on an ocean liner — except where, as a concession to snobbishness, a Louis XVI salon or a Pompeian lounge has been added — there is absolute fitness, expressiveness, naked beauty, in the aspect of the ship as a whole, precisely and lovingly shaped for speed and grace, her funnels dominating with the feel of engines below, with the clean sea-faring finish everywhere apparent, long unornamented stretches of deck, the clean-cut equipment of such working parts as the captain's bridge. These liners have become immense hotels with mechanical means for sea-going. If the designer of a theatre could think of his problem as directly and honestly as that, would we not have a building quite as expressive of stage needs and audience needs as the ship is of sea-going and passenger-comfort?

If the designer of a theatre, with a passion for building and a knowledge of stage requirements, but without the architect's stylistic training, could be set down to make plans for a theatre with no other inspiration than that gained from a thorough examination of a giant passenger aëroplane, would he not give us a building more usable, more expressive, more stirringly creative than anything we have now? Even from contemplation of the plumbing that will go into his building he might learn something salutary about honesty, fitness to purpose, and craftsmanlike finish.

The gain by stripping ornament from the outside and inside of the building is, of course, a negative one in itself — but an extremely important first step. Beyond the stripping process, after getting back to the beginning of naked construction, one will probably find in the early examples of a new theatre architecture these qualities analogous to those of the designed machine: love of the clean line, mass outline for expressiveness of purpose — and the mass-creation here is almost the sculptor's problem — joy in the feel of the material, whether it be concrete, stone, iron-and-glass, or cut

Staatliches Bauhaus in Weimar 1919–1923

The State Theatre at Jena, as remodelled by Walter Gropius and A. Meyer of the school of modernist designers known as "the Weimar Bauhaus group." One of the most interesting European examples of the present period of "stripped architecture", absolutely without ornament but with indications of new decorative values, which may forerun a real machine-age architectural "style." The accentuation of straight lines and angles, the importance of sculptural mass design, and the reliance on flat walls, interesting for their texture, are all typical of the anti-operatic school of theatre design.

metal, and sheer surfaces (although decoration will come, appropriately, imaginatively, as an enrichment). Outwardly there will be reflection of both the engineering of the building and its uses.

The common idea that modernism in art means getting away from *everything* that is accepted or "normal" is, of course, wrong. In theatre architecture to be modern means to stick to a very great deal that engineering has brought to the present structure. Under its ornament and disguising façades, the investigator will find that the current playhouse has its mass-outline that is characteristic — and that in the hands of genius this becomes arresting and interesting. Here the three-part character of the building determines the honest design: audience space, acting space, and a section with "the works" and the dressing rooms. The problems of hanging the balcony over the orchestra without post-supports, and of sloping the orchestra floor without adding dangerous stairs — these problems of auditorium engineering, if confessed, may be made assets rather than liabilities. Granted that one wants a stage for backdrops and flats, the present stage machinery is all to the good — and here one seldom does see disguise. But Constructivism, the machine-age setting, may render much of the line and tackle unnecessary. Perhaps a walled-in space will be all that a repertory of shows needs. That and light. In the machine-age an adequately illuminated stage, not to say a luminous stage, is characteristic and right. Constructivism is anti-decorative and anti-pictorial. It is skeleton-engineering applied to stage setting, and is conceived entirely in response to the uses to which the stage-space is to be put. Probably its anti-decorative bias is too consciously stressed at present; but it provides a new honest starting-point for the "decorators" and an extension of the idea into the other parts of the theatre can only prove beneficial.

Examples for illustration stop largely at the "stripped-architecture" period. That is, when I look around for examples of modernist architecture in play-houses, I find only a house or two in which ornament has been cut away successfully, with little further progress toward typical expressiveness of the theatre machine. The State Theatre at Jena, as rebuilt by Walter Gropius, is as successful as any, if one judges by the photographs. Of course Van de Velde had worked along that road, with his famous Cologne "Werkbund" Theatre, where the labor-society idea as well as the articulated three-part theatre structure did get successfully into the plan and aspect of the building. There, too, the tri-partite stage was exemplified, and it may be that one of the keys to the future lies in that. At any rate the platform stage, the naked architectural non-pictorial stage, is in my estimation likely to return — and its honest confession of purpose, its truth to acting, its freedom from concession to the painting art, is in line with modern ideas of building integrity. Thus Copeau's and Jouvet's stages have been as interesting as any developed in the last hundred years; and Perret, who followed Van de Velde in designing the Théâtre des Champs-Élysées in Paris, followed also with a tri-partite stage at the Exposition Theatre built in Paris for the Exposition des Arts Décoratifs — a building that came as close as any to a typical early-

machine-age expression.   But it, too, is at the "stripped"
stage of development.

As yet unbuilt, but more of a thrust toward the
future, is the design of Frank Lloyd Wright for the
Barnsdall Theatre in Los Angeles.   Here there is clear
thinking through to a solution of the play-producing
problem as one mind sees it; a creative use of materials;
a near approach to a decorative mode appropriate to
the building's uses and the spirit of the times.

Really the heart of the problem is in two things, and
the architect will learn about it in these ways: by a
reëxamination of the *use* of the theatre building and
by an understanding and appreciation of machinery.
Starting there, his imagination will supply what of
decorative values is necessary over and above constructive honesty if he is the poet he should be.

My own idea of an honest theatre building for these
times embraces at the back an arrangement of dressing
rooms, work rooms, and storage rooms equipped with
every modern appliance of sanitation and service to
actor and mechanic, the whole light and airy but com-
pact; a large cleared dark stage space with flexible
lighting equipment, with adaptable platform stage and
"constructions" as frankly architectural as the Elizabethan stage or Copeau's but with more reliance on
lighter materials and open space as developed by the
Constructivists; and an auditorium and lobbies that
confess their engineering, that provide mechanical
comfort for audiences, that gain their warmth and
atmosphere by simplicity of line, material-interest,
precision of craftsmanship, and color.

GRUB–STREET THEATRES

By Lewis Mumford

THE search for new forms and vivid modes of expression has touched every part of the modern theatre in America, except the building itself. While stage settings have, in the hands of Robert Edmond Jones and Norman Bel Geddes, become more structural and architectonic, the buildings themselves have remained little more than a weak sort of stage-setting, thought out in one of the current fashions that sweep over the draughting room, and leave a froth of vapid designs in their wake.

There are plenty of prosaic reasons for this failure in theatre-design; and it will perhaps be well to take a look at them, before we begin to seek a basis for a new theatre architecture. In the first place, the ordinary commercial theatre is a job which the respectable architect, until recently, could scarcely be brought to undertake. Theatres were designed on the Grub-Street principle, and what was called decoration, the pseudo-baroque contortions in plaster and gilt that used to span the proscenium arch and dribble down from the ceiling and wall, were furnished by the cubic foot, along with real, hand-painted murals depicting

"Nymphs at Play", or "The Spirit of the Drama." Of the few improvements that have been made in theatre design, the support of the balcony by steel trusses instead of columns was an inevitable result of modern technology, whilst the widening of the orchestra, with the abolition of the deep, under-the-balcony seat, was made possible by the replacement of the old-fashioned stage setting, with its numerous lateral exits.

There is still another reason why scarcely a single distinguished architect in America has been tempted by the theatre; and this is the fact that, however excellent an elevation may be when it leaves the architect's hands, the chances that the whole effect will be ruined by placards, billboards, elephantine marquees, and a terrific spatter of electric advertisement are at least a hundred to one: so why should the architect bother to begin with? The Times Square Theatre in New York is an excellent example of what happens to the architect's front when the press agent and the advertising manager are done with it. The only way that the architect could meet this problem would be by outdoing the manager, and creating a façade which, in its inception, would be sheer advertisement.

A long time ago I suggested that the architect's salvation, with respect to the commercial theatre, was to design the façade with the marquee and the announcement signs as the central element; I pointed out that it was futile to design a respectable piece of picture-book architecture with the stinging certainty that, bad as it was, it would be covered up by something even worse as soon as the architect took his hands off the job. So far, I regret, no one has taken this advice seriously. Architecture is still one thing; and metal awnings and electric signs are another; and while this is so, both the signs and the architecture remain uninteresting, or something worse than that.

And now a final reason for the mean quality of most of our theatre architecture. This is the fact that in our large cities the exorbitant rise of ground rents has necessitated a cramping and stingy treatment of the various elements of the theatre: a setback from the street, a reasonably spacious foyer, an attempt to model the building in the mass — none of these things has been possible. The result has been, as far as the elevation goes, façaderie; and as for the interiors, a general tightening and scamping on all the essentials. A little of the gilt and gimcrackery has disappeared in the process; but that has been a negative gain, rather than an opening for a more exhilarating effort at form. While these economic forces remain in existence, the province of the architect must be correspondingly small. All that one can ask is that, within this province, he should not waste what opportunities remain. This brings us to our clean slate. What *are* the opportunities?

As for the exterior treatment of the theatre, it is plain that none of the Renaissance, Baroque, or Colonial precedents is of any use at all, except to disguise the architect's lack of interior resources. Our architects are all so thoroughly obsessed with the notion of dignity that they design theatres given over to revues as if they were funeral parlors, and, by the same token, they wall a stage which may serve "The Master Builder" or "Goat Song" behind a façade appropriate to a bonding

Peter A. Juley

The fine façade of the new Ziegfeld Theatre in New York, designed by Joseph Urban and sketched by Hugh Ferriss. The playhouse marks a distinct departure from the ginger-bread architecture which is so commonly used for our theatres, achieving a striking effect by the strength with which masses are handled and the simplicity of the decorative motifs. Containing an elliptical auditorium and an unusually well-equipped stage that is backed by a permanent cyclorama, the building makes excellent use of space. The walls are decorated with murals instead of with the usual moldings and hangings.

house or a bank; whereas it is plain that farce and tragedy and all that lies between represent, in one way or another, an intensification of life, and this drabness, this dullness, this dingy prudence is the very essence against which the theatre, in all its aspects, is a protest.

The remedy is plain; let the architect be content, on the outside, with a blank wall, and the fewest possible openings: no brummagem decoration, no fake balconies, and, above all, no windows to admit, during the performance, the clatter and scream of the streets. My own appreciation of the mechanical substitutes we use to take the place of sunlight and fresh air is very far this side of idolatry; but plainly, a theatre is a place where a thorough artificial ventilating system should be installed, so as to remove the necessity for windows or for the periodical opening of doors.

As for the necessary doors and openings, and the lobby itself, here is a place where a few intense gestures in ornament would be welcome; and here is where we need the originality in ornamental design that the late Louis Sullivan brought to architecture, that Mr. Claude Bragdon exhibited once upon a time in the Song and Light Festival, and that would flourish more freely, with the help of our original artists, if the architect could only manage to make a holocaust of the books and plates from which he is tempted to crib and pick and steal his ornamental motifs. Mr. Eli Kahn, the architect, induced Mr. Gaston Lachaise, the sculptor, to model the bronze elevator doors and the letter-box in a loft building; and there are a score of artists in New York who would welcome a similar chance to create expressive designs for doors, panels, grilles, pavements, and wall surfaces. This method of decoration would be great fun; and the cost of genuine art, curious to say, is scarcely more than the cost of the orthodox daubery and finery, as conceived by the senior draughtsman.

Now, what shall we say of the decoration of the interior? Of the necessary rooms — the rest rooms, the foyer, and the offices — one can only ask that the same sort of taste which would do away with attempts to reproduce "periods" in architecture should govern the interior too. The American architect can get a great deal of encouragement in the design of carpets, furniture, and fixtures from some of the Dutch, French, and Austrian work which was shown in the Exhibition des Arts Décoratifs; in any event, we are getting past the period when, like Gilbert's æsthete, we thought that art stopped short in the cultivated court of the Empress Josephine. This still leaves us, however, with the main decorative problem unsolved: that of the theatre itself, the walls of the auditorium, the frame of the stage, the ceiling.

In this province, it seems to me, we have hardly begun to appreciate the possibilities of decorative and constructive effects. Each play exists in an atmosphere, and establishes, more or less definitely, a mood. The time spent before the play opens, and that occupied in the intervals, may either establish this atmosphere and mood or nullify it; and what will happen in this period will depend, in some part, upon the form and decoration of the theatre itself. It is not merely that a great mass of brilliant ornament creates a rim of confusion about the picture upon which the spectator is focussing, although this happens, often enough, when one's attention is slightly lagging; it is even more that the right sort of form keeps one, spiritually, within the framework of the performance, while the wrong sort misses this opportunity or works against it. How quickly the mood of the revival of "East Lynne" was established by the cartoon on the curtain; it awakened the appropriate preparatory response. But the curtain is only one element in the scheme; and there is no reason why this effort should end with the curtain. The stage designer creates, at will, an atmosphere of intimacy, for example, by diminishing the size of his frame and reducing the scale: why should the architect not take a hint from this practice, and create a theatre capable of being adapted directly to the play in hand? I am suggesting in other words that the practices of modern scenic art can be applied to the decoration of the theatre as a whole; since, given a sufficient storage room, there is no reason why the interior decorations should not be changed to harmonize with the play that is presented.

This would, of course, be unthinkable if we conceived "decoration" in the ancient form of plaster cupids, moldings, cornucopias, and the sort of mural which would almost win the Prix de Rome; but as soon as we think of interior decoration in terms of the stage itself, it resolves itself largely into an arrangement of planes, prisms, and lights; and, given a theatre architectonically worked out, the alteration of these elements would, on the whole, be simpler than the shift of settings in the short time interval demanded by the actual performance. Some of the materials necessary, such as light, are used now with complete imbecility, as in the vacuous changes of light that are cast around a big moving picture auditorium during the music. Plainly, however, light might be significantly used to lessen the amount of distraction, and the shift in moods, between the acts; or again, it might be employed to establish a tonal contrast. As theatres are now conceived and decorated — even the chaste and neutral "better ones" — this sort of mobile decoration is impossible, without a complete rebuilding, such as was effected in the Geddes production of "The Miracle"; a modern scheme of internal construction would be conceived, on the contrary, with this possibility continuously in view. At times, the director might keep the conventional breaks and distractions; but the frame would always be ready for dynamic use.

The other great unused resource in theatre design is the modulation of space. One breathes differently, feels differently, thinks differently in a room where one can almost touch the ceiling than one breathes, thinks, and feels in a room with a ceiling or roof that climbs into a spacious obscurity. This is an effect which might be varied quite easily in a theatre where the balcony was kept fairly low and small. We are beginning to rebel against the convention of seeing plays "in the flat": the revival of the apron and the use of the central stage are indications of a new attitude towards the spatial relations of the audience, the scene, and the actors. When the drama is less an external performance, and more an interior process, with the spectator intimately participating, the two-dimensional stage is unsatisfactory, and means must be found for bringing the play, more or less literally, out into the audience. One of the ways of achieving this is to throw the spectator, as soon as he takes his seat, into an environment which reflects or echoes or continues that of the play itself.

This is not an esoteric doctrine; it is a commonplace. No one would think of putting on "The Cherry Orchard" in the Hippodrome; but in slightly less violent ways, this is what we are doing all the time. To build theatres which may be adapted to the audience and the play is only, on the other hand, to bring the new art of stage design into a wider sphere of application. It is time that our architects brooded a little over this possibility. By the use of curtains, partitions, and painted screens the form of the theatre, and the color-patterns of its surfaces, could be altered conveniently — and with no vast outlay — in a way that would express or deliberately form a contrast to the dominant mood of the play. At the very least, this mode of decoration, with its strict and essential simplicity, would be a great relief from the ostentatious or humdrum ornament that afflicts us today; and, in a magnificent moment, it could rise to its full opportunity.

In sum, scenic design has little enough to learn from current architecture; but I think that our theatre architecture might borrow more than a word or two from modern stage design. Our architects have been quick enough to learn how to put up a false front: now, by a paradox, our decorators can show them the elements of constructive æsthetics! I have a feeling that Mr. Norman Bel Geddes might put them right.

NEW PATHS AND BYWAYS

NEW PATHS AND BYWAYS

GRANVILLE-BARKER once said that the greatest contribution which America had made to the theatre was in dilating the region of its preparation, in pushing back the study not only of the drama but of playwriting, acting, design, and the subsidiary arts into the schools and, accordingly, into the lives of the country's youth. Certainly the schools of America and the colleges have added to our professional theatre much of its best dramatic writing, its most complete human equipment, and of its finest audience. Yet it is not only in the schools that the new contribution to the theatre can be measured, but in the Little Theatres of every professional and amateur complexion, in the increasing skill of those most democratic of artists, the "vaudevillians" (often likened to the players of the Commedia dell' Arte), in the development of a drama of Negro life, in the marionette shows and the mask makers, on all the byways of theatre interest.

LITTLE THEATRE BACKGROUNDS

By KENNETH MACGOWAN

ABOUT the little theatre movement of America there is the atmosphere of the unique. Across a country four thousand miles wide somewhere in the neighborhood of fifteen thousand amateur actors provide amusement for an audience whose size can only be estimated by multiplying five hundred producing organizations by whatever figure you may care to set as their average clientele. If you guess their patronage at five hundred per bill, your estimate will be two hundred and fifty thousand; with only a very little recklessness, you can push the little theatre audience of the United States up to half a million. All the professional producers of Broadway and the Road do not mount so many plays in any season as these five hundred little theatres with their two to twenty bills a year.

If you put the American mania for statistical extravagance firmly in its place, you still find certain things that seem to cut off our little theatre movement from any theatrical phenomenon of the past. It is ninety-nine per cent amateur, and it dedicates itself above all things to the newer arts of scenic design and atmospheric lighting.

And yet these symptoms of American geography, American megalomania, and American enthusiasm for the newest in current fashions should blind no one to the fact that our little theatre has an ancestry of almost forty years on the continent of Europe, and is only a part — a current phase — of a long story of theatrical rebellion. It is a story in which the amateur actor, the subscription audience, and the small auditorium have always played a part.

Free Theatre, Independent Theatre, . . . Literary Theatre, Art Theatre, . . . National Theatre, Stage Society, Repertory Theatre, . . . Little Theatre, Chamber Theatre, Intimate Theatre — behind all the twists of phrase which set them off into families there is a common note of rebellion. Strindberg set it down on paper in the eighties. With these words he called into being those rebel playhouses which almost invariably included among the plays of their first seasons the "Ghosts" of the other great Scandinavian playwright:

"Let us have a free theatre where there is room for everything but incompetence, hypocrisy, and stupidity! . . . where we can be shocked by what is horrible, where we can laugh at what is grotesque, where we can see life without shrinking back in terror if what has hitherto lain veiled behind theological or æsthetic conceptions is revealed to us."

It was against the conventional drama and the conventional acting of the Parisian boulevards that André Antoine — clerk in the gas company and amateur actor — launched the Théâtre-Libre, ancestor of all the little theatres of the world. On March 30, 1887, in a small hall above a café on Montmartre, Antoine and his friends put on their first bill of modern one-act plays. The actor who spoke the prologue forgot his lines, and there were many hitches about the scenery; everything was quite in the soon-to-be-established tradition of the little theatre. But actors appeared as human beings in plays of recognizable milieu, they smoked cigarettes, they even turned their backs on the audience, and through their agency the way was opened for distinguished realistic playwrights like Brieux, De Curel, Porto-Riche, and Lavedan.

Brother to the Théâtre-Libre and great-uncle to the American little theatre, the Freie Bühne appeared in Berlin in 1889. Amateurs and critics — Maximilian Harden and Otto Brahm, for example — mingled with professionals in its leadership, and Ibsen, Hauptmann, and Tolstoy were given to an audience of subscribers only.

In England George Moore, arch-realist, began to talk of a free theatre in 1891, and before spring had come John T. Grein, the critic, launched the Independent Theatre, with that performance of "Ghosts" which permitted the reviewers of the London stage to make consummate asses of themselves. The membership in Grein's society included George Meredith, Thomas Hardy, Arthur Wing Pinero, and Henry Arthur Jones; the next year Grein produced Shaw's first play — written for this theatre — "Widowers' Houses", and not so many years after its founding in 1900 the London Stage Society, which replaced the Independent Theatre, was putting forth Granville-Barker, Somerset Maugham, Arnold Bennett, and St. John Hankin as

well as Shaw, Maeterlinck, Hauptmann, Ibsen, and the
rest. Other acting societies followed — the Play Actors, the Oncomers, the Drama Society, the Pioneer
Players, etc. — and soon Barker was worming his way
into the commercial and professional theatre to give
London Galsworthy and Masefield.

In 1897 Russia created the greatest of modern acting
companies out of a dramatic school maintained by
Nyemirovitch-Dantchenko, and a little theatre headed
by an amateur actor called Stanislavsky. It took
about a dozen years for the amateur reformers of the
London stage to break into the professional theatre.
I cannot say how long the Moscow Art Theatre was
a-borning in Russian little theatres, but the strength
of that special and finely amateur impulse was evident
when, at the height of its success and in the midst of a
world war, the Stanislavsky company began the organization of its four Studio Theatres where new talent
meets special audiences.

In all these efforts the same spirit of amateurism, the
same system of subscription, the same parallels with
our own little theatre movement are clear enough.
The cause is rebellion against the commercial stage.
The guiding spirit is amateur. The economic system
is based on the subscription audience. And the playhouse is usually a small and cheap one, or an ordinary
theatre rented economically for occasional performances. The difference between these European theatres
of reform and our own are two: The policies of the
European theatres succeeded in breaching the walls
of the professional houses, and establishing their
leaders — Antoine, Brahm, Barker — as directors of

commercial playhouses, just as their amateur ventures died; and the chief aim and artistic outcome of these efforts was the development in each country of new playwrights with a distinctly native quality. Our little theatres have their effect upon Broadway, but the necessities of the smaller cities, deserted by good road companies, keep them alive even when their actors or directors move on into new work. As for their product, it is not as yet — worse luck! — a brilliant group of such playwrights as the free theatres of Europe produced; but the rebellion of today is against the realism that the free theatres fostered, and imagination in production, settings, and lights opens the way for imagination in playwriting.

Later European efforts than those I have chronicled also link up with our little theatre movement. Within half a dozen years of the founding of the Théâtre-Libre Paul Fort in the Théâtre d'Art and Alexandre Lugné-Poë in the Théâtre de l'Œuvre were cultivating Shelley, Maeterlinck, and Verlaine, and setting their faces against realism. When, fourteen years later, Jacques Rouché founded in 1907 the Théâtre des Arts, and began the exploitation of French stage designers, and when in 1913 Jacques Copeau made a group of amateurs into a fine acting company on the naked stage of the Vieux-Colombier there had already developed in Germany a unique figure — Max Reinhardt — out of a unique aspect of the rebellious and amateur little theatre movement.

However professional Reinhardt may appear as actor and director, it is highly significant that the first theatre over which he exercised complete control was

One of the advantages of the Little Theatre is that it serves as a laboratory of not too costly experiment in new forms, and a testing place of tradition. In them even the production of Shakespeare is not allowed to become hardened by convention. Above is a design for "Twelfth Night" which Alan Crane and Anna Wille worked out for Richard Boleslavsky's production of "Twelfth Night", at the Laboratory Theatre in New York. The director tried to recreate the festival spirit of the comedy, and the designer, with his vivid and flashing colors, coöperated with him.

called the Kleines Theater, that he worked in the
Freie Bühne, and that he bridged the gap between
volunteer work with the Freie Bühne and the management of the Kleines Theater by an adventure in the
kind of cabaret management of which we have caught a
glimpse in Balieff's Chauve-Souris. From 1900 to
1902, while Reinhardt was still a member of Brahm's
company at the Deutsches Theater, he was creating in
Die Brille and Schall und Rauch two cabarets amateur
in spirit and emolument, and exclusive in their special
audience. From these efforts, which were vivid and
imaginative in quality, it was natural that Reinhardt
should venture into the production of short, picturesque
plays, and finally into the management of a theatre
where vivid realism and imaginative drama utilized
the services of the new stagecraft and took advantage
of the intimacy of a small auditorium. Oddly enough,
the first plays that Reinhardt attempted in Schall und
Rauch were by the same Strindberg who sounded the
trumpet call of the free theatre and who founded in
Stockholm in 1907 a tiny Chamber Theatre in partner-
ship with August Falk.

Of the European backgrounds of our little theatres
there remain only the English and Irish ventures which
have brought forward the phrase "repertory theatre"
as a misnomer for a resident stock company. However professional some of these companies became, the
people who served the oldest of them all and the woman
who gave them all their financial impulse were amateurs. In 1894 a certain Miss A. E. F. Horniman, who
bore significantly the name of a popular brand of tea,
put up the money for Florence Farr to produce "Arms

and the Man" in London. In 1904 this same woman bought the Mechanics Institute Hall in Dublin, turned it into the Abbey Theatre, and presented it rent free for six years to the Irish National Dramatic Society. This organization, which had come to life through the energies of two amateur actors, W. C. and Frank Fay, which had enlisted W. B. Yeats from the moribund Irish Literary Theatre of 1899, and which had brought to itself John Millington Synge and Lady Gregory, developed in half a dozen years into a professional theatre that sent us the Irish Players, created a dramatic literature of real distinction, and, inspired by Gordon Craig, embarked on significant experiments in the new stagecraft.

Turning to England again, Miss Horniman began in Manchester a dramatic movement which even the war has been unable completely to destroy. In 1907 she set up in the Midland capital the Manchester Repertory Company, at the beginning under the direction of B. Iden Payne, later of Lewis Casson. In 1909 Glasgow created the Scottish Repertory Theatre; in 1911 the Liverpool Repertory Theatre came into being under the direction of Basil Dean. The Birmingham Repertory Theatre followed in 1913 under the leadership of John Drinkwater and Barry Jackson. These theatres and certain others that imitated them employed many professional players and turned their first energies to the calling forth of new playwrights; yet their relationship is closer, perhaps, to our little theatres than to any other of the rebellious experiments of Europe.

Though the "provinces" of England could be pocketed in Texas, they correspond fairly closely in their theatrical life to the present state of the far-flung touring system of the United States. London is an exaggerated Broadway. In 1907, when the successes and the stars of a New York season were certain to spend a year at least visiting Boston, Baltimore, St. Louis, Des Moines, Denver, and stands between, it was a rare play that came to Manchester or Birmingham with any members of the original London cast, and it was only the most obviously popular pieces which went on tour. In the repertory theatres of the provinces a considerable impulse came originally from playwrights or the hope of playwrights, but the necessities of play-starved audiences had as important a part in calling forth new theatres as they had in our American provinces.

And today, when most of the pioneers are gone, the provincial repertory theatres that remain do so largely in response to a need for dramatic entertainment and not because of a creative impulse among the artists. Play-producing societies like the Stage Society still continue to render their special service and theatres like the Maddermarket at Norwich and a few others form a link between the older and the newer experimental theatres.

By a terrific effort the history of the rebel theatre in the United States can be forced back to 1892 and the abortive Theatre of Arts and Letters. A little less energy discovers it at work in 1906 and 1907 with the founding in Chicago of three institutions of which two quickly passed away — the New Theatre under the direction of Victor Mapes, the Robertson Players under the direction of Donald Robertson, and the

Hull House Theatre under the direction of Laura Dainty Pelham. The years 1909 to 1911 marked the rise and fall of the New Theatre in New York under the direction of Winthrop Ames, and 1911–1912 the brief resurgence of Donald Robertson in the Drama Players. But for practical purposes the true start of dramatic reform in the United States must be reckoned with 1911, when Thomas H. Dickinson founded the Wisconsin Dramatic Society, and 1912, when Mrs. Lyman Gale's Toy Theatre of Boston and Maurice Browne's Little Theatre of Chicago came into existence. After these beginnings came the Arts and Crafts Theatre of Detroit, and the Little Theatre of Philadelphia, the 47 Workshop of Harvard, the Little Country Theatre of North Dakota, the Dramatic Workshop of Carnegie Institute of Pittsburgh, and a long line of experiments that had at their forefront the Washington Square Players, the Neighborhood Playhouse, the Provincetown Players, the Portmanteau Theatre, the Vagabond Players of Baltimore, the Carolina Playmakers, the Pasadena Community Theatre, the Ram's Head Players, the Cleveland Playhouse, the Dallas Little Theatre, Le Petit Théâtre du Vieux Carré of New Orleans, the enterprises of Sam Hume, Irving Pichel, and Maurice Browne on the Pacific Coast, not to mention the Canadian ventures, the Vancouver Little Theatre, the Hart House Theatre of Toronto, and the Home Theatre of the Canadian Players.

It seems to me that the impulses and results of the American little theatres are clear enough. Except for a small group of educational enterprises they have come into existence for one of two reasons, and they have continued successfully when both these motives were present. Europe knows these motives. In varying degree they were behind the rebel theatres that began with Antoine.

One motive is an audience that needs and to some extent demands more or better entertainment than its professional theatres provide. In Europe in the nineties it was the degrading "Sardoodledum" of the commercial playhouses that left audiences unsatisfied; in England in the first decade of the twentieth century and in America in the second decade it was the decay of the touring system outside of the theatrical capitals.

The other motive behind the American little theatre as well as its Continental forerunners is the creator who cannot find an opening in the professional theatre. Everywhere the amateur actor has always insisted on exhibiting his charms, but in the serious theatre of which I am writing a new type of truly creative amateur appeared. In Europe he was the director or the playwright, and the outcome of his efforts was new drama. In America he has been the director or the scenic designer, and the result has been new and imaginative beauty in production. The difference is only a difference of the times. The rebellion of the eighties and the nineties looked towards the intellectual, the literary, and the realistic. The rebellion of today is looking towards the imaginative, the picturesque, the expressionistic, and it takes the visual path first, the written path later.

One type of little theatre distinguishes our movement from the movement of Europe. This is the scholastic. The vigor of the dramatic interest of America finds its sharpest index in the hundreds of courses in play-writing, play producing, acting, and design given at our leading universities. These courses have a practical outlet in the producing theatres of men like Baker, Arvold, Koch, Stevens, and others whose number and activity increase each year. Even the acting schools begin to see the light and give their pupils the practical experience of appearing frequently in first-rate plays under the general conditions of little theatre performances.

Within the last few years an entirely new phase of development has opened up for the little theatres which, like Pasadena and Cleveland, have grown large enough and sure-footed enough to venture upon new theatre buildings, with complete and modern professional equipment offering great opportunity not only to little theatre directors of professional quality, but to progressive professional actors and to playwrights who prefer to have their own roads.

A fine amateurism is at the heart of all this effort, both here and abroad, but in this amateurism certain curious distinctions between the movement in Europe and in America appear. In the European ventures, particularly in the English repertory theatres, the actors were sometimes professionals, though the directors were invariably amateurs. The American movement began on a wholly amateur basis, and almost (though of course not quite) all of its actors remain amateurs. The directors, on the other hand, have frequently developed into professionals, like Browne, Hume, Pichel, Hinsdell, Dean, McConnell, and others, who shift from little theatre to little theatre.

Clifford Norton

An older generation in "the provinces" can remember distinguished players from Daly's and the Empire coming regularly, if somewhat belatedly to their doors. To-day the price of rents and railroads has changed that and the "road" is reported dead. It is dead only to the trade theatre, however, as the new Cleveland Playhouse is evidence. Under the direction of Frederic McConnell this theatre, with its mixed professional and amateur company, presents one of the most distinguished repertories ever offered in the country. Above, McConnell's own setting for "The Sunken Bell."

In Europe the directors passed from their amateur first ventures into important posts in the professional theatre. Antoine became head of the State-subventioned Odéon. Rouché is now the director of the Paris Opéra. Reinhardt conquered the whole German theatre. Dean and Drinkwater found openings in London, and Payne in America. Stanislavsky and Copeau quickly solidified their beginnings into the finest professional theatres of their two nations. Perhaps the fact that most of these men worked in the capitals of States was at the bottom of this swift development; certainly it was this fact which accounted for the rapid growth of three New York ventures, the Washington Square Players-Theatre Guild, the Neighborhood Playhouse, and the Provincetown Players. In the bulk of the little theatres of the United States it is not the directors but the actors, designers, and occasional playwrights who pass on from the amateur to the professional playhouse. It is to these graduates that we look for the justification of the ideals and the practice of the rebellious little theatres in the professional playhouse, slowly but surely being conquered for art.

dawn of the "synthetic theatre" with the singing, dancing actor, and the plastic stage, the versatile gifts of the Negro actor seem peculiarly promising and significant.

Unfortunately it is the richest vein of Negro dramatic talent which is under the heaviest artistic impediments and pressure. The art of the Negro actor has had to struggle up out of the shambles of minstrelsy and make slow headway against very fixed limitations of popular taste. Farce, buffoonery, and pathos have until recently almost completely overlaid the folk comedy and folk tragedy of a dramatically endowed and circumstanced people. These gifts must be liberated. I do not narrowly think of this development merely as the extension of the freedom of the American stage to the Negro actor, although this must naturally come as a condition of it, but as a contribution to the technical idioms and resources of the entire theatre.

To see this rising influence one must of course look over the formal horizons. From the vantage of the advanced theatre, there is already a significant arc to be seen. In the sensational successes of "The Emperor Jones" and "All God's Chillun Got Wings" there have been two components, the fine craftsmanship and clairvoyant genius of O'Neill and the acting gifts of Charles Gilpin and Paul Robeson. From the revelation of the emotional power of the Negro actor by Opal Cooper and Inez Clough in the Ridgeley Torrence plays in 1916 to the more recent half-successful attempts of Raymond O'Neill's Ethiopian Art Theatre and the National Ethiopian Art Theatre of New York, with Evelyn Preer, Rose McClendon, Sidney Kirkpatrick, Charles

Olden, Francis Corbie, Julius Bledsoe, and, more lately, in the production of Paul Green's "In Abraham's Bosom", an advanced section of the American public has become acquainted with the possibilities of the Negro in serious dramatic interpretation. But the real mine of Negro dramatic art and talent is in the sub-soil of the vaudeville stage, gleaming through its slag and dross in the unmistakably great dramatic gifts of a Bert Williams, a Florence Mills, or a Bill Robinson. Give Bojangles Robinson or George Stamper, pantomimic dancers of genius, a Bakst or an expressionist setting; give Josephine Baker, Eddie Rector, Abbie Mitchell, or Ethel Waters a dignified medium, and they would be more than a sensation, they would be artistic revelations. Pantomime, that most essential and elemental of the dramatic arts, is a natural *forte* of the Negro actor, and the use of the body and voice and facile control of posture and rhythm are almost as noteworthy in the average as in the exceptional artist. When it comes to pure registration of the emotions, I question whether any body of actors, unless it be the Russians, can so completely be fear or joy or nonchalance or grief.

With his uncanny instinct for the theatre, Max Reinhardt saw these possibilities instantly under the tawdry trappings of such musical comedies as "Eliza", "Shuffle Along", and "Runnin' Wild", which were in vogue the season of his first visit to New York. "It is intriguing, very intriguing," he told me then, "these Negro shows that I have seen. But remember, not as achievements, not as things in themselves artistic, but in their possibilities, their tremendous artistic possibilities. They are most modern, most American, most expressionistic.

They are highly original in spite of obvious triteness, and artistic in spite of superficial crudeness. To me they reveal new possibilities of technique in drama, and if I should ever try to do anything typically American, I would build it on these things.

I didn't enthuse. What Negro who stands for culture, with the hectic stress of a social problem weighing on the minds of an over-serious minority, could enthuse! "Eliza", "Shuffle Along", "Runnin' Wild" — when I had come to discuss the possibilities of serious Negro drama, of the art-drama! I didn't outwardly protest, but raised a brow already too elevated perhaps and shrugged the shoulder that carries the proverbial racial chip.

Herr Reinhardt read the gestures swiftly. "Ah, yes — I see. You view these plays for what they are, and you are right; I view them for what they will become, and I am more than right. I see their future. Why? Well, the drama must turn at every period of fresh creative development to an aspect which has been previously subordinated or neglected, and in this day of ours, we come back to the most primitive and the most basic aspect of drama for a new starting point, a fresh development and revival of the art — and that aspect is pantomime, the use of the body to portray story and emotion. And your people have that art — it is their special genius. At present it is prostituted to farce, to trite comedy — but the technique is there, and I have never seen more wonderful possibilities. Yes, I should like to do something with it."

With the New Russian Theatre experimenting with the "dynamic ballet" and Meierhold's improvising or creative actor, with Max Reinhardt's own recently founded International Pantomime Society, with the entire new theatre agog over "mass drama", there is at least some serious significance to the statement that the Negro theatre has great artistic potentialities. What is of utmost importance to drama now is to control the primitive language of the art, and to retrieve some of the basic control which the sophisticated and conventionalized theatre has lost. It is more important to know how to cry, sob and laugh, stare and startle than to learn how to smile, grimace, arch, and wink. And more important to know how to move vigorously and with rhythmic sweep than to pirouette and posture. An actor and a folk art controlling the symbolism of the primary emotions has the modern stage as a province ripe for an early and easy conquest. Commenting on the work of the players of the Ethiopian Art Theatre, discerning critics noticed "the freshness and vigor of their emotional responses, their spontaneity and intensity of mood, their freedom from intellectual and artistic obsessions." And almost every review of Paul Robeson's acting speaks of it as beyond the calculated niceties, a force of overwhelming emotional weight and mastery. It is this sense of something dramatic to the core that flows movingly in the blood rather than merely along the veins that we speak of as the racial endowment of the Negro actor. For however few there may be who possess it in high degree, it is racial, and is in a way unique.

Without invoking analogies, we can see in this technical and emotional endowment great resources for the theatre. In terms of the prevalent trend for the serious development of race drama, we may expect these resources to be concentrated and claimed as the working capital of the Negro theatre. They are. But just as definitely, too, are they the general property and assets of the American Theatre at large, if once the barriers are broken through. These barriers are slowly breaking down both on the legitimate stage and in the popular drama, but the great handicap, as Carl Van Vechten so keenly points out in his "Prescription for the Negro Theatre", is blind imitation and stagnant conventionalism. Negro dramatic art must not only be liberated from the handicaps of external disparagement, but from its self-imposed limitations. It must more and more have the courage to be original, to break with established dramatic convention of all sorts. It must have the courage to develop its own idiom, to pour itself into new moulds; in short, to be experimental.

This development may have to await the expected growth of the serious, worth-while drama of Negro life, which for all the dramatic intensities of Negro experience has lagged lamentably until recently. There are many reasons for this; foremost, of course, the fact that drama, unless it develops in its own native soil, is the child of social prosperity and of cultural maturity. Negro life has only recently come to the verge of cultural self-expression, and has barely reached such a ripening point. Further than this, the quite melodramatic intensity of the Negro's group experience has defeated its contemporaneous dramatization; when life itself moves dramatically, the vitality of drama is often sapped. But there have been special reasons. Historical controversy and lowering social issues have clouded out the dramatic colors of Negro life into the dull mass contrasts of the Negro problem. Until lately not even good problem drama has been possible, for sentiment has been too partisan for fair dramatic balancing of forces and too serious for either æsthetic interest or artistic detachment. So although intrinsically rich in dramatic episode and substance, Negro life has produced for our stage only a few morally hectic melodramas along with innumerable instances of broad farce and low comedy. Propaganda, pro-Negro as well as anti-Negro, has scotched the dramatic potentialities of the subject. Especially with the few Negro playwrights has the propaganda motive worked havoc. In addition to the handicap of being out of actual touch with the theatre, they have had the dramatic motive deflected at its source. Race drama has appeared to them a matter of race vindication, and pathetically they have pushed forward their moralistic allegories or melodramatic protests as dramatic correctives and antidotes for race prejudice.

A few illuminating plays, beginning with Edward Sheldon's "Nigger" and culminating in "All God's Chillun Got Wings" and " In Abraham's Bosom " have already thrown into relief the higher possibilities of the Negro problem play. Similarly, beginning with Ridgeley Torrence's "Three Plays for a Negro Theatre" and culminating in "Emperor Jones" and "The No 'Count Boy", a realistic study of Negro folk-life and character has been begun, and with it the inauguration of the artistic Negro folk play. The outlook for a vital and characteristic expression of Negro life in drama thus becomes more promising.

NEW PATHS AND BYWAYS

The path of this newly awakened impulse is however by no means as clear as its goal. Two quite contrary directions compete for the artist's choice. On the one hand is the more obvious drama of social situation, focussing on the clash of the race life with its opposing background; on the other the apparently less dramatic material of the folk life and behind it the faint panorama of an alluring race history and race tradition. The creative impulse is for the moment caught in this dilemma of choice between the drama of discussion and social analysis and the drama of expression and artistic interpretation. But despite the present lure of the problem play, it ought to be apparent that the real future of Negro drama lies with the development of the folk play. Negro drama must grow in its own soil and cultivate its own intrinsic elements; only in this way can it become truly organic, and cease being a rootless derivative.

Of course the possibilities of Negro problem drama are great and immediately appealing. The scheme of color is undoubtedly one of the dominant patterns of society and the entanglement of its skeins in American life one of its most dramatic features. For a long while strong social conventions prevented frank and penetrating analysis, but now that the genius of O'Neill has broken through what has been aptly called "the last taboo", the field stands open. But for the Negro it is futile to expect fine problem drama as an initial stage before the natural development in due course of the capacity for self-criticism. The Negro dramatist's advantage of psychological intimacy is for the present more than offset by the disadvantage of the temptation

Probably no American play has been the subject of more successful experiment, in design and production, than Eugene
O'Neill's study in fear, "The Emperor Jones", still considered
by many as the most finished if not the most ambitious, of his
plays. With the design above, Aaron Douglass, a young
Negro artist, adds his contribution to the settings for the scene
of the tropical jungle closing in on the defeated Brutus Jones.

to counter partisan and propagandist attitudes. The white dramatist can achieve objectivity with relatively greater ease, though as yet he seldom does, and has temporarily an advantage in the handling of this material as drama of social situation. Proper development of these social problem themes will require the objectivity of great art. Even when the crassest conventions are waived at present, character stereotypes and deceptive formulæ still linger; only genius of the first order can hope to penetrate to the materials of high tragedy — and, for that matter, high comedy also — that undoubtedly are there. For with the difference that modern society decrees its own fatalisms, the situations of race hold tragedies and ironies as deep and keen as those of the ancient classics. Eventually the Negro dramatist must achieve mastery of a detached, artistic point of view, and reveal the inner stresses and dilemmas of these situations as from the psychological point of view he alone can.

The folk play, on the other hand, whether of the realistic or the imaginative type, has no such conditioned values. It is the drama of free self-expression and imaginative release, and has no objective but to express beautifully and colorfully the folk life of the race. At present, too, influenced perhaps by the social drama, it finds tentative expression in the realistic genre plays of Paul Green, Willis Richardson, and others. But in all of these plays as yet, there still comes the impression that the drama of Negro life has not become as racy, as gaily unconscious, as saturated with folk ways and the folk spirit as it could be, as it eventually will be. Decidedly it needs more of that poetic strain whose counterpart makes the Irish folk drama so captivating and irresistible, more of the joy of life even when life flows tragically, and, even should one phase of it remain realistic peasant drama, more of the emotional depth of pity and terror. This clarification will surely come as the Negro drama shifts more and more to the purely æsthetic attitudes. With life becoming less a problem and more a vital process for the younger Negro, we shall leave more and more to the dramatist not born to it the dramatization of the race problem and concern ourselves more vitally with expression and interpretation. Others may anatomize and dissect; we must paint and create. And while one of the main reactions of Negro drama must and will be the breaking down of those false stereotypes in terms of which the world still sees us, it is more vital that drama should stimulate the group life culturally and give it the spiritual quickening of a native art.

The finest function, then, of race drama would be to supply an imaginative channel of escape and spiritual release, and by some process of emotional reënforcement to cover life with the illusion of happiness and spiritual freedom. Because of the lack of any tradition or art to which to attach itself, this reaction has never functioned in the life of the American Negro except at the level of the explosive and abortive release of buffoonery and low comedy. Held down by social tyranny to the jester's footstool, the dramatic instincts of the race have had to fawn, crouch, and be amusingly vulgar. With the fine African tradition of primitive ritual broken and with the inhibitions of Puritanism snuffing out even the spirit of a strong dramatic and mimetic heritage, there has been little prospect for the development of strong native dramatic traits. But the traces linger to flare up spectacularly when the touch of a serious dramatic motive once again touches them. One can scarcely think of a complete development of Negro dramatic art without some significant artistic reëxpression of African life, and the tradition associated with it. No set purpose can create this, only the spontaneous play of the race spirit over its own heritage and traditions. But the deliberate turning back for dramatic material to the ancestral sources of African life and tradition is a very significant symptom.

It may seem a far cry from the conditions and moods of modern New York and Chicago and the Negro's rapid and feverish assimilation of all things American. But art establishes its contacts in strange ways. The emotional elements of Negro art are choked by the conventions of the contemporary stage; they call for freer, more plastic material. They have no mysterious affinity with African themes or scenes, but they have for any life that is more primitive and poetic in substance. So, if, as seems already apparent, the sophisticated race sense of the Negro should lead back over the trail of the group tradition to an interest in things African, the natural affinities of the material and the art will complete the circuit and they will most electrically combine. Especially with its inherent color and emotionalism, its freedom from body-hampering dress, its odd and tragic and mysterious overtones, African life and themes, apart from any sentimental attachment, offer a wonderfully new field and province for dramatic treatment. Here both the Negro actor and dramatist can move freely in a world of elemental beauty, with all the decorative elements that a poetic emotional temperament could wish. No recent playgoer with the spell of Brutus Jones in the forest underbrush still upon his imagination will need much persuasion about this.

More and more the art of the Negro actor will seek its materials in the rich native soil of Negro life, and not in the threadbare tradition of the Caucasian stage. In the discipline of art playing upon his own material, the Negro has much to gain. Art must serve Negro life as well as Negro talent serve art. And no art is more capable of this service than drama. Indeed the surest sign of a folk renascence seems to be a dramatic flowering. Somehow the release of such self-expression always accompanies or heralds cultural and social maturity. I feel that soon this aspect of the race genius may come to its classic age of expression. Obviously, though, it has not yet come. For our dramatic expression is still too restricted, self-conscious, and imitative.

But when our serious drama shall become as naïve and spontaneous as our drama of fun and laughter, and that in turn genuinely representative of the folk spirit which it is now forced to travesty, a point of classic development will have been reached. It is fascinating to speculate upon what riotously new and startling things may come from this. Dramatic maturings are notably sudden. Usually from the popular sub-soil something shoots up to a rapid artistic flowering. Of course, this does not have to recur with the American Negro. But a peasant folk art pouring out from under a generation-long repression is the likeliest soil known

THE NEGRO AND THE THEATRE

for a dramatic renascence. And the supporters and exponents of Negro drama do not expect their folk temperament to prove the barren exception. While the deliberate turning back for dramatic material to the ancestral sources of African life and tradition is a significant symptom, no set purpose can create this artistic rebirth, but only the spontaneous play of the race spirit over its own heritage and tradition.

THE THEATRE AND THE UNIVERSITY

By George Pierce Baker

Thirty years or more ago American universities offered courses in Shakespeare and his contemporaries timorously for the first time. Taking courage from the eager interest of their students, they moved on to the drama of the Restoration and the Eighteenth Century. Soon the inevitable happened. Courses in contemporary English drama appeared, whose teachers had the temerity to try to judge the current drama as the critics of the press always have. However, even these courses were successful. Then youth took control, saying, "All this study of the history of the drama stirs us to expression. Help us to write the plays we feel we must write." Thus came courses in dramatic technique. Their students, believing they were helped by them, have pressed steadily for a greater development of this technical work. It would be bromidic to dwell on the admitted effect of all this in a wider reading of plays, in the appearance and rapid growth of experimental theatres, and in the coming to the professional theatre of many college graduates.

What, however, is not bromidic and needs to be said is that many of the historical courses are still given with little or no emphasis on the plays as plays, but rather on characterization and beauty of prose or verse — on matters which could be as well illustrated by the reading of some poems or of most novels and short stories. I believe that in all colleges where work in the drama is offered there should be an introductory course in the appreciation of the drama, open to as many students as possible, and offered in as many different ways as the special abilities of the teachers in charge may determine. Some of these students will inevitably go on to courses dealing with the drama of special periods or countries. In fairness to them and for the betterment of dramatic taste in the country at large, such courses should be given with their main emphasis on plays as something to be acted — something to be judged with accuracy only when seen. These courses should make theatre-going for the college graduate more intelligent and more pleasurable by giving him not only understanding of plays as plays but also catholicity of taste. In the next twenty-five years I am sure that our colleges will do more and more to enrich the later lives of graduating youth by implanting not only a general love of the fine arts but also that grounding in the elements of technique sure to make any art more pleasurable.

All this concerns, however, the general student. What does the university owe the student to whom it has offered a course in the writing of plays? More than anything else it owes him a place where plays may be seen under fitting conditions—in other words, a theatre.

The would-be dramatist needs knowledge of the acted drama, — of many kinds, of many countries, of many periods. It is lack of proper standards which most often defeats him. Examine a pile of manuscript plays submitted in any competition or for the reading of any theatre manager. Throw out swiftly the plays obviously hopeless. What remains? The larger part — much the larger — will be plays well put together, perhaps, but so reminiscent of this or that recent success on Broadway, this or that well-known play of continental Europe, that it is nearly impossible to believe there was any impulse in the writer forcing him to composition — except a desire for immediate monetary gains. Watch the vogue in plays on Broadway. Any success in a new direction, however slight, means play after play of similar kind. Don't blame the manager wholly for this. Whatever his responsibility may be, a greater must rest on the would-be dramatists, young and old, who think that success lies in imitation. Ideas and form such workers copy well, but the individualizing something which turns a play into a work of art is lacking. What these people must be taught (if they are to become more than entertainers of the passing moment) is that they must first have thought or felt something strongly enough to be compelled to try to phrase it so as to create understanding through the emotional response of their audiences. Not to rephrase for the general public what has already been generally approved but to try to find the form which will convey to the general public what the writer is determined to convey, — that is the attitude to be developed.

Standards — informative, steadying standards — are what our young workers in the theatre need. They face audiences which in spite of a growing understanding of the theatre are still preponderantly made up of people who blindly follow their emotional responses along the lines of least resistance. This means liking what is tritely theatrical rather than humanly right, liking that which is easiest to feel, and consequently to understand. It is easier as an auditor to respond to signals, symbols for mirth or pity, than it is, through sympathetic understanding of a character or of the author's point of view, to feel amusement or pain to which most people are ordinarily insensitive. The dramatist must study the public early and late, not to truckle to its desire for signals and symbols but in order to learn how he may induce it to feel what he wants it to feel, and feeling, to understand. For all this a theatre is necessary.

Youth bluffs. The finer the spirit of the young artist the more unsure and secretly timid he is in trusting his instincts for expression. Basically he has a deep reverence for the best accomplishments of the past, even if he feels he cannot be satisfied to express himself in the same terms. In the great rhythm of emotional life he is too liable to mistake what is commonplace for something highly individual, merely because of its momentary intensity for him. What is really finely individual in his feeling and thinking about life, as he has read of it or experienced it, he too often passes over as of no consequence. He exults when he can sweep down the broad currents companioned by the multitude, oblivious that he may be lost in the crowd. He forgets that what the isolated thinker, the lonely traveller, brings back to the great world may open up a new field of science or reveal a new continent.

He needs to learn that form is not rigid, is not a fashion, a moral or an artistic obligation, but something an artist chooses after much selective thought as the best medium for the expression to which he finds himself compelled. Youth has too often a marvelous faith in the effectiveness and finality of five acts, four acts, three, or one; in prologues or epilogues; in scenes replacing acts, etc. Instead of talking of all this, how better prove to him that all have their wise and their unwise uses than by demonstrating it to him in a theatre?

Just as the playwright should understand that rightness of form is relative to the purpose of the individual dramatist, so, too, he should be taught catholicity of taste. Nearly every beginner pins his faith to the kind of work he does best. He is the uncompromising realist, romanticist, expressionist — what you will, or rather what he wills. He who has watched a generation of playwrights will be sure, however, that nothing is more common than for the realist to turn romantic, for the youthful cynic to discern, with the passing of the years, poetry — even beauty — where at first he saw only harsh realism and squalor. A theatre makes it possible to illustrate the rightness of each kind of work — to show the worker that artistic truth lies in no one form, idea, or message, but in the content that is the dramatist's individual contribution, and that the finest truth lies in the perfect inter-adjustment of thought, emotion, and form.

Many a playwright of experience is curiously unable to judge his own work. Subject his manuscript to discussion by sympathetic fellow workers and he will

George Pierce Baker, to whose teaching and inspiration much of the younger accomplishment in the theatre must be credited, has, after many years of experimental work in the 47 Workshop at Harvard, been rewarded by a theatre of his own. The theatre is not at Harvard, however, but at Yale University. Messrs. Blackall, Clapp and Whittemore, the architects, were more than usually successful in adapting the Tudor Gothic style, in harmony with the other university buildings, to the needs of the new University Theatre and workshops. The theatre is not only good architecture, but good theatre.

undoubtedly gain, but what will transform him is to see his manuscript in course of production and, above all, tried out before an audience accustomed to seeing plays in process of development. From criticisms he can glean at the performances, from written comments such as university audiences provide, he will see his play from many angles, through many preconceptions and prejudices. Through these same audiences he will begin to sense the chief characteristics of the greater audiences he must eventually face. More than that, he will come to understand how it is that what is for him sound, moving, and climactic in his writing may be none of these for the audience at which he aims. He begins to see his work, not any less as the artist, but as the artist interpreting to his public.

Perhaps it is characteristic of artists in general, certainly it is of workers in the theatre, to wish to be high specialists. Playwrights will work with endless patience on their manuscripts, but when they have watched one set of rehearsals they rebel at more — unless the plays be their own. They do not like to know intimately what goes on behind the curtain if it means shifting scenery or helping the chief electrician. They do not willingly take courses in designing scenery, costumes, or properties, unless they have some special gift in such matters. Yet as soon as a dramatist understands what all these branches may contribute to that curiously complicated result — a produced play — his writing gains in producibility. He prepares intelligently for each complementary worker to do his part — though he does not attempt to do the work for him. He becomes one of a corps — a commanding officer, if you like — and not an individual insisting on pet ideas, who complicates a group. The arts of the theatre, if studied separately, are likely to have the importance of each so over-emphasized that when a student thus trained must share in a difficult production there is wastage, confusion, — and temperament!

For instance, scenery as scenery is bad. It is right when it creates or emphasizes a mood, defines place or background, or sets off the costume play. Old-fashioned settings, new-fashioned settings, flats, curtains, stylized sets — none is always or generally right; each has its place. Beginners — particularly in this country — and some teachers want a royal road to treatment of a production. There is none. He who casts always to type is no better, no worse, than he who will not cast to type. A good production is the smooth working unit, under a wise and skilled hand, of many complementary forces. Even a slight over-emphasis on scenery or lighting, over acting, movement or gesture over speech, of atmosphere over characterization, may send a play scuttling down to its doom. As has already been pointed out, a good producer needs training in his attitude toward his fellow-workers. He needs it, too, toward play, author, and actors. The ancient idea that the most important step to becoming a director is to be a stage-manager emphasizes a part as the whole and is pretty well exploded. Being a stage-manager is good for what it gives, but it will make a director only of him who from birth was so intended. Why should youth stumble along the slow and painful road of stage-managership when all the necessary rudiments may be taught in a university theatre?

Such a theatre must be both conservative and flexible. Most of its students will later, in one way or another, live and work in the regular theatre world. Therefore it is important that they be trained under theatre conditions not more exacting than those ordinarily found in the commercial theatre. At the same time, they must not be trained so steadily with special devices for settings, lightings, etc., that they will find themselves at a loss when they become partners in productions touring the country. Here lies the danger in the training given by some experimental theatres. Students should be taught so that they can give the best production possible under the physical conditions of the stage on which they may work. On the other hand, the theatre in which they work should be sufficiently flexible to permit all kinds of experimentation.

There must be much opportunity for the electrician, that wizard of the present-day stage. When we speak of the electrician in the theatre, we still think too much in terms of candles and gas, just as in the moving picture we are still too much under the spell of the regular theatre. The university theatre should not only train young electricians to lighting as real, as delicate, as suggestive as possible, but should abet them in all desired technical and imaginative experiments. Many an electrician thinks technically in watts and amperes, but not in terms of the imagination. Others riot in imagination, but are not properly based technically. Here, as elsewhere in the theatre, the leap inspired by imagination should be taken from a sure footing in technique.

Places these university theatres should be where sound theory is drawn from past and present practice without limiting initiative or imagination, where beliefs are established which will sustain the young artist against unthinking conservatism till he proves his fitness or unfitness in his chosen field.

What is the hardest test the untrained, ambitious worker in any of the theatrical arts must face? When he is told that this or that can not be done because it has not been done, would not work if tried. When he is told that plays must contain this or that, must be written thus and so. To stand against obvious experience consciously inexperienced oneself, that is exceedingly difficult. What is strengthening is to have worked in a group which has demonstrated again and again by work done in common that doing again what has been done may mean perfecting form and finish. It is in experiment that advance lies. Not only rudimentary training but beliefs which will sustain a worker through times of doubt or crisis, this the university theatre must provide as far as possible.

WRITING FOR PUPPETS

By Alfred Kreymborg

If, in those moments of detachment which come least of all to active and most of all to reflective people, one is able to see oneself as an infinitesimal individual in an environment of time and place in which the proportionate part one plays is so insignificant as to appear grotesquely ridiculous, one is assuredly an appropriate instrument for puppets to serve unselfishly, faithfully, entirely. Let such a person decide upon some pages of autobiography; let him make from these a play for puppets which shall animate their sightless eyes, deaf ears, rigid mouths, and bloodless appendages with confession. Given the necessary patience, they will respond (in so far as they are made capable of reacting) to whatever mood, thought, or record he wishes to realize.

Notwithstanding its miniature proportions, the puppet theatre is absolute in its properties, harmonious in its values of light and shade. Its frame is high and broad and deep enough to admit the whole gamut of a chosen activity. At the same time it is sufficiently restricted to restrain and compose the movement inside a form as completely alive and impersonally cool as a Shakespearean sonnet, a Rembrandt etching, a Villon ballade, a Bach fugue, an Æsop fable. The theatre is magic enough on the one hand and real enough on the other to accommodate fancied replicas of the sun and moon, of mountains, caves, forests, seas; and it has room for all the animals of Noah's ark — providing the animals come in patterns of ones and twos and not in unconscious herds. This embryonic theatre is so microscopically true that the elements engaged in interpreting a confession are given a dramatic share in artificial time, space, and dynamics commensurate with the share allotted to people by the familiar fate which directs the strings that keep the universe in motion. A puppeteer is to puppets what the hidden hand is to people. People see a little more and guess a little more than puppets; otherwise, they are equally helpless; and out of this mutual helplessness is derived that curious bond which lifts a man into an actor or a doll into an animated reproduction.

The carved puppets — whether man, beast, or bird, fish, snake, or insect, tree, sprite, or hobgoblin, creatures of reality or fancy — will attempt everything asked of them and will succeed to the full extent of the power which inhabits or inhibits them. They are perfect as far as their creators can perfect them; and fail only when the potter fails. You may amplify them to the capacity of a full confession; or reduce them to the shyness of reticence. They are cunning, dull, brave, afraid, impudent, grave, tragic, droll, superb, childish, normal, abnormal — in accordance with the personality of the manipulator. Carve them into Faust and Mephisto, Puck and Oberon and Bottom, Tartuffe, Cleon, Œdipus, Electra; and they will play these

314

characters miraculously well or feebly and poorly to a degree for which they, personally, are certainly not responsible. If shortcomings intervene, the crime is yours alone. You cannot blame the actors, the stage manager, the prompter, the electrician. You cannot say the stage was too much thus and so, the properties inadequate, the acoustics discordant, the audience unresponsive, the critics a pack of thieves, and your friends a nodding crew of hypocrites. You had no human beings to deal with. You engaged no *tenori robusti*, *bassi profundi*, *soprani temperamenti*. You yourself wrote or selected the play, designed and built the theatre, shaped and strung the puppets, manipulated and spoke for them. They can only do what you do.

In such intimate relations, the ideals, responsibilities, and methods of composing for puppets are correspondingly severe. Moved to the expression of some phase of experience, determining the elements which shall incorporate and develop a theme, and concentrating them into the parts to be interpreted by dolls, one is bound, if one is faithful to one's view of the truth or the fancied truth, to see oneself and one's contacts as a series or group of puppets set off, enhanced, or repressed by the surrounding environment, and to do so, if possible, in the guise of a detached critic seizing and dispassionately commenting upon the antics of a foreign, though familiar, entity. If one is a comedian, one sees other folk in a similar plight; they excite a fellow-feeling; one would share one's experience with them, compare notes, even though the instinct of loving and sympathizing with them, and sharing confidences only prove another form of self-pity and self-preservation. And so one writes for puppets as nearly akin to people as it is possible for puppets to be.

Although one tries to do this simply, clearly, directly, one does not eschew subtlety. One hides the beggar in the background. One warns him to keep his hand behind him and his tin cup among his rags. Even though the author open himself wide, let this or that impersonation of himself sing, his relation to the mendicant must be folded in secrecy. The creatures who infest the song or crowd the stage are so many puppets of himself. If John Doe eyes the program, or listens to the characters calling each other by name, he probably learns to recognize Mr. Incognito, Mrs. Thingum-bob, and Punch and Judy, in their resemblances, however faint or indistinct, to himself and his own affairs. They look and act not a little like himself and his friends and acquaintances. They are droll. He likes them, applauds them. Not all that they do. No. He could have improved on this; he would hardly have done that. But he would have kissed Judy, as Punch did. And he would most certainly have thwacked the devil. After the final curtain, he is enough like Punch to emulate a part of him. On the way home, he resolves to kiss Mrs. John Doe not once, but twice — once for good measure. That play was all the better for being inspirational. But alas, poor Punch. Never — alas, Mr. Author. And so in return — thank you, whispers the beggar — and hands the receipts to his master.

A puppet play, then, has for its interpreters a tireless troupe of docile nonentities who will enter into what is

Probably nowhere in the world is there a puppeteer who has achieved quite what Richard Teschner has in Vienna. All of human beauty, with something added, is in his figures and composition.

required of them at any time of day, with or without
rehearsal, under the most harrowing conditions, if
necessary, and in serene opposition to obstacles which
would cause most human actors to go on strike. In
the course of your production, you may make certain
demands with respect to the technical aspects of your
work. You may have selected a commonplace theme
containing folk-like ingredients. It is possible that the
language you employ is an improvisation on everyday
speech and, in the play of one character upon another,
particular phrases are not only repeated, but heightened
and developed and stylized toward a clearly defined
ritual composed of interdependent voices acting and
reacting upon one another like instruments in a trio,
quartette, or quintette. On the stage, the movement
of the puppets will coincide with the speech of the
recurrent voices, and provide for the eye an impression
identical with the appeal made to the ear. It may be
that this ritual introduces symphonic problems of pitch
and tempo. Certain lines may lie in the soprano or
tenor register; others in the mezzo, still others in the
bass; and, in accordance with the action at a given
moment, those characters which have been driven by
an allegro pace may have to retard their voices, while
those which have indulged an adagio are forced to
accelerate theirs. Naturally, the puppeteers will have
to sound the pitches and the rubati; meanwhile, the
puppets must not lag behind. Their gestures will beat
time in visual fidelity to the varying timbres and tempi.
The voices will chant to a given quartette; the puppets
will play it. When the two elements work in complete
understanding, not even a wiseacre will be able to detect

the slightest discrepancy : Speech and movement, voice and doll will belong to the same entity. A skilled puppeteer will have the finger of a musician. If he wears a doll on his fingers (finger up each arm, and one up the head), he will play upon the air as he might on a keyboard, flute, or string; and the head and hands of the doll will beat out the tune upon space. Burattini, the traditional Italian puppets, are the best of instruments for such a performance. They are as much a part of the puppeteer as his fingers are. Strings are intermediaries; they are subject to entanglement; and, like divers, marionettes can never be trusted absolutely; they don't always feel and respond to the tug of a string; puppeteer and marionette frequently disagree. In this respect, marionettes resemble the human actor, and the puppeteer (unless he is old and wise and patient) is liable to fall into the temper of a stage manager. If one has a musical idea in mind, it is therefore best to employ one's fingers and the dolls that fit them.

Puppet plays, puppets, and puppet theatres have the additional value of serving as miniature models for the human play, actor, and theatre. There is no more intimate way of testing a drama to be performed, let us say, in a Broadway theatre, than to build a toy stage and to try out each and every line and situation, the play and interplay of pantomime, the values of light and shade, and the proportionate part to be devoted to the scenic background. The puppet performance will design a blue print in accordance with which the final structure is to be erected. Inasmuch as it is easier to detect a flaw in a lyric than an epic, in a miniature than a fresco, in a dialogue than a five-act tragedy, in a prose poem than a novel, in a prelude than a symphony, the faults of a play or a production will be clearer to the eye and ear in a puppet performance than in the highly complex machinery of the larger, human theatre; and infinitely more time will be saved in the correction or eradication of each sinner.

Moreover, the actor, if he loves his profession more than himself, if he gives himself to an ensemble rather than the exposition of his particular individuality, if he desires to enter and maintain a part, in preference to flirting with the limelight, if he be willing to subject rather than object himself — such an actor will learn something from the puppet (as he did in some of the earliest Oriental theatres). He will recognize just how much and how little he is concerned in the performance *en masse;* and when his cues are called on the human stage, he will deliver what has been allotted to him with every sense modestly alive to the harmony he must serve and preserve in connection with every other actor, personality, and thing in the surrounding scene. Goethe has said somewhere that no play is perfect until it can be successfully performed by puppets; and in this connection, it will be recalled that the author of *Faust* found his inspiration for that lifelong composition in the performances of the traditional folk-play of that name given by strolling puppet companies during his childhood.

Puppets are never a tedious people. This is another — and perhaps their greatest blessing. They are too shy and too profoundly considerate to ask their audience always to sit through five, four, or three acts.

One act will do, one scene, one dialogue. They can show what the author has to tell in less than three hours, two hours, one. Less than half a dozen minutes will suffice for the dramatization of a lyric mood. If you insist on Goethe's own *Faust*, they will accommodate you, especially when it comes to demons and the supernatural agencies of a Walpurgis revel. They are not timid about attempting Puck and the fairies; they fly through space a little more naturally and with less machinery and fright than human actors. If they fall and crack, there's not so much ado.

If you haven't the cosmic mood and the sustained patience for "Faust" or "A Midsummer Night's Dream" (as they have in Germany); if you belong to a nervous, energetic era like the present; if yours is, now and then, at least, a staccato character, and you have to release the ego in short, brilliant movements, running an entire gamut in a minute or two, there are plenty of shadows for the purpose; and you don't have to go to Java for the figures. If one is a child of a youthful country, with a long future and not much of a past, one is addicted to lyrism at the start. One is fed on pubescent illusions; one cannot see macrocosm for the microcosm; one has a tendency — if one writes at all — to compose crisp, romantic dialogues. One likes to see them acted. One has them produced — not on Broadway, which is still harnessed to the five-act, four-act, three-act tradition of an older civilization — but in out-of-the-way places where people are not as yet grown up; where they are primitive, unsophisticated, and easily led astray; where they are children who require but a hint to urge the imagination on a journey. The play may be over in a wink; neverthe-less, such childish folk may be depended upon. They will develop the overtones, the undertones, the echoes. Suppose you give the thing a title: an especially common name like "Springtime." It is possible that you are old (if not in years, then in mood). At the moment, you may hanker after youth. A crooked willow and a sprightly birch may appeal to you as tem-porary symbols. Let a puppet play the willow and another play the birch. Set them going — lay a stream between — with a mocking water-sprite for the ques-tioner and a slow, dreamy answer for the willow. Assuredly, the birch is silent. And there are doubts concerning his hearing capacity.

> Willow, Why do you bend so low
> with your staring into the stream?
> *Only to see how deep it is!*
>
> Fool, Do you think you 're beardless still
> and meditating suicide?
> *Only to find if one might wade!*
>
> Lilies and cat-tails belong to the young,
> and the water is cold this time of year?
> *Only to touch my love over there!*
>
> Your love?   Your love?   And which is she?
> That wrinkled, gnarled, old-bandy-leg?
> *The one with gay white limbs!*
>
> Dotard, What could she see in you?
> She 'd yank your beard and laugh away?
> *She 's nodding her head at me!*

COMMEDIA DELL' ARTE AND
AMERICAN VAUDEVILLE

By Vadim Uraneff

"No one fails to understand that in the Commedia dell' Arte the Italians of the sixteenth century gave to future generations a hint as to the possibilities of the Art of the Theatre. The hint was never taken by those of the subsequent centuries. I believe and hope that this century will see a revival of this independent spirit of the Theatre. I even believe that the spirit has begun to stir again in its ancient bones."

Gordon Craig in "The Mask" of 1912-1913.

Commedia dell' Arte — which influenced the European theatre for centuries; which developed the most extraordinary comedians, famous throughout the Renaissance world, which set the actor free of his bondage to the author and created improvisation, on the stage: this is the art whose revival is the dream of Gordon Craig, of Copeau, and of Meierhold, the most famous authorities of the modern theatre.

There are books available in every language on Commedia dell' Arte, and the latest researches together with the material left by its contemporaries afford a clear understanding of the matter to those who wish to study it. Commedia dell' Arte is described here only so far as may be necessary to draw a parallel between the Italian theatre of the sixteenth and seventeenth centuries and the American theatre of today, only in so far as may be necessary to prove that in America the spirit and the art of Commedia dell' Arte could be reproduced better than anywhere else by emphasizing certain qualities already present and active in the American theatre. By American theatre I mean that branch of the purely commercial theatre which has grown up in response to the demands of the great American public and which appeals directly to popular audiences. The most typical, vital, and perfect expression of that theatre is vaudeville. A comparison between American vaudeville and the theatre of the Italian Renaissance reveals the opportunity of a movement of great possibilities, with productions of native quality and with distinctive achievements in the realm of pure theatricality.

"Commedia dell' Arte all' improvise" grew out of the performances of strolling players and assumed its form in the latter half of the sixteenth century. In the early days Italian comedy belonged exclusively to the people. The players gave their shows in the streets, in the suburbs, or in booths erected in the market places during the street fairs. Persecuted by the church and ignored by the over-refined society of the day, they had the love of the populace from the beginning and always retained it.

Side by side with this gay popular art there existed in Italy a literary theatre, independent of the public taste and patronized by the Princes and great lords of the day. It was for this theatre that the sophisticated poets of the Renaissance wrote their plays, but the theatre was to them merely a medium for spoken poetry and they ignored the fundamental laws of dramatic art. This attitude brought about, as might be expected, a complete degeneration of the theatre of their day. The cultured society of the Renaissance with its inherent craving for genuine theatricality, turned to the art of the people for relief. By that time the traditions of the popular theatre had become established, and it possessed actors with a very special and remarkable technique. So its appeal was immediate and the theatre of the booths and barns was transferred to a new social environment. There, literary influence, material prosperity, and the amateur acting in vogue all conspired to change the character of the performances. After two hundred years of existence, Commedia dell' Arte was celebrated throughout Europe; the apogee of its fame was the end of the seventeenth century. In its final form undoubtedly superior in every way to the productions of the market place, Commedia dell' Arte would nevertheless have been impossible to realize had it not been for the roots planted in the soil of the country, the traditions established in the popular theatre and the incomparable actors, the result of an incomparable training.

The most important factor in its evolution was that for centuries it had developed entirely by pressure of popular taste, in a theatre where the primitive spectator was the ultimate judge. The primitive spectator, having no knowledge of other forms of art, is always a peculiarly sensitive critic of the theatre, because a feel-

Francis Bruguière

Whoever knows Charlie Chaplin knows the leading
figure in America's Commedia dell'Arte, but there
are, in vaudeville and revues especially, many
other clever mimes and improvisers like Al Jolson,
Eddie Cantor, the Marx Brothers, to fill the places
of Arlechino, Mezzetino and the rest. Some years
ago Vadim Uraneff tried a production of "The Show
Booth", a play after the manner of the Commedia,
by Alexander Blok, to emphasize this quality. For
James Watts as the Clown, Robert Edmond
Jones designed this traditional costume translated
into the language of the expressionistic stage.

ing for the essentially theatric is not dulled in him by influences and associations foreign to histrionic art. There can be no doubt of the supreme value of such a process of "natural selection" in type, story, and setting, as a foundation for a National Theatre, in developing theatrical traditions and as a basis for a technique in acting.

A stylized setting for Commedia dell' Arte. Each character has his own entrance. The three center doors were for the servants, the first Zanni, the second Zanni, Arlecino, and Smeraldina or Columbina. The two center side doors were for the lovers. The large side doors were the doors of two houses, the one on the right the house of Dottore, on the left that of Pantalone. Dottore and Pantalone, however, did not make their appearance from the doors of their own houses, these being reserved for the girls, but came from the forward wings.

In the Commedia dell' Arte this process of selection naturally and gradually resulted in that stylization of form, mise-en-scène, material, and character which has become, for us, its most characteristic feature.

The schematic drawing reproduced from Meierhold's magazine, "The Love of the Three Oranges", shows the conventional architectural set of the Commedia dell' Arte performance. So definitely stylized a set naturally gave a very definite and stylized design to the mise-en-scène.

The plays used by the actors of Commedia dell'

Arte were also stylized to a great extent. A written scenario was always provided which contained certain

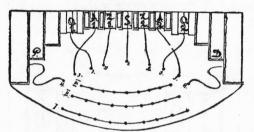

basic situations which had proved irresistible to an audience. A particularly successful improvisation was used again and again, and the "lazzi" or jokes were repeated as long and as often as they met with response. By col-

Every play opened with the appearance of all the characters, who came through their traditional entrances in a stylized manner, each with his stylized walk. They lined up in a traditional arrangement, made three stylized bows and made their exit, each to his own door. The first appearance was called the Parade.

lecting those situations which were most successful, that famous scenario, " Scene of the Night ", was constructed which was the basis of all scenarios used by the Commedia dell' Arte.

The most charac-teristic and stable feature of Com-media dell' Arte is, however, the presence of defi-nite stage charac-ters that may be grouped into a small

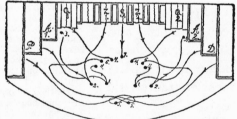

The first of a series of stylized arrangements for the Commedia dell' Arte " Scene of the Night," showing how complicated and yet how simple some of their forms were.

number of popular theatric types. Each of these had its particular qualities and limitations, its distinctive costume, carriage, and gesture. A characteristic mask was invariably worn by each type and only one rôle was assumed by an actor during his lifetime. At seventy, one famous old actor was still playing the lover.

The four main personages were Pantalone and Dottore, old men, and the first and second Zanni who went by various names at different times, though the first Zanni was usually Brighella and the second Arlechino. There were other fixed characters, such as Pulcinella, a Captain — always of Naples; a Spanish Captain, Smeraldina, and Tartaglia and Mezzettino. It was largely to this feature of stylized traditional characters that improvisation was due at that time. Indeed, without traditional impersonation, improvisation could hardly be achieved, which may explain why, since the passing of Commedia dell' Arte, no theatre has succeeded in throwing off the literary yoke and freeing the actor from the written word.

It must be clear that the revival of anything like Commedia dell' Arte in form or in spirit is impossible and all attempts in that direction are vain, until a country affords conditions similar to those which brought to life that theatre in Italy; until there exists a popular theatre with traditions developed through a long period and with actors of a special technique; and until there are associated with this theatre and these actors certain definite theatrical types registered in the mind of the spectator, as a basis for the actor's improvisation.

These indispensable conditions are present at this moment in no other place than American vaudeville. When I say American vaudeville I do not mean those numbers imported to the vaudeville stage from musical comedy, revue, farce, or the legitimate drama. I mean, paradoxically enough, those "vaudeville" numbers and actors, some of which and some of whom — perhaps the most representative and best of them — are to be found in the field of musical comedy, revue or burlesque, although wherever they are, they retain their vaudeville spirit. It is difficult to explain in a few words just what are the characteristics of the genuine vaudeville spirit. But here are some of the fundamentals:

1. The actor is always in the foreground, the literary form is calculated with a view to the individual possibilities of the actor. The interest of the act never depends on the plot, for it is the actor that counts.

2. Acting does not aim to give the illusion of life on the stage, but is in a style of exaggerated parody. It has a tendency to solve theatrical situations by physical action, even, where necessary, by acrobatic stunts. In accordance with the non-representational spirit of acting, the face is treated in make-up like a mobile mask. The vaudeville performer knows that the theatre is three dimensional in spirit. That is why most vaudeville acting is done as near the audience as the apron of a vaudeville stage will allow.

3. A meticulous regard for never stepping out of an assumed character is a cardinal point. No joke even, no matter how effective and clever it may be, is ever used by a true vaudeville performer if it is not strictly in his character.

4. Stylization in gesture, pose, mise-en-scène, and make-up follows as a result of long experimentation

328

before the primitive spectator whose power as a judge is absolute.

5. The actor works with the idea of an immediate response from the audience; and with regard to its demands. By cutting out everything — every line, gesture, movement — to which the audience does not react and by improvising new things, he establishes unusual unity between the audience and himself.

All these points apply equally to Commedia dell' Arte and vaudeville.

To assemble a complete collection of American theatrical types already fixed in the mind of the primitive spectator, to complete the parallel with Commedia dell' Arte, one must not limit oneself to vaudeville, but include other forms of the commercial theatre — musical comedy, farce, burlesque, the moving picture. There we find the business man, the sailor, the black face comedian, the sweetheart, the chorus girl, the "sissy." Just as in Commedia dell' Arte, each type has its characteristic appearance; its characteristic walk, costume, gestures, and movements. Its traditional make-up, as, for instance, that of the black-face, is quite as artificial as the mask of the Italian. Some of these types are almost identical with the personages of Commedia, others have been transformed under the influence of our more complex modern life among sky scrapers, aeroplanes, electric signs, and machinery. Others have disappeared, and new ones have taken their places.

There is an absolute identity between the Pantalone of Commedia and the Business Man of the American theatre and of eternity. Perucci (writing in Naples, in 1699) gives the characteristics of Pantalone as a surly merchant thus: "He is calculating and suspicious but sometimes naïvely credulous. He is shrewd, and at the same time good-natured. His appearance is impressive. He is ridiculous in his love of adventure, and often is the rival of his son. Of course he always loses the lady, and gets a good scolding for his adventures from his wife." It is evident that he corresponds closely to the Business Man of American vaudeville and musical comedy.

The first Zanni, a comical servant, very quick and very cunning, noted for his shrewdness and native wit, who purposely promotes the intrigue in Italian comedies, was the most popular character in Commedia, and is equally popular today in its reincarnation. He was called by various names — usually Brighella or Pedrolino (who later became the French Pierrot). Several American comedians, among others Fred Stone and Jim Barton, give striking examples of the comic and dynamic aspect of this character. Of the second Zanni, Arlechino, who later became the French Harlequin, Perucci says: "In the valley of Bergamo, there are people of the simplest and funniest type, and all who have talked to them can but agree that they are charming in their simplicity. It seems as if nature, herself, brought them to life in order to amuse people. They play with their hands, answer at the wrong time, talk and have discourse with themselves, become panic stricken without cause, do not understand Latin words, or else interpret them upside down." What is this character but our black face? It might have been written about Frank Tinney.

COMMEDIA DELL' ARTE

A new type strangely popular in our time is the effeminate or "sissy" portrayed so amazingly by Eddie Cantor and the late Dooley Brothers. The characters most closely resembling this were Tartaglia and Mezzettino.

Columbina or Smeraldina, who is the ancestor of Columbine, was different from her French successor (as, it may be mentioned in passing, were most of the Italian characters). The former was a woman servant delightfully grotesque and slightly vulgar, the friend of both "Zannis" who helped them in developing intrigues and who always ended the play. James Watts is a perfect example of this type in our contemporary theatre.

Finally, I must speak of one incomparable American artist who, being the most representative of the spirit of Commedia dell' Arte, needs no comparison with it. Charlie Chaplin, with his extraordinary technique, with his power of getting the most subtle things over to the most primitive audience, with his instantaneous appeal, has nothing to learn from the history of Commedia dell' Arte. Although his tricks and situations are never twice the same, his masklike make-up and his characteristic walk are unvarying. In other words, he is always true to the great school of acting of the Italian improvisational comedy.

It must be evident from what has been said that America has every requisite for a brilliant revival of Commedia dell' Arte. All that is required to complete it are native American productions with scenarios constructed from the material now in use in American vaudeville stylized to meet the stylization of character and with a mise-en-scène in the spirit of the whole.

THE END

INDEX

333

INDEX

334

INDEX

335

INDEX

INDEX

INDEX

INDEX

339

INDEX

340

INDEX